ENGLISH SYNTAX AND ARGUMENTATION

MODERN LINGUISTICS SERIES

Series Editors

Professor Noël Burton-Roberts
University of Newcastle

Professor Maggie Tallerman
University of Newcastle

Each textbook in the **Modern Linguistics** series is designed to provide a carefully graded introduction to a topic in contemporary linguistics and allied disciplines, presented in a manner that is accessible and attractive to readers with no previous experience of the topic, but leading them to some understanding of current issues. The texts are designed to engage the active participation of the reader, favouring a problem-solving approach and including liberal and varied exercise material.

Titles published in the series

English Syntax and Argumentation (3rd Edition)   Bas Aarts
Phonology   Philip Carr
Linguistics and Second Language Acquisition   Vivian Cook
Sociolinguistics: A Reader and Coursebook
Nikolas Coupland and Adam Jaworski
Morphology (2nd Edition)   Francis Katamba and John Stonham
Semantics   Kate Kearns
Syntactic Theory   Geoffrey Poole
Contact Languages: Pidgins and Creoles   Mark Sebba

Further titles in preparation

Modern Linguistics Series
Series Standing Order
ISBN 0–333–71701–5 hardcover
ISBN 0–333–69344–2 paperback
(outside North America only)

You can receive future titles in this series as they are published by placing a standing order. Please contact your bookseller or, in the case of difficulty, write to us at the address below with your name and address, the title of the series and the ISBN quoted above.

Customer Services Department, Palgrave Ltd
Houndmills, Basingstoke, Hampshire RG21 6XS, England

English Syntax and Argumentation

Third Edition

Bas Aarts

First edition published 1997
Second edition published 2001
Third edition published 2008

First pblished 1997 by
PALGRAVE MACMILLAN

Palgrave Macmillan in the UK is an imprint of Macmillian Publishers Limited,
registered in England, company number 785998, of Houndmills, Basingstoke,
Hampshire RG21 6XS.

Palgrave Macmillan in the US is a division of St Martin's Press LLC,
175 Fifth Avenue, New York, NY 10010.

Palgrave Macmillan is the global academic imprint of the above companies
and has companies and representatives throughout the world.

Palgrave® and Macmillan® are registered trademarks in the United States,
the United Kingdom, Europe and other countries.

ISBN-13: 978–0–230–55120–6 hardback
ISBN-10: 0–230–55120–3 hardback
ISBN-13: 978–0–230–55121–3 paperback
ISBN-10: 0–230–55121–1 paperback

This book is printed on paper suitable for recycling and made from fully
managed and sustained forest sources. Logging, pulping and manufacturing
processes are expected to conform to the environmental regulations of
the country of origin.

A catalogue record for this book is available from the British Library.

A catalog record for this book is available from the Library of Congress.

10 9 8 7 6 5 4
17 16 15 14 13 12 11 10

Printed and bound in China

To my family and friends

Contents

Preface to the First Edition

This book grew out of a need for an introductory text that teaches students not only English syntax but also the basics of argumentation. It is inspired by current Chomskyan theory, but it is not an introduction to it. However, having worked their way through this book, students should be able to progress to a more advanced study of syntax, descriptive or theoretical.

I would like to thank the following people for having read an earlier version of the book or parts of it: Flor Aarts (who also helped correcting proofs), Valerie Adams, Judith Broadbent, Dick Hudson, Gunther Kaltenböck, Andrew Spencer, and the students who took part in the Modern English Language seminar at University College London.

Special thanks are due to Noël Burton-Roberts for his advice, extensive comments and support. Naturally, all blunders, bloopers and other blemishes are entirely due to me.

B.A.

Preface to the Second Edition

This new edition is a completely revised and corrected version of the first edition. The most obvious change is that Chapter 7 of the first edition (on X-bar syntax) has been split into two, giving more prominence to clauses in a new Chapter 8 (entitled 'More on clauses'). In addition, the book contains many new exercises, which are now graded in terms of level of difficulty. I am grateful to colleagues and students who used the first edition of this book, and gave me very valuable feedback preparing the present edition. In particular, I would like to thank Kersti Börjars, Ilse Depraetere, Nik Gisborne, Sebastian Hoffman, Hans-Martin Lehmann, Magnus Ljung, Gergana Popova, Mariangela Spinillo and Gunnel Tottie, as well as students at UCL, the Universidad de La Laguna, the University of Sofia, and the University of Zürich.

B.A.

Preface to the Third Edition

This new edition incorporates a number of corrections and changes in terminology. For example, I now use *determinative* as a form label, rather than *determiner*. I have added a new chapter on grammatical indeterminacy which has been informed by my research on syntactic gradience. Furthermore, I have reorganised Chapter 15 (formerly Chapter 14) by moving one of the case studies to the new Chapter 14, and by adding a new case study. I have also written a number of new exercises, while removing others that didn't 'work'.

I am again extremely grateful to a number of colleagues for sending me corrections and suggestions for changes. Among them are Dong-hwan An (who translated the second edition into Korean), Gunnar Bergh, Myong-Hi Chai and three anonymous readers. For advice, comments, suggestions and corrections I'm very grateful to Maggie Tallerman, the new editor for the Modern Linguistics series, to Sonya Barker at Palgrave Macmillan, as well as to my copy editor Penny Simmons. Finally, I would like to thank my students at UCL, past and present, who have always been a tremendous pleasure to teach, and students from elsewhere who have written to me with corrections and comments.

University College London   B.A.
b.aarts@ucl.ac.uk

The Scrabble tiles on the cover design are reproduced by kind permission of J. W. Spear and Son PLC, Enfield EN3 7TB, England.

Part I
Function and Form

1 Introduction

Along with sleeping, eating and drinking, talking is one of the most common of human activities. Hardly a day goes by when we don't talk, if only to ourselves! When we speak, we utter a stream of sounds with a certain meaning, which our interlocutors can process and understand, provided they speak the same language of course. Naturally, language also exists in written form. It then consists of a string of letters which form words, which in turn make up sentences. Why is the study of language worthwhile? Well, first and foremost the capacity for using language is uniquely human, and if we know how language works we get to know something about ourselves. Other animals also communicate with each other, to be sure, but their communicative and expressive powers are very limited. Thus, while dogs and cats can signal pleasure by wagging their tails or purring, there's no way for them to tell you something more complicated, for example that although they are generally content, they wouldn't mind if you turned the heating up a little. By contrast, we humans can communicate just about any meaning we wish, however complex, using language. As an example, consider the utterance *Had Nick been here on time, we would not have missed the train*. This is a perfectly straightforward and easily intelligible sentence, though to understand it we have to do a bit of mental computing by creating in our minds a 'picture' of a situation that did *not* obtain, a situation in which Nick *was* on time, and we did *not* miss our train. Or consider the sentence *I went to a conference on language in France*. Have you noticed that it's ambiguous? Under one reading I went to a conference on language which took place in France; under the second reading I went to a conference which was about 'language in France', which could have taken place anywhere. This is called a *structural ambiguity*, because we can group the words together differently to bring out the two meanings. There are of course many other reasons to be fascinated by language. If you're a student of literature, you cannot really grasp the totality of meaning that a work of literary art communicates without knowing how language works. And if you're interested in interpersonal relationships you might wonder why there are so many ways to ask someone to open the window: 'Open the window!', 'Can you open the window (please)?', 'Could you open the window (please)?', 'I was wondering whether you could possibly open the window?' and 'I'm hot'. The last example is especially interesting, because at first sight it's a simple statement about one's physical condition. For the hearer to get to the meaning 'open the window, please', some mental computation is again involved. I could continue endlessly to give more examples to illustrate the many fascinating aspects of the field of language studies, called *linguistics*. In this book we focus on the *structure* of English. Now, if you have thought about language, you will have realised that whether it is spoken or written, it is not a hotchpotch of randomly distributed elements. Instead, the linguistic ingredients that language is made up of are arranged in accordance with a set of rules. This set of rules we call the *grammar* of a language. Grammar is a vast domain of inquiry and it will be necessary to limit ourselves to a subdomain. In this book we will only be concerned with the part of grammar that concerns itself with the structure of sentences. This is called *syntax*.

How can we go about describing the structure of sentences? Well, before we can even start, we will need to specify what we mean by 'sentence'. This is not as straightforward a question as it may seem, and linguists have come up with a variety of definitions. In this book we will say that a sentence is a string of words that begins in a capital letter and ends in a full stop, and is typically used to express a state of affairs in the world. This definition is not unproblematic, but will suffice for present purposes.

Let's now see what kinds of issues syntax deals with. First of all, one of the principal concerns of syntax is the *order* of words. In English we cannot string words into a sentence randomly. For example, we can have (1), but not (2) or (3):

(1)   The President ate a doughnut.
(2)   *The President a doughnut ate.
(3)   *Doughnut President the ate a.

NB: An asterisk (*) placed before a sentence indicates that it is not a possible structure in English.

The contrast between (1) and (2) shows that in English the word that denotes the activity of eating (*ate*) must precede the word (or string of words) that refers to the entity that was being eaten (*a doughnut*). Furthermore, if we compare (2) and (3) we see that not only must *ate* precede *a doughnut*, but we must also ensure that the two elements *the* and *a* precede *President* and *doughnut*, respectively. It seems that *the* and *President* together form a unit, in the same way that *a* and *doughnut* do. Our syntactic framework will have to be able to explain why it is that words group themselves together. We will use the term *constituent* for strings of one or more words that syntactically and semantically (i.e. meaningwise) behave as units.

Consider next sentence (4):

(4)   The cat devoured the rat.

It is possible to rearrange the words in this sentence as follows:

(5)   The rat devoured the cat.

Notice that this is still a good sentence of English, but its meaning is different from (4), despite the fact that both sentences contain exactly the same words. In (4) the agent (perpetrator) of the attack is *the cat* and the undergoer (victim) is *the rat*. In (5) these roles are reversed. Our rules of syntax must be set up in such a way that they can account for the fact that native speakers of English *know* that a reordering of elements like we have in (4) and (5) leads to a difference in meaning.

However, not all reorderings lead to a difference in meaning. An alternative ordering for (4) is given in (6) below:

(6)   The RAT, the cat devoured.

Sentences of this type are commonly used for contrast. For example, (6) might be uttered in denial of someone saying *The cat devoured the mouse*. Again, the syntactic rules of our grammar must be able to characterise the regrouping that has transformed (4) into (6), and they must also be able to explain why in this case there is no change in meaning.

The examples we have looked at so far make clear that syntax deals with the way in which we can carve up sentences into smaller constituent parts which consist of single words or of larger units of two or more words, and the way in which these units can be combined and/or rearranged.

Let us look at some further simple sentences and see how we can analyse them in terms of their constituent parts. Consider (7) below. How could we plausibly subdivide this sentence into constituents?

(7)   The President blushed.

One possible subdivision is to separate the sentence into words:

(8)   The — President — blushed

However, clearly (8) is not a particularly enlightening way to analyse (7), because such a dissection tells us nothing about the relationships between the individual words. Intuitively the words *the* and *President* together form a unit, while *blushed* is a second unit that stands alone, as in (9):

(9)   [The President] — [blushed]

We will use square brackets to indicate groups of words that belong together. One way in which we can also *show* that the string *the President* is a unit is by replacing it with *he*:

(10)   [He] — [blushed]

The subdivision in (9) makes good sense from the point of view of meaning too: the word-group *the President* has a specific function in that it refers (in a particular context of utterance) to an individual whose job is Head of State. Similarly, the word *blushed* has a clear function in that it tells us what happened to the President.

Let us now turn to a slightly more complex example. Consider the sentence below:

(11)   Our vicar likes fast cars.

If we want to set about analysing the structure of this sentence, we can of course divide it up into words, in the way we did in (8), as follows:

(12)   Our — vicar — likes — fast — cars

But again, you will agree, this is of limited interest for the same reason as that given above: an analysis into strings of individual words leaves the relationships between words completely unaccounted for.

Exercise

Can you think of a different way of analysing this sentence into subparts which accounts for our intuition that certain words belong together?

Intuitively the words *our* and *vicar* belong together, as do *fast* and *cars*. The word *likes* seems to stand alone. We end up with (13):

(13)   [Our vicar] — [likes] — [fast cars]

Again, just as in (10), we can also *show* that the bracketed strings behave as units, by replacing them:

(14)   [He] — [likes] — [them]

An analysis along the lines of (13) of a simple sentence like (11) has been widely adopted, but there are in fact reasons for analysing (11) differently, namely as in (15):

(15)   [Our vicar] — [[likes] — [fast cars]]

Like (13), (15) brings out the fact that *our* and *vicar* belong together, as do *fast* and *cars*, but it also reflects the fact that *likes* forms a constituent with *fast cars*. Why would that be? There are a number of reasons for this which will be discussed in detail in later chapters, but we will look at one of them now. Notice that *like* requires the presence of a constituent that specifies what is being liked. In (11) that constituent is *fast cars*. The sentence in (16), which provides no clue as to what is being liked by the vicar, is *ungrammatical*, i.e. not part of the grammar of English.

(16)   *Our vicar likes.

Likes and *fast cars* are taken together as a constituent in (15) to bring out the fact that there is a close bond between *like* and the constituent that specifies what is being liked (i.e. the constituent that is required to complete the meaning of *like*). Notice that *blush* in (7) does *not* require the presence of another constituent to complete its meaning.

Much of this book, especially Part III, will be concerned with finding reasons why one analysis is to be preferred over another in much the same way that reasons have been given for preferring (15) over (13). Giving motivated reasons for adopting certain structures and rejecting others is called *syntactic argumentation*. One aim of this book is to train you in the art of being able to set up a coherent syntactic argument. We will almost exclusively be concerned with the syntax of English, not because other languages are not interesting, but because studying the syntactic properties of other languages requires a wider framework than we can deal with here. The general syntactic framework I have adopted is inspired by the theory of language developed by the American linguist and philosopher Noam Chomsky over the last fifty years. The main aim of the book is to make you familiar with the basics of English syntax and, as noted above, with the fundamentals of syntactic argumentation. A further aim is to enable you to move on to more advanced books and articles on theoretical syntax.

Key Concepts in this Chapter

linguistics
structure
grammar
syntax
constituent
syntactic argumentation

2 Function

In the last chapter we saw that sentences are not random collections of words, but strings of words which are organised according to certain rules. It is the task of syntax to give an account of those rules. We saw that sentences can be analysed into subparts which we referred to as constituents. In this chapter we will look at how these constituents *function* in the sentences of which they are a part.

2.1 Subject and Predicate

Consider again the pair of sentences below, which we first came across in Chapter 1:

(1)   The cat devoured the rat.
(2)   The rat devoured the cat.

The structure of these sentences can be represented as in (3) and (4) below using brackets:

(3)   [The cat] [devoured [the rat]]
(4)   [The rat] [devoured [the cat]]

As we have already seen, these sentences contain exactly the same words, but differ quite radically in meaning. This meaning difference comes about as a result of the different roles played by the various constituents. In (3) and (4) distinct entities, namely *the cat* and *the rat*, respectively, carry out the action denoted by the word *devoured*. We will call words that denote actions *verbs*. Also, notice that we could say that (3) is concerned with telling us more about the cat, while (4) is concerned with telling us more about the rat. We can now define the *Subject* of a sentence as the constituent that on the one hand tells us who performs the action denoted by the verb (i.e. who is the *Agent*), and on the other hand tells us who or what the sentence is about. So to find out what is the Subject of a particular sentence we can ask 'Who or what carried out the action denoted by the verb?' and also 'Who or what is this sentence about?' The answers to these questions will pinpoint the Subject.

The second bracketed units in the sentences in (3) and (4) are *devoured the rat* and *devoured the cat*, respectively. These constituents tell us more about the Subject of the sentence, namely what it was engaged in doing (or, to be more precise, what its *referent* was engaged in doing). In (3) the Subject (*the cat*) was engaged in eating a rat, whereas in (4) the Subject (*the rat*) was engaged in eating a cat. We will use the term *Predicate* for the unit in a sentence whose function is to specify what the Subject is engaged in doing. The notion Predicate is therefore a second type of grammatical function. In any given sentence the Predicate is everything in the sentence except the Subject.

Exercise

In each of the following sentences determine what is the Subject and what is the Predicate:

(i)   The police arrested the bank robber.
(ii)   This factory produces a revolutionary new type of fax machine.
(iii)   That stupid waiter gleefully spilt soup all over my trousers.
(iv)   The stuntman smashed sixteen cars in five minutes.
(v)   She probably painted the President's portrait at the palace.

The Subjects are: *the police, this factory, that stupid waiter, the stuntman* and *she*. The Predicates are: *arrested the bank robber, produces a revolutionary new type of fax machine, gleefully spilt soup all over my trousers, smashed sixteen cars in five minutes* and *probably painted the President's portrait at the palace*.

You will no doubt have noticed that the subdivision of sentences into Subjects and Predicates is very rough-and-ready and can be established quite mechanically. You will also have noticed that the strings of words you identified as Predicates in the exercise above differ in their internal structure. We will need to account for these different internal structures and this we will do in later chapters.

Just now we saw that the Subject of a sentence is often defined as the unit that indicates who or what is engaged in carrying out the action specified by the verb, and also as the unit that tells you what the sentence is about. In each of the sentences we looked at so far the referent of the Subject was indeed engaged in performing the action denoted by the verb, and the Subject also indicated what the sentence was about. However, referents of Subjects need not always be *doing* something. Consider the sentences in (5)–(8) below and think about the question why they are problematic for our initial definition of the notion Subject:

(5)   *My brother* wears a green overcoat.
(6)   *The committee* disliked her proposal.
(7)   *The girl with the red hat* stood on the platform.
(8)   *This car* stinks.

Although the italicised Subjects do have a relationship with their Predicates, their referents cannot be said to be instigating any kind of action: 'wearing a coat', 'disliking a proposal', 'standing on a platform' and 'stinking' are not activities. What these sentences show, then, is that Subjects can also precede *stative* Predicates. The Predicates we have encountered up to now, by contrast, were *dynamic*.

Our initial definition of the notion Subject turns out to be problematic in another respect: in addition to the referent of a Subject sometimes not performing any kind of action, Subjects can be elements that are meaningless, and cannot therefore be said to tell us what the sentences of which they are the Subject are about. Consider the following:

(9)   *It* is raining in England.
(10)   *It* was hot.
(11)   *There* were three lions in the cage.
(12)   *There* exist ways of making you talk.

The element *it* in (9) and (10) is often called *weather it*, because it is used in expressions which tell us about the weather. It is also called *nonreferential it*. This second term brings out the important fact that this element does not refer to anything in the way that *referential it* in (13) does:

(13)   Where did I put my hat? Ah, I put *it* in the car.

Here *it* refers back to the string of words *my hat*, which in its turn refers to a concrete object in the real world.

There in sentences (11) and (12) is called *existential there* because it is used in propositions that have to do with existence. Existential *there* should be kept apart from *locative there* which, as the name implies, specifies a location, as in (14):

(14)   I saw the cat a minute ago. *There* it is!

Nonreferential *it* and existential *there* are said to be meaningless because all they seem to be doing in the sentences in which they occur is fill the Subject slot. It would be odd to say that *it* and *there* tell us what (9)–(12) are about.

What emerges from (5)–(12) is that although our earlier (semantic) definition of Subject is practical and useful, we must use it only as a general guideline. If we want to define the notion Subject more precisely, we will need to do so in structural terms, i.e. in terms of syntactic configurations.

The first thing to note about the Subjects of the sentences we have looked at so far is that they predominantly consist of groups of words whose most important element denotes a person (*that stupid **waiter**, the **stuntman**, **she**, my **brother**, the **girl** with the red hair*), an animal (*the **cat**, the **rat***), a group of people (*the **police**, the **committee***), an institution (*this **factory***) or a thing (*this **car***). Anticipating the discussion in the next chapter, we will call such words *nouns*. Furthermore, we will refer to groups of words such as *the cat, that stupid waiter, the girl with the red hair*, etc. as *Noun Phrases (NPs)*. The generalisation we can now make is to say that Subjects are usually Noun Phrases.

Secondly, in straightforward run-of-the-mill sentences, i.e. those that are used to make a statement, the Subject is the first NP we come across.

Thirdly, Subjects are obligatory.

Fourthly, Subjects determine the form of the verb in such cases as the following:

(15)   She never *writes* home.
(16)   James always *sulks*.
(17)   This book *saddens* me.
(18)   Our neighbour *takes* his children to school in his car.

We say that the verbs (*write, sulk, sadden, take*) in these sentences *agree* with the Subjects (*she, James, this book, our neighbour*). This agreement is visible through the *-s* ending on the verbs. Such agreement occurs only if we have a third person singular Subject. Such a Subject does not denote the speaker or the hearer (i.e. a third person is not me or you), but someone (or something) else. Any Subject other than a third person singular Subject takes what is called the *base form* of the verb, i.e. a form of the verb that has no endings:

(19)   I *like* tea.
(20)   You *like* tea.
(21)   We *like* tea.
(22)   They *like* tea.

Here we have Subject-verb agreement as well, though it is not visible as an ending on the verb.

Before presenting a fifth characteristic of Subjects, compare the sentences in (23)–(26) with those in (27)–(30):

(23)   This teacher is a genius.
(24)   The kids have arrived safely.
(25)   Your brother can be serious.
(26)   Our parents should inform the police.

(27)   Is this teacher a genius?
(28)   Have the kids arrived safely?
(29)   Can your brother be serious?
(30)   Should our parents inform the police?

(23)–(26) are straightforward sentences, each of which makes a statement about some state of affairs in the world. The sentences in (27)–(30) are concerned with asking questions. More specifically: they are used to ask questions which elicit either a 'yes' or a 'no' response. Now, the fifth characteristic of Subjects is that in sentences which are used to ask questions with 'yes' or 'no' as an answer, the Subject changes position: the verb is then in the initial slot of the sentence and the Subject is in the second slot. I will return to questions in Chapter 4.

Finally, we can identify the Subject of a sentence by adding a so-called *tag question* to it. A tag question, as the name implies, is a short question that is tagged onto a statement. One of its uses is to seek the hearer's confirmation of what is being stated. If we add tag questions to (23)–(26) we derive (31)–(34):

(31)   *This teacher* is a genius, isn't *she*?
(32)   *The kids* have arrived safely, haven't *they*?
(33)   *Your brother* can be serious, can't *he*?
(34)   *Our parents* should inform the police, shouldn't *they*?

The generalisation is that the Subject of a sentence is identified by the unit which is being referred back to by means of words like *she, they, he, they* in a tag question. As we will see in the next chapter, these words are all *pronouns*, so another way of expressing the generalisation above is to say that a tag question must contain a pronoun that identifies the Subject of the sentence it is tagged onto.

The six tests we have just looked at are all *distributional* tests. This means that they define the notion of Subject by referring to syntactic positions and environments in sentences, rather than to rather vague semantic notions.

In most cases, if we apply the semantic and syntactic criteria discussed above *in conjunction* we can unambiguously identify the constituent that functions as Subject in a particular sentence. If we apply only the semantic criteria, this can lead to an incorrect identification of some constituent as Subject, or we may possibly not even be able to identify a Subject at all. We have already come across some examples of this happening. In (5)–(8) above, if we were to use only our semantic characterisation of the notion Subject as the unit in the sentence that refers to the entity that performs the action denoted by the verb, then we would be led to conclude that these sentences do not contain a Subject. The reason is that they do not contain a constituent that can be said to refer to an entity that performs an action. In (9)–(12) the units we identified as Subjects again do not refer to entities that do something, and additionally, unlike the Subjects in (5)–(8), can also not be said to be the topics of the sentences in which they occur. However, if we also apply one or more of the distributional tests we discussed, then we have no problems in identifying the Subjects of sentences. Take example (5), repeated here:

(35)   My brother wears a green overcoat.

My brother is the Subject of this sentence for the following reasons:

(i)   This constituent is a Noun Phrase.
(ii)   It is the *first* NP in the sentence.
(iii)   It is obligatory: **wears a green overcoat* is not a possible sentence
(iv)   *My brother* is a third person singular phrase and the verb *wear* agrees with it, witness the *-s* ending.

(v)   In a question *my brother* swaps places with an inserted verb *does*: *Does my brother wear a green overcoat?* (I will have more to say on the insertion of *do* in the next chapter.)

(vi)   If we add a tag question to (35) we must include a pronoun (in this case *he*), and this pronoun refers back to *my brother*: *My brother wears a green overcoat, doesn't **he**?*

Let's look at a further example that might at first sight appear to be problematic as regards finding its Subject. Consider (36):

(36)   Last night, the teachers were very drunk.

Exercise

What do you think is the Subject of the sentence in (36)?

First of all, notice that the referents of the NPs *last night* and *the teachers* are not engaged in doing something. We cannot therefore use agenthood as a diagnostic for subjecthood. Furthermore, despite the fact that arguably 'last night' is what the sentence is about, and despite the fact that this string of words is not only an NP, but also the *first* NP in the sentence, the Subject is in fact the NP *the teachers*. The following are the reasons for this:

(i)   The NP *the teachers* is obligatory, the NP *last night* is not: **Last night were very drunk./The teachers were very drunk.* The fact that *last night* can be left out indicates that this NP plays a peripheral role in the sentence. Further evidence for the peripherality of *last night* lies in the fact that it is followed by a comma. This comma indicates a pause in the pronunciation of the sentence and sets *last night* apart from what follows. Subjects are never peripheral; they play an integral part in every sentence. Notice also that *last night* can be moved to the end of the sentence: *The teachers were very drunk last night.*

(ii)   It is the plural NP *the teachers* that determines the form of the verb *be*. We can't have a singular verb-form: **Last night the teachers was very drunk.* If *last night* had been the Subject, the verb-form *was* would have been expected.

(iii)   In a yes/no interrogative sentence it is the NP *the teachers* that swaps places with *were*: *Last night, were the teachers very drunk?*

(iv)   In the tagged version of (36) *they* refers back to *the teachers* not to *last night*: *Last night, the teachers were very drunk, weren't **they**?* The tag *wasn't it?* in which *it* would refer back to *last night* is impossible: **Last night the teachers were very drunk, wasn't **it**?*

Exercise

Using one or more of the criteria we have discussed, find the Subjects of the sentences below:

(i)   My friend travelled around the world on a bicycle.
(ii)   It was freezing cold in Moscow.
(iii)   The supporters of the football club down the road destroyed our fence.
(iv)   In the Middles Ages people often burnt books.
(v)   There is a rat in the room.
(vi)   Yesterday at midnight Harry fell down the stairs.

The Subjects are the following phrases: *my friend, it, the supporters of the football club down the road, people, there, Harry.*

2.2   Predicator

So far we have looked at the way in which the bracketed strings in (37) and (38) function:

(37)   [The cat]   [devoured the rat].   = (1)
       Subject   Predicate

(38)   [The rat]   [devoured the cat].   = (2)
       Subject   Predicate

We should now take a closer look at the elements *inside* the Predicate. Can we assign further functions to them? Yes, we can. In each of the Predicates above there is a verb, *devoured*, and a Noun Phrase, namely *the rat* and *the cat*, respectively. Here we will concentrate on the function of the verb. We will say that *devoured* in (37) and (38) functions as *Predicator*. Predicators are pivotal elements which specify what we could call the bare-bone content of the sentences in which they occur, that is, the main action or process denoted by the verb. As their name suggests, Predicators are in the business of *predicating* something, i.e. saying something of something else. Thus, the bare-bone content of (37) and (38) is 'devouring'. This devouring activity is predicated of the Subjects of these sentences, which specify who was engaged in the activity of devouring. The NPs that specify what was being devoured have a function we haven't discussed so far, and we turn to it in the next section. Be careful to distinguish Predicates from Predicators.

We can now refine (37) and (38) as follows:

(37′)   [The cat]   [devoured the rat]
        Subject   Predicator
                         |—Predicate——|

(38′)   [The rat]   [devoured the cat]
        Subject   Predicator
                         |—Predicate——|

2.3   Direct Object

After our discussion of Subjects, Predicates and Predicators we now turn to a fourth type of grammatical function: the *Direct Object (DO)*. Consider the following sentences:

(39)   His girlfriend bought this computer.
(40)   That silly fool broke the teapot.
(41)   Our linguistics lecturer took this photograph.
(42)   My sister found this book.

The Subjects of these sentences are the first NPs in each case: *his girlfriend, that silly fool, our linguistics lecturer* and *my sister*. The Predicates are: *bought this computer, broke the teapot, took this photograph* and *found this book*. The Predicators are: *bought, broke, took* and *found*.

We now assign the function of Direct Object to the NPs *this computer, the teapot, this photograph* and *this book*.

How can we characterise the notion Direct Object? In semantic terms Direct Objects are said to be constituents that refer to entities that *undergo* the activity or process denoted by the verb. In (39) the referent of the NP *this computer* undergoes a buying activity, in (40) the referent of the NP *the teapot* undergoes a breaking process, in (41) the referent of *this photograph* undergoes a picture-taking process, and, finally, in (42) the referent of *this book* undergoes a process of being found.

The characterisation of Direct Objects I have just given is in terms of the kind of role they play in sentences: in the same way that Subjects typically play an *agentive* (i.e. instigator) role, Direct Objects have a *Patient* role (though of course not in the medical sense!). As we have just seen, what this means is that the referent of the constituent that we can identify as Direct Object typically undergoes the action or process denoted by the verb. However, although this semantic characterisation is useful, and in most cases enables us to find the Direct Object of a sentence, we will also need to define DOs syntactically, i.e. in terms of their structural properties.

So what can we say about the structural properties of Direct Objects? Well, like Subjects, DOs are often Noun Phrases (though not exclusively, as we will see in Chapter 5). Secondly, their usual position, as (39)–(42) show, is after the main verb. Thirdly, Direct Objects have a strong relationship with the verb that precedes them. Recall my discussion in Chapter 1 of the sentence in (43):

(43)   Our vicar likes fast cars.

We saw that the verb *like* requires the presence of a Noun Phrase. We can now be a little more precise and say that *like* requires a *Direct Object Noun Phrase*. In (39)–(42) we have the same situation: each of the verbs in these sentences requires the presence of a Direct Object. If the DO is left out, the results are bad:

(44)   *His girlfriend bought.
(45)   *This silly fool broke.
(46)   *Our linguistics lecturer took.
(47)   *My sister found.

We will say that a verb that requires a Direct Object to complement its meaning is a *transitive verb*.

Not all verbs are transitive. We also have *intransitive verbs*. These are verbs that do not need a following constituent to complete their meaning. Below are some sentences whose main verb is intransitive:

(48)   William blushed.
(49)   Sean cried.
(50)   Thomas slept.
(51)   Lee dreamt.
(52)   Garry jumped.

Unlike in the case of (44)–(47), we do not have a sense of incompleteness with these sentences.

Some verbs appear to be able to function both transitively and intransitively, as the sentences in (53) and (54) show:

(53)a   Harold moved the table.
    b   Harold moved.

(54)a   Jake walked the dog.
    b   Jake walked.

Saying that in each case the verb can function both transitively and intransitively amounts to saying that we have two different verbs *move* and two different verbs *walk*. Following dictionary practice, let's call these two sets of verbs *move$_1$/move$_2$*

and *walk₁*/*walk₂*. *Move₁* and *walk₁* in (53)a and (54)a are transitive, whereas *move₂* and *walk₂* in (53)b and (54)b are intransitive. Positing the existence of two verbs *move* is not implausible given the fact that the meaning of *move* in (53)a is different from the meaning of *move* in (53)b, witness the fact that we can substitute another verb, for example *displace*, for *move* in (53)a, but not in (53)b: *Harold displaced the table/*Harold displaced*. A change of meaning can also be detected in contrasting (54)a with (54)b. We can replace *walk* in (54)a by the near-equivalent *escort*, but not in (54)b: *Jake escorted the dog/*Jake escorted*.

Consider now (55) and (56):

(55)a   Goneril was reading a book.
   b   Goneril was reading.

(56)a   Pat was eating a sandwich.
   b   Pat was eating.

Here again we might surmise that we have two verbs *read* and two verbs *eat*. However, more plausibly, we might say that although the Direct Object is missing in (55)b, it is nevertheless felt to be there. After all, Goneril must have been reading *something*. The same is true for (56)b. Rather than positing the existence of two different verbs in (55) and (56) we will say that the Direct Objects here are *understood* or *implicit*. This solution is preferable because in the a- and b-sentences of (55) and (56) the meanings of *read* and *eat* stay constant.

So far we have seen that Direct Objects are constituents that are closely related to the verb that precedes them. A fourth syntactic characteristic of DOs is brought out by comparing the a-sentences below with the b-sentences:

(57)a   His girlfriend bought *this computer*.
   b   *This computer* was bought by his girlfriend.

(58)a   That silly fool broke *the teapot*.
   b   *The teapot* was broken by that silly fool.

(59)a   Our linguistics lecturer took *this photograph*.
   b   *This photograph* was taken by our linguistics lecturer.

(60)a   My sister found *this book*.
   b   *This book* was found by my sister.

What is happening here? Clearly, in each of these cases the a-sentence is related to the b-sentence. The question is: how? We will refer to the a-sentences as being *active*, and to the b-sentences as being *passive*. Active sentences present their Subject as being actively engaged in something, whereas passive sentences present their Subject as undergoing something. (This, incidentally, is another reason for not defining Subjects exclusively as Agents.) As for the syntactic differences between active and passive sentences, notice that the italicised Direct Objects of the a-sentences are the Subjects of the b-sentences. This is quite a regular alternation in English, so much so that linguists have attempted to set up a rule to capture it. The basic insight of this rule is the observation that if we turn an active sentence into a passive sentence, the Direct Object of the active sentence becomes the Subject of the passive sentence. Furthermore, the Subject of the active sentence ends up in a phrase introduced by the word *by*. Notice that in each of the passive sentences a form of the verb *be* has appeared (in the guise of *was* in these particular cases).

Exercise

Produce passive versions of the following active sentences:

(i)   We drank this bottle of coke.
(ii)   My son found a wallet.
(iii)   The inspectors checked the tickets.
(iv)   This store sells only silk shirts.

You should not have experienced any problems in producing the passives of these sentences. They are: *This bottle of coke was drunk by us, A wallet was found by my son, The tickets were checked by the inspectors* and *Only silk shirts are sold by this store.*

We saw above that Direct Objects complete the meaning of the verbs that precede them. Another way of putting this is to say that Direct Objects function as *Complements* to verbs. When we talk about Complements we're using a cover term to denote any constituent whose presence is required by another element. As we saw in sentences like (39)–(42) and (44)–(47), Direct Objects are required to the extent that they typically complete the meaning of an active verb. They are not the only units that can function as Complements of verbs, though. I will now discuss an additional type of Complement, *Indirect Objects.*

2.4   Indirect Object

In this section we will be looking at a further type of verbal Complement: *Indirect Objects (IOs)*. In the sentences below the IOs have been italicised:

(61)   We gave *the boys* the CDs.
(62)   The publisher sent *her* a review copy of the book.
(63)   She lent *the student* a diskette.
(64)   My father always told *us* stories.

When we discussed Subjects and Direct Objects in the previous sections, we saw that Subjects typically have the role of *Agent* and that Direct Objects typically have the role of *Patient/Undergoer*. In (61)–(64) the typical role associated with the italicised Indirect Objects is *Goal/Receiver* or *Beneficiary*. Notice that (61)–(64) also contain Direct Objects, namely the phrases *the CDs*, *a review copy of the book*, *a diskette* and *stories*. Verbs that take a Direct Object *and* an Indirect Object are called *ditransitive verbs*.

Apart from their semantic properties, Indirect Objects have a number of syntactic characteristics.

Firstly, they are usually Noun Phrases.

Secondly, they cannot occur without a following Direct Object. Compare the sentences in (65)–(68) with those in (61)–(64): if we leave out the Direct Objects the sentences become ungrammatical.

(65)   *We gave the boys.
(66)   *The publisher sent her.
(67)   *She lent the student.
(68)   *My father always told us.

Of course, (65)–(66) *are* possible, but only if we interpret the NPs following the verbs as Direct Objects.

Thirdly, Indirect Objects always precede Direct Objects. We cannot have the sentences in (69)–(72) where the order of IOs and DOs has been reversed:

(69)   *We gave the CDs the boys.
(70)   *The publisher sent a review copy of the book her.
(71)   *She lent a diskette the student.
(72)   *My father always told stories us.

Notice that we can 'repair' the sentences in (69)–(72) by adding the word *to*:

(73)   We gave the CDs *to the boys*.
(74)   The publisher sent a review copy of the book *to her*.
(75)   She lent a diskette *to the student*.
(76)   My father told stories *to us*.

A final syntactic characteristic of Indirect Objects is that, like DOs, they can become the Subjects of passive sentences. Compare (77)–(80) with (61)–(64):

(77)   *The boys* were given the CDs by us.
(78)   *She* was sent a review copy of the book by the publisher.
(79)   *The student* was lent a diskette by her.
(80)   *We* were always told stories by our father.

Notice that the Subject of the active sentence again ends up in a *by*-phrase. The Direct Objects stay in place.

Now, compare (77)–(80) with (81)–(84):

(81)   *The CDs* were given to the boys by us.
(82)   *A review copy of the book* was sent to her by the publisher.
(83)   *A diskette* was lent to the student by her.
(84)   *Stories* were always told to us by our father.

Here the Direct Objects of (61)–(64), rather than the Indirect Objects, have become the Subjects of passive sentences. In passivising (61)–(64) to become (81)–(84), not only have the Direct Objects of active sentences become the Subjects of passive sentences, another change has occurred: the Indirect Objects have ended up in phrases beginning with *to*: *to the boys*, *to her*, *to the student* and *to us*. The generalisation is that if we passivise the Direct Object of a sentence which also contains an Indirect Object, then the Indirect Object ends up in a *to*-phrase.

2.5   Adjunct

We turn now to a final grammatical function. Consider the following sentences:

(85)   The bus stopped *suddenly*.
(86)   Shakespeare wrote his plays *a long time ago*.
(87)   They went to the theatre *in London*.
(88)   He hates maths *because he can't understand it*.

The italicised strings of words in these sentences have the function of telling us about the *how*, *when*, *where* or *why* of the situations expressed by the respective sentences. Constituents that have this function we will call *Adjuncts*. We can test to see if a particular sentence contains an Adjunct by asking *how?*, *when?*, *where?* or *why?* For example, if we want to know what is the Adjunct in (85) we ask 'how did the bus stop?'. The answer is 'suddenly', and this phrase therefore functions as an Adjunct. Similarly, in (86) we can ask 'when did Shakespeare write his plays?'. The answer is 'a long time ago'. Adjuncts are always optional, and express peripheral information.

Another characteristic of Adjuncts is that they can be 'stacked', which means that more than one of them can appear in a sentence:

(89)   *Last year* I saw this film *several times*.

Finally, Adjuncts are mobile, as the following examples show:

(90)   *Greedily* André ate all the biscuits.
(91)   André *greedily* ate all the biscuits.
(92)   André ate all the biscuits *greedily*.

Notice, though, that the position between the main verb and Direct Object is excluded:

(93)   *André ate *greedily* all the biscuits.

In Chapter 7 we will distinguish between sentence-level Adjuncts and phrase-level Adjuncts.

Key Concepts in this Chapter

Functions:

Subject
Predicate
Predicator
Complement
   Direct Object
   Indirect Object
Adjunct

In this book all function names will be written with a capital letter. Remember that functional labels are mutually exclusive: if a string of word is a Subject, it cannot also be a DO, or an Adjunct or anything else.

Exercises

NB: In this book the exercises are graded, such that the starred ones are slightly more difficult.

1.   Assign function labels (Subject, Direct Object, Adjunct, etc.) to the italicised phrases in the following sentences:

    (i)   *Greg* opened *a can of Coke*.
    (ii)   *She* arrived *last week*.
    (iii)   You will need *a comprehensive travel insurance*.
    (iv)   Who *said* that?
    (v)   Benny *worked* in a shoe factory *when he was a student*.
    (vi)   *Who* will do the cleaning?
    (vii)   *The lecturer from France who talked about Wittgenstein yesterday* left.

2.   Construct sentences containing:

    (i)   a Subject, a Predicator, an Indirect Object and a Direct Object
    (ii)   a Subject, a Predicator, a Direct Object and an Adjunct

(iii)   a Subject, a Predicator and an Adjunct
(iv)   a Subject and a Predicator

3. In the text we said that Subjects are obligatory. In this context, discuss the sentence in (i) below:

(i)   Read Chapter 5 for tomorrow's class.

Is this an exception? Motivate your answer.

(Sentence (i) is an *imperative* which will be discussed further in Section 4.3)

4. True or false? In the sentence This summer all the students will have vacation jobs in their home towns:

(i)   the Subject is *this summer*
(ii)   *this summer* is an Adjunct
(iii)   *vacation jobs* is an Indirect Object
(iv)   *all the students* is the Subject
(v)   *in their home towns* functions as Adjunct
(vi)   the Direct Object is *vacation jobs*

5. Underline the Adjunct(s) (if any) in the sentences below:

(i)   Gradually, the train accelerated.
(ii)   It finally hurtled through the landscape at great speed.
(iii)   Then, suddenly there was a loud bang at the back of the train.
(iv)   It startled all of us.
(v)   It turned out that there had been an animal on the tracks.
(vi)   Why does this happen each time I travel?

*6. Consider the sentence in (i):

(i)   In August we always go *to France*.

What would you say is the function of the italicised string? Give reasons for your answer.

*7. In the text we saw that there are reasons for saying that the verb *move* in (i) below is different from the verb *move* in (ii):

(i)   Harold moved the table.   (= 53a)
(ii)   Harold moved.   (= 53b)

The reason for having two verbs was that *move* in (i) means 'displace', whereas it means something like 'stir' in (ii). However, you may want to argue that *move* in fact is exactly like *read* and *eat* discussed in the same section, if we simply assume that *move* in (ii) involves an implied DO, namely *himself*. Sentence (ii) above would then mean 'Harold moved/displaced himself'. Is this a plausible line of reasoning? Give reasons for your answer.

*8. Why is assigning the grammatical function of Direct Object to the italicised strings in the sentences below problematic? Is there another function we can assign instead?

(i)   This computer weighs *twenty kilograms.*
(ii)   Each of these oranges costs *ten pence.*
(iii) The information booklet contains *four pages.*
(iv)   That jacket suits *you.*

*9. Apply the criteria for subjecthood presented in Section 2.1 to the sentence in (i) below:

(i)   There is a rat in the kitchen.

You will have reached the conclusion that the Subject is *there*. How can we square this conclusion with the fact that it doesn't make sense to say that *there* 'is' in the kitchen, whereas it *does* make sense to say that *a rat* 'is' in the kitchen? In other words, wouldn't it make more sense to say that *a rat* is the Subject in (i)?

Further Reading

For other overviews of grammatical functions consult a major grammar of English, such as Quirk et al. (1985), Huddleston (1984) or Huddleston and Pullum et al. (2002). You will also find the reference works listed at the end of this book useful. When you consult these books, be aware of the fact that there are variations in the use of grammatical terminology. For example, Quirk et al. use two additional functional labels, namely Subject Complement and Object Complement, which we have not adopted (see Chapter 10). Also, the term 'Adjunct' is used by them in a narrower sense than in this book. For them an Adjunct is one type of *Adverbial*, along with Disjuncts, Conjuncts and Subjuncts. Huddleston (1984) uses the term 'Adjunct' more or less in the same way as I have done here, but there are differences too.

In Section 2.1 I assumed that 'weather *it*' is meaningless. Not all linguists would agree with this; see, for example, Bolinger (1977) for a diverging view.

3 Form: Words, Word Classes and Phrases

In this chapter we'll take a closer look at the smallest building blocks of syntax, namely words. We will see how they can be grouped into word classes and how they form phrases, which in turn combine into sentences. In the next chapter we will look at clauses and the way these too combine into sentences, but in a different way from phrases. Some of the concepts and ideas introduced in this chapter will only be dealt with in a preliminary way, and will receive more attention in later chapters.

3.1 The Notion 'Word'

So far I have only mentioned words in passing. You may have thought this strange, because surely the most obvious way to divide a sentence up is into words. This is true, but as we will see later in this chapter, it is not the most interesting way to do it. Trying to define the notion 'word' is not easy. This may surprise you, as words seem to be straightforward enough entities. To give you some idea of the problems we might encounter in trying to characterise words as linguistic units, consider (1)–(3) below:

(1)   dog, dogs
(2)   eat, eats
(3)   duty-free

Nobody would have any hesitation in calling what we have in (1) two separate words. *Dogs* is different from *dog*, because it looks different: it has an -*s* ending added to it. However, if you think about it, there is also a sense in which *dogs* is the *same* word as *dog*, in that it is simply its plural. Let us say that *dog* and *dogs* belong to the same *lexeme*, or dictionary entry. This reflects the sense in which they are the same word. At the same time they are different *word-forms* or *orthographic words*. We can make the distinction clear by drawing an analogy: a Boeing 747 and a Boeing 767 are the same to the extent that they are both aeroplanes, but they are different to the extent that the 747 has a different shape and size from the 767. Thus, the 747 and the 767 both belong to the 'aeronautic lexeme' *aeroplane*, but at the same time are different 'aeroplane-forms'. We can make the same point for *eat* and *eats* in (2): both of these belong to the verbal lexeme *eat*, but are different verb-forms. What about (3)? Here we seem to have two words *duty* and *free*, but they are so closely linked in many contexts (cf. *duty-free shop, duty-free alcohol, duty-free allowance*, etc.) that they feel like one word, hence the hyphen. We need not worry about these problems inordinately, as they really belong to the domain of *morphology*, the study of the internal structure of words. For our purposes it will do to use 'word' in the sense of 'word-form', unless stated otherwise. We can then say that the sentence in (4) below consists of nine words:

(4)   The President regularly eats big doughnuts in his limousine.

Rather than counting the words contained in (4) (which in itself is not very interesting), it is far more worthwhile to investigate how these words could be said to be syntactically different from each other. Intuitively, the word *regularly* is different from the word *eats* and this word is different again from *doughnuts*. But how are they different? To explain the differences linguists have proposed various ways of classifying words. The kind of classification that is chosen depends on one's aims. For example, lexicographers (people who write dictionaries) are interested in arranging words alphabetically, and pairing them off with their pronunciation and meaning (and sometimes etymology). If we are interested in the history of a language, we might want to group words into an *open class* (i.e. a class of words that is constantly enlarged as time goes by) and a *closed class* (i.e. a class of words that is static, in that no new members are added to it). In this book we will be using a system of word classification that goes back to the ancient grammarians. It groups the words of languages into *word classes* (also called *parts of speech*). We will make use of the following word classes:

noun
determinative
adjective
verb
preposition
adverb
conjunction
interjection

The word classes are notions of *form*, as opposed to the *functional* notions we looked at in the preceding chapter. Let us now take a closer look at each of the word classes listed above in turn.

3.2   Nouns and Determinatives

Traditionally nouns are defined as words that denote people, animals, things or places. This definition enables us to identify *Jim, dog, aeroplane, teacher, chair, London*, etc. as nouns. A description like this is called a *notional definition*, because it offers a characterisation, in this case of a word class, in terms of concepts of meaning. A problem with the notional definition of nouns is that it leaves a great number of words unaccounted for, which could also be said to belong to the class of nouns, but which do not denote people, animals, things or places. These include words that denote abstract ideas or concepts (e.g. *death, sincerity, success*), emotional states (e.g. *happiness, love*), bodily sensations (e.g. *dizziness, pain*) and a host of others. Of course, we could keep on extending our notional definition in such a way that eventually all these words would be incorporated into the class of nouns. However, our definition would then become so stretched and vague that we would end up with little more than a list of nouns. It should be obvious that a list cannot serve as a definition of the concept noun. Why not? Well, for one, lists are seldom very interesting by themselves. What we would want to know is *why* a particular item is on a list together with other items, and why other items are not on the list. In the case of nouns we would want to know why all the italicised words above are on the list of nouns, but not, say, *hot, eat* or *through*. The problem with lists, then, is that they have no explanatory value. A related serious problem with lists is that they lead to circular reasoning: why is *car* a noun? Because it is on the list of nouns. Why is it on the list? Because it's a noun. This gets us nowhere. A far better approach is to characterise nouns using *formal* and *distributional* criteria. Under this view we look at the shape words can take, at where they can occur in sentences, and at the way they behave and function in sentential patterns. Let's see how this works by discussing a few examples. Consider the words in (5), (6) and (7) below:

(5)   alliance, defiance, reliance
        bachelorhood, fatherhood, preacherhood
        abolition, demarcation, indication
        darkness, kindness, wildness
        lectureship, tutorship, studentship

(6)   actor – actors
        door – doors
        lamp – lamps
        room – rooms
        table – tables

(7)   man – man's
        pub – pub's
        sister – sister's

The items in (5) show that different words can have similar endings, or *suffixes* as they are known in morphology. Suffixes, and their positional counterparts *prefixes*, belong to the class of *affixes*. Thus, to return to (5), notice that all the words in the first set of three words have the suffix *-ance*. The words of the

second set all end in -*hood*, whereas those of the third, fourth and fifth sets end in
-*tion*, -*ness* and –*ship*, respectively. These are only five of quite a number of typical
noun endings. The point here is that sometimes, by looking at the morphological
make-up of words, we can tell to which word class they belong. The words in (6)
and (7) illustrate a similar point: in (6) we have plural endings, indicating that we
have more than one item of a kind, whereas in (7) we have *genitive* endings which
usually, though not exclusively, indicate possession (e.g. *the man's clothes, the pub's
clientele, my sister's cat*). Plural and genitive endings are also typical of nouns.

It turns out, however, that morphological criteria are only of limited value.
For example, many nouns do not end in any of the typical nominal suffixes such
as -*ance*, -*hood*, -*ion*, -*ness* (e.g. *arm, book, rain, lamp*); some take an irregular
plural ending (e.g. *child – children, ox – oxen*), etc.

If semantic (i.e. notional) and morphological criteria are inadequate, then it
seems that what we have left are distributional criteria. As we will see, these are
in fact the most reliable. Recall that when we talk about distributional criteria,
we are referring to the way in which words, in this particular case nouns, behave
syntactically in sentences, i.e. the patterns they typically occur in. For example,
we might observe that all the words we have labelled as nouns can be preceded by
words such as *the, a, this/these, that/those*, etc. These words belong to the class
of *determinatives* which specify more precisely the meaning of the nouns they
precede. Here's a list of the most common determinatives in English with a few
examples:

determinative	example
the/a	*the/a camera*
this/these	*this film/these films*
that/those	*that dog/those dogs*
which	*which house?*
whose	*whose neighbours?*

Nouns can also be preceded by *adjectives*; for example, *nice, difficult, strong* (as
in *a nice person, a difficult problem, a strong box*). These are words that in some
way qualify the nouns they precede (see Section 3.3 below). What we are doing,
then, is defining a word class by characterising the environments that the members of that class (in this case nouns) typically occur in. As users of the language
we know when a particular word is a noun simply by virtue of its occurring in a
particular syntactic context. To give a further example, no word class other than
a noun could occur in the blank of the sentence *the . . . was wheel-clamped by the
police*. Of course, the fact that the word *car* or *motorcycle* can occur in this slot,
and that therefore they are nouns, is not something we consciously realise when
we hear this sentence, but it *is* something that must somehow be registered in
our brains in order for us to process the sentence mentally. We can illustrate
the idea of definition through context further by using an example from the real

world (as opposed to from the mental world to which the word classes belong). Consider the word *skyscraper*. We call buildings skyscrapers because of the form they take (they are usually tall and slender structures), but also, and especially, in relation to their physical environment: a skyscraper is only a skyscraper in relation to other less tall buildings. In fact, we could go so far as to say that the idea of a skyscraper only exists in relation to these other buildings: there would be no skyscrapers if there were no small buildings such as houses or churches. The same point holds true for grammatical concepts such as nouns and the other word classes: they only exist in relation to other words around them. There is no point in calling a word a noun, except to make clear the relationship that particular word has to other words in the sentence which behave differently.

I will now discuss ways in which we can set up a number of subclasses within the class of nouns. The table below shows the various different types of English nouns and examples of each of them. This classification is a common, though not uncontroversial, one.

Noun subclasses

Common nouns:

countable	*book, cat, fork, train*, etc.
non-countable	*butter, flour, jam, soap*, etc.

Proper nouns:

Jack, London, Cathy, Sarah, etc.

Pronouns:

general personal pronouns	*I/me, you/you, she/her, he/him, it/it, we/us, they/them*
	Note: The first form is the subjective form, the second the objective form.
'possessive' personal pronouns	*my/mine, your/yours, her/hers, his/his, our/ours, their/theirs*
	Note: The first form is the dependent form (before nouns; e.g. *my house*), functioning as Specifier (see Chapter 7). The second form is the independent form (occurring elsewhere; e.g. *the house is mine*).
reflexive personal pronouns	*myself, yourself, herself, himself, itself, ourselves, themselves*
reciprocal personal pronouns	*each other, one another*
demonstrative pronouns	*this/these, that/those*, e.g. *I like that.*
	Note: *This/these* and *that/those* are dependent forms when they occur before nouns (e.g. *this/that house*) belonging to the class of determinatives. They then function as Specifiers (see Chapter 7).
relative pronouns	*that*, e.g. *the book that I bought*

	who, e.g. *the woman who bought the CD*
	which, e.g. *the pen which he bought*
	Note: *Which* is a determinative functioning as a Specifier (see Chapter 7) when it occurs before a noun, e.g. *Which apple did you eat?* The same is true for *whose*, e.g. *Whose book is that?*
interrogative or *wh*-pronouns	*what*, e.g. What *did you eat?*
	which, e.g. Which *did you eat?*
	why, e.g. Why *did you eat it?*
	where, e.g. Where *did you eat it?*
	Note: *what* and *which* when they occur before a noun (*what/which book*) are determinatives, functioning as Specifiers (see Chapter 7).

As the name suggests, common nouns are ordinary, everyday nouns. Some of them can be counted (*one book/two books, one cat/three cats*, etc.), but others as a rule cannot (**one butter/*two butters, *one flour/*three flours*, etc.), and this accounts for the subdivision of the class in the table above. Proper nouns are names of people, places and even objects. In English they do not normally take a preceding determinative or modifying element (**the Jack, *a Sarah*), nor a plural ending (**the Janets*). I say 'normally' because in certain circumstances we can say, for example, *He's not the Jack I used to know* or *Would all the Janets in the room please raise their hand*). Proper nouns are examples of what are called *referring expressions*. This is because when they are uttered in a particular context, they uniquely refer to one individual (or place or object) in the world of discourse.

Pronouns are special, in fact so much so that some grammarians have argued that they ought to be put into a class of their own. Why should that be? Consider the word *pronoun* a little more closely. It is made up of two parts: *pro* and *noun*. The word *pro* is Latin for *for* and so really what *pronoun* means is 'for a noun' or 'instead of a noun'. In other words, the label *pronoun* suggests that these words function as noun substitutes. And this indeed seems to be the case, as an example will make clear. Consider the following sentence:

(8)   Jim walked into the room and everybody stared at *him*.

Notice that here the personal pronoun *him* can refer either to Jim or to some other male individual mentioned in a preceding (but here omitted) context. However, the most likely interpretation of this isolated sentence is to take the pronoun to refer to *Jim*. We can now say that *him* substitutes for *Jim*. For this reason (8) could also have been read as in (9) (assuming that there is only one *Jim*):

(9)   Jim walked into the room and everybody stared at Jim.

However, although (9) is perfectly intelligible, it is stylistically very clumsy, and this is precisely because we've used the name *Jim* twice. In order to avoid this repetition, we use the pro-noun *him*. Pronouns derive their referential content from nouns. In (8) *Jim* is a referring expression. In order to be able to interpret the pronoun *him* we need to link it to *Jim* (*him* is then said to be *bound* to *Jim*), or to some other male person, identified by the context of utterance.

So far so good, but matters are a little more complicated than I have made them out to be. I've been cheating a little by offering sentence (8) as an example of pronouns as noun substitutes. To see why, consider (10) below:

(10)   The exhibition was a success. It ran for six months.

Exercise

Which expression does the pronoun *it* refer to here?

If your answer to this question was *exhibition* then you were wrong, because in fact *it* refers back to *the exhibition*, i.e. a determinative + noun sequence. Such determinative + noun sequences, as we already saw briefly in Chapter 2, are called *Noun Phrases (NPs)*, so really pronouns are strictly speaking not pro-nouns, but pro-NPs (even in (8), as we will see in a moment). The concept 'phrase' is extremely important in syntax and I will discuss some of the properties of phrases in general later on in the book. Here we'll take a closer look at Noun Phrases.

We can define Noun Phrases as strings of words whose central element is a noun. All the following are therefore NPs:

(11)a   the *hats*
    b   the blue *hats*
    c   the blue *hats* on the shelf

In each of these strings of words the central element is the noun *hats*. Let's refer to this central element in a phrase as its *Head*. Notice that this word is spelt with a capital letter, indicating that it is a functional notion. Heads function as the central elements of phrases.

As you can see from the examples in (11), Noun Phrases can become very long, indefinitely long in fact, if we keep adding elements. But they can also consist of only a Head, as in (12):

(12)   [$_{NP}$ *Hats*] have always been fashionable.

Here we have an NP consisting of an unadorned plural nominal Head.

At this point you may be wondering why I am labelling *hats* in (12) as a Noun Phrase, rather than as a simple plural noun. The motivation for this is distributional: it is because the slot in (12) in which *hats* occurs can be filled by what is clearly an NP that we also want to call *hats* in (12) an NP. We can substitute any of the NPs in (11) for *hats* in (12). (13) shows two further possibilities of expanding the NP *hats*:

(13)a   *These hats* have always been fashionable.
   b   *Hats that you buy at Harrods* have always been fashionable.

In (13)a the Head is preceded by a determinative ('only the hats here in front of us are fashionable'), while in the b-sentence a further specification has been added to the Head noun ('not just any old hat is fashionable, only hats that you buy at Harrods'). As we saw in the previous chapter, the sentence-initial (Subject) position in which these NPs occur is a typical Noun Phrase position. So, on the grounds that we can expand *hats* in (12) into a larger string of words which is clearly an NP, and because it occurs in a typical NP position, we say that *hats* too is not just a noun, but a Noun Phrase.

We turn now to a word class that often plays a role in Noun Phrases: adjectives.

3.3   Adjectives

We have already come across a few adjectives as words that can modify nouns: a **beautiful** spring, a **careless** attitude, a **constructive** criticism, an **unsavoury** lecturer, a **green** car, an **impertinent** remark, etc.

As with nouns, adjectives can sometimes be identified through certain formal characteristics: in the examples above the suffixes *-ful*, *-less* and *-ive* are typical adjectival affixes, among others, as is the prefix *un-*. The adjectives *green* and *impertinent*, however, make clear that not all adjectives have such endings.

Most adjectives are gradable, i.e. they can be preceded by words such as *very*, *extremely*, *less*, etc. (cf. *very helpful*, *extremely nasty*, *less interesting*) which indicate the extent to which the adjective applies to the word it combines with. Exceptions are normally adjectives denoting material (e.g. *wooden*, cf. **a very wooden floor*), nationality (e.g. *Russian*, cf. **an extremely Russian book*), and a few others, though see Exercise 11!

Adjectives can also take *comparative* and *superlative* endings. The comparative form of an adjective indicates the greater extent to which the normal form of the adjective, called the *absolute form*, applies, while the superlative form indicates the maximal extent (cf. *big–bigger–biggest*). Here are some further examples:

(14) **Absolute form**	**Comparative form**	**Superlative form**
great	great*er*	great*est*
full	full*er*	fulle*st*
good	better	best

You will have noticed that the forms *good–better–best* are exceptional. This is because there is no resemblance between the absolute and the other forms of the adjective. We speak of *suppletion* when grammatically related words bear no physical resemblance to each other, while this is the norm for other words related in the same way.

Not all gradable adjectives are able to form comparative and superlative forms with *-er* and *-est*. Some adjectives form comparatives and superlatives *analytically*. What this means is that there is no single word-form for the comparative and superlative. Instead, the words *more* and *most* are used. This is the case for quite a few adjectives. Examples are *beautiful, eager, hopeless, interesting, practical*, etc. The general rule is that adjectives with two or more syllables take analytical comparative and superlative forms. We will return to comparative and superlative forms later in the chapter, when we come to discuss adverbs.

We now turn to the distributional characteristics of adjectives. The first thing to notice is that adjectives typically occupy two positions in English: the *attributive position* and the *predicative position*. When an adjective precedes a noun in a Noun Phrase, it is said to occur in attributive position. It then supplies more information about the character, nature or state of the noun. We've already come across examples of adjectives modifying nouns at the beginning of the section. In English some adjectives follow the noun they modify, as in (15) below:

(15)   The *person* **responsible** will be punished.
       We went to a meeting attended by the *Attorney* **General**.
       Mr Bisibodi is the *Governor-***elect** of this province.

This post-nominal attributive position is the norm for adjectives in the Romance languages; for example, Portuguese, Italian, Spanish and French.

When an adjective follows a so-called *linking verb* or *copula*, it is said to occur in predicative position. There is only a small set of linking verbs in English. Here is a selection of them, with some example sentences:

(16)   *appear, be, become, feel, look, remain, seem, smell, sound*
(17)   This academic appears pretty unintelligent.
       She is crazy.
       This fabric feels soft.
       These apples smell strange.
       The music sounds great!

We say that the adjectives in (17) are *predicated of* (i.e. are employed to say something about) the referent of another constituent, namely *this academic, she, this fabric, these apples* and *the music*, respectively.

Like nouns in Noun Phrases, adjectives function as the Heads of *Adjective Phrases (APs)*. Examples of APs are given in (18) below. In each case the Head is italicised.

(18)   *happy*
       extremely *happy*
       happy to be here
       extremely *happy* to be here

The strings in (18) show that an AP can consist of only a Head, or of a Head preceded by a modifying word, or of a Head followed by a *Complement* (see Chapter 2), or a combination of the last two possibilities.

It is important that you are aware of the fact that Adjective Phrases can occur *within* Noun Phrases. Consider the following:

(19)   the happy actor

Quite clearly, this string is an NP since its central element, its Head, is a noun (namely *actor*). But what about the status of the word *happy*? Well, you might want to say that this is obviously an adjective. And so it is, but it is also an Adjective *Phrase*! To be precise, it is an AP which consists of only an adjective which modifies the noun *actor*. But why is *happy* an Adjective Phrase, and not just an adjective? The reason is that we can substitute what is clearly an Adjective Phrase for the bare adjective in (19), as has been done in (20):

(20)   [$_{NP}$ the [$_{AP}$ *extremely happy*] actor]

Here *happy* is preceded by a modifying word, namely *extremely*. As we saw in (18) above, a string like *extremely happy* is an AP. The reasoning now runs as follows: because *happy* in (19) can be replaced by *extremely happy*, which is clearly an AP, the word *happy* must also be an AP:

(21)   [$_{NP}$ the [$_{AP}$ *happy*] actor]

3.4   Verbs

Consider the two sentences below:

(22)   Every day our Head of Department *devours* three pizzas.
(23)   The builders *worked* for many days.

The italicised words in (22) and (23) are *verbs*. In Chapter 2 we tentatively defined verbs as action words. Here we must be more precise. Notice first of all that the endings *-s* and *-ed* have been appended to the words *devour* and *work*. Such endings are called *inflections*. They encode grammatical properties. The *-s* ending signals that the verb is in the *present tense*, and we therefore call it a present tense inflection, while the *-ed* ending encodes a *past tense* and is called a past tense inflection. Any word that can take a tense inflection is a verb. Tense is a grammatical notion which refers to the way language encodes the semantic notion of time.

Verb endings do not only signal tense. The *-s* ending on the verb *devour* is referred to as the *third person singular ending* of the present tense. We already came across this term in Chapter 2. Let us take a closer look here at the system of 'person' in grammar. There are three 'persons', both in the singular and the plural:

(24)   **singular**   **plural**

	singular	plural
1st person:	I	we
2nd person:	you	you
3rd person:	he/she/it	they

Singular or plural referring expressions (e.g. *John, Kate, Paris, The Canary Islands*, etc.) are also third person. We now say that in (22) there is *agreement* between the 3rd person singular form *Our Head of Department* and *devour*. This agreement is signalled by the *-s* ending that is added to the verb. In the present tense, English, unlike some of the world's other languages, really only has one ending for most verbs, and that is the third person singular ending *-s*. The verb-forms for the other persons are all the same, as (25) below shows for the verb *devour*:

(25)   I devour   we devour
       you devour   you devour
       he/she/it *devours*   they devour

The form of the verb other than the third person singular is often referred to as the *base form*. The verb *be* is an exception to the general pattern in that in the present tense singular it has special forms for all three persons:

(26)   I *am*   we *are*
       you *are*   you *are*
       he/she/it *is*   they *are*

A verb that carries tense is called a *finite verb*, whereas a verb that doesn't carry tense is a *nonfinite verb*. All the verb-forms in (25) and (26) are finite verb-forms. We have to be careful, though, because for most verb-forms tense is usually not visibly marked, except in the third person singular, as is clear from the present tense forms of the verb *devour* in (25). In the past tense for most verbs all the verb-forms are the same, singular and plural, as (27) shows for *devour*:

(27)   I *devoured*   we *devoured*
       you *devoured*   you *devoured*
       he/she/it *devoured*   they *devoured*

What about nonfinite verb-forms? These I will discuss in a moment, after considering the different types of verbs that English possesses.

The verbs in (22) and (23) are called *main verbs* or *lexical verbs*. These are verbs which can stand on their own in a sentence, without another verb preceding or following. Verbs that cannot occur independently, but instead function as 'helping verbs', are called *auxiliary verbs*. (This term derives from the Latin *auxiliari*, 'to help') Consider (28):

(28)   Jeremy is laughing.

The main verb in this sentence is the *-ing* form of the verb *laugh*. It is preceded by the auxiliary *is* (the third person singular form of *be*). In what sense do auxiliaries 'help' main verbs? An auxiliary helps a main verb to the extent that it adds more specific meaning to it. Put differently, an auxiliary specifies from what point of view we should view the meaning expressed by the main verb. Thus, in (28) the auxiliary indicates that the laughing is ongoing, i.e. that it takes place over a certain stretch of time.

Exercise

Is the verb *be* an auxiliary in the sentence below?

(i)   He is friendly.

Be cannot be an auxiliary verb here, because it is the *only* verb in the sentence. It is therefore a main verb. Auxiliary verbs, by definition, are helping verbs, and must therefore accompany another verb, namely a main verb. Depending on context, the verb *be* functions as a main verb or as an auxiliary verb.

Before further elaborating on the role of auxiliary verbs, we will make a subdivision in the class of auxiliaries. This class can be subdivided into four groups:

modal auxiliaries
aspectual auxiliaries
*the passive auxiliary **be***
*the dummy auxiliary **do***

Here's an overview of the different types of auxiliary verbs with some example sentences in which they appear in italics:

Modal auxiliaries: *can/could, may/might, must, ought to, shall/should, will/would,*

(29)   We *can* dance until midnight.
(30)   You *may* take two courses if you wish.
(31)   You *must* comply with the regulations.
(32)   They really *ought to* leave.
(33)   We *shall* write to you as soon as possible.
(34)   He *will* survive.

Aspectual auxiliaries: *be, have*

(35)   These students *are* always complaining.
(36)   Shelley *has* broken two wine glasses.

The passive auxiliary: *be*

(37)   This doughnut *was* eaten by our Head of Department.

The dummy auxiliary: *do*

(38)   *Do* you like eating doughnuts?

Let's be a little more specific about the way in which auxiliary verbs can be said to 'help' the main verbs they precede. I start with the modal auxiliaries (or *modals* for short). A quick glance at the sentences in (29)–(34) reveals that each of them contains one of the following elements of meaning: 'ability', 'permission', 'possibility', 'obligation', 'necessity', 'intention', 'prediction', etc. These are called *modal* meanings which are concerned with expressing situations that do not obtain at the present moment, but will, could, must or should obtain in the future. Thus, the verb *can* in (29) expresses the fact that the people referred to as *we* have the ability to dance until midnight, or, alternatively, because (29) is in fact ambiguous, that they have permission to dance until midnight. In (30) permission is given to take two courses, whereas in (31) somebody is being obliged to comply with the regulations. (32)–(34) express necessity, futurity and prediction, respectively. We could say, informally, that the modals *colour* the meaning of the verbs they precede. Modals are always finite (i.e. they carry tense) and they do not take typical verb endings such as the third person singular present tense *-s* ending or the past tense *-ed* ending. Most of the modal verbs *do* have past tense forms, as the pairs of modal verbs above show, but these past tense forms are not formed by simply adding an *-ed* ending to the base form of the modal.

Let us now turn to the aspectual auxiliaries. These verbs encode *aspect*, a concept which refers to the way the meaning of the main verb is viewed in time. The main categories of aspect in English are *progressive aspect* and *perfective aspect*. The first type of aspect has already been exemplified in (28). In this sentence Jeremy's laughing is presented as an ongoing process. (35) is a further example. Here the act of complaining expressed by the main verb is viewed as taking place over a stretch of time: it has a certain duration.

Perfective aspect is illustrated by (36). This time the auxiliary encodes the fact that the breaking of the glasses took place in the past and has *current relevance*. What this means is that when we utter (36) we are indicating to our interlocutor that Shelley's breaking of the glasses is somehow important at the time of utterance. The notion of current relevance becomes clearer if we contrast a sentence containing a past tense form with a sentence containing a perfective auxiliary.

(39)   Shelley broke two wine glasses last month.
(40)   Shelley has broken two wine glasses.   (= (36))

The past tense in (39) is used simply to record *when* Shelley broke two wine glasses, whereas the perfective form is used to indicate that Shelley broke two wine glasses quite recently, and that this event is still relevant (the pieces of glass might still be lying on the floor). Notice that we cannot say *Shelley has broken two wine glasses last month.*

Exercise

Why not? That is, why can't we combine perfect aspect (*has broken*) with a definite time reference (*last week*)?

The reason is that in the sentence *Shelley has broken two wine glasses last week* there is a clash between the meaning expressed by *has broken*, namely that the situation has current relevance, and the meaning expressed by *last month*, which suggests that the event is over and done with.

    The difference between the past tense and the present perfect can be shown on 'time lines':

(41)   ———X————|————
(42)   ———X————>|————

In both sentences 'X' indicates the moment when Shelley broke the glasses and 'I' indicates the present moment. In (42) the arrow indicates that the relevance of this event extends to the present moment.

    We distinguish the *present perfect*, as in (40), from the *past perfect*, as in the sentence below:

(43)   By the time we arrived, Shelley *had broken* two wine glasses.

This time the auxiliary *have* is in the past tense. What (43) means is that Shelley broke the wine glasses prior to a reference point in the past ('the time we arrived'), and that this event was still relevant at the reference point. The time line for (43) is as in (44):

(44)   ———X—>x————|————

As before, 'I' indicates 'now', while 'X' indicates the breaking of the glasses, which is still relevant at reference point 'x' ('the time we arrived').

Exercise

In the following sentence we also have a form of the verb *have*. Is this an auxiliary verb? If not, why not?

(i)   Larry has ninety-four CDs.

Because there is only one verb in this sentence, *has* cannot be an auxiliary. It is therefore a main verb. So *have*, like *be*, can function as an auxiliary verb or as a main verb. The modals, by contrast, can only function as auxiliary verbs.

Let us now turn to the remaining types of auxiliary verbs in English: the passive auxiliary and the dummy auxiliary. The first of these is illustrated below:

(45)   Billy wrecked the garden shed.
         >
       The garden shed *was* wreck*ed* by Billy.

As you will remember from Chapter 2, we call the first sentence of the pair in (45) an *active* sentence, while the second is a *passive* sentence. We will not concern ourselves here with the different ways in which we use active and passive structures in particular situations, but will concentrate instead on the syntactic differences between actives and passives. Notice that the Direct Object of the first sentence (*the garden shed*) is in Subject position in the second sentence, and that the Subject of the first sentence appears in a phrase introduced by *by* in the second sentence. This quite regular alternation between active and passive sentences I have already described. Apart from the fact that the Subject and Object of the first sentence in (45) have moved, another important and necessary change has occurred in turning the active structure into a passive one, and that is the introduction of an auxiliary verb, namely the passive auxiliary verb *be*. This auxiliary is always followed by a main verb ending in *-ed* which we will label the *past participle* form of the verb. Note that for many verbs the past tense form (cf. (27)) and the past participle form are identical. This is not true for most irregular verbs (*see–saw–seen; sing–sang–sung*).

Before turning to the last type of English auxiliary, notice that if we want to form the negative counterparts of sentences containing either a modal auxiliary, an aspectual auxiliary or a passive auxiliary, we simply add the negative particle *not* after the first auxiliary:

(46)   We *will **not**/won't* dance until midnight
(47)   These students *are **not**/aren't* always complaining.
(48)   This doughnut *was **not**/wasn't* eaten by our Head of Department.

Notice that *not* can be separate from the auxiliary, or tagged onto it. (In the latter case we say that it is *cliticised* onto the auxiliary.)

We now turn to our last auxiliary type: the dummy auxiliary *do*. Notice that if we want to form the negative counterpart of a sentence that does not contain an auxiliary verb, then we cannot simply add *not*, as the contrast between (49)a and (49)b shows. Instead, we need to insert a form of the verb *do* ((49)c):

(49)a   Jon cycles to work every day.
   b   *Jon not cycles to work every day.
   c   Jon *does not/doesn't* cycle to work every day.

The process of inserting *do* is called ***do*-support** in the linguistic literature. As we have already seen, in forming negative sentences *do*-support is not necessary if the sentence in question already contains an auxiliary verb.

   Do is also used to form the interrogative versions of sentences that do not contain an auxiliary verb:

(50)   Jon cycles to work every day.
    >
    Jon *does* cycle to work every day.
    >
    Does Jon cycle to work every day?

(50) shows that to form the interrogative version of a sentence that does not contain an auxiliary verb, we first insert *do* before the main verb and then we invert this verb with the Subject. This inversion process is called *Subject-auxiliary inversion*. *Do*-support is not necessary in forming the interrogative versions of sentences that already contain an auxiliary, as (51)–(53) show.

(51)   Jon will ride a bike all his life.
    >
    Will Jon ride a bike all his life?

(52)   Jon is always riding his bike in his spare time.
    >
    Is Jon always riding his bike in his spare time?

(53)   Jon has cycled to work since he got his first job.
    >
    Has Jon cycled to work since he got his first job?

The third use of the dummy auxiliary is in contexts where auxiliaries get 'stranded'. To illustrate this, consider the sentences below:

(54)   Does Jon cycle to work every day? He *does*.
(55)   Jon cycles all the way to work every day, and so *does* Tim.

Here, in the strings *He does* and *so does Tim* the auxiliary occurs without its main verb. This property has rather opaquely been referred to as *code*. (56)–(61) show that the other auxiliary types also display the phenomenon of code:

(56)   Will Jon ride a bike all his life? He *will*.
(57)   Jon will ride a bike all his life, and so *will* Harry.

(58)   Is Jon always riding a bike in his spare time? He *is*.
(59)   Jon is always riding his bike in his spare time, and so *is* Harry.

(60)   Has Jon cycled to work since he got his first job? He *has*.
(61)   Jon has cycled to work since he got his first job, and so *has* Harry.

There is a fourth use of the dummy auxiliary, and that is in so-called emphatic contexts. Imagine a situation in which someone has just denied the truth of the sentence *Jon cycles to work every day*. If we are nevertheless convinced that this statement is true, we might indignantly respond by saying:

(62)   Jon DOES cycle to work every day!

Here the capital letters indicate the heavy stress with which the auxiliary is pronounced. Again, in sentences that already contain an auxiliary *do*-support is not required to create emphasis:

(63)   Jon WILL cycle to work every day!
(64)   Jon IS cycling to work every day!
(65)   Jon HAS cycled to work since he got his first job!

Exercise

Consider the following sentences:

(i)   Kathy did her homework.
(ii)   Francesco did today's dinner.

Is the verb *do* in these sentences an auxiliary verb? If not, why not?

The verb *do* in these sentences is the only verb, and for that reason cannot be said to be a 'helping' verb. We must therefore regard *do* in (i) and (ii) as main verbs.

From the observations on the behaviour of the auxiliary verb *do* we can make a generalisation regarding the auxiliary verbs collectively. What distinguishes auxiliaries from main verbs is that they can:

1   carry the *negative* enclitic particle *not*
2   *invert* with the Subject

3 manifest *code*
4 carry *emphatic* stress

1–4 are referred to as the *NICE properties*. NICE is an acronym which is made up of the first letters of each of the italicised properties above.

You may have wondered why *do* has constantly been referred to as a *dummy* element. The reason is that it doesn't really by itself carry any meaning, but is inserted simply to aid main verbs in forming negative or interrogative sentences, and also to allow code and emphasis.

So far we've looked at sentences which contain only one auxiliary verb, but it is quite common for auxiliaries to combine. Here are a few examples of some of the possible combinations:

(66)   The company *is being* taxed three times this year.
(67)   The company *has been* taxed three times this year.
(68)   The company *has been being* taxed three times this year.
(69)   The company *will have been being* taxed three times this year.

In (66) there are two auxiliaries: the progressive auxiliary *be* and the passive auxiliary *be*. In (67) the perfective auxiliary *have* combines with the passive auxiliary *been*. In (68) we have perfective, progressive and passive auxiliaries. And finally, in (69) we have no fewer than four auxiliaries: the modal *will* combines with the perfective, progressive and passive auxiliaries. In each case the verb-form *taxed*, as we have seen, is the past participle of the main verb *tax*. Structures like (68) and (69) are rare in English.

From the sentences above a number of important facts emerge. First of all, notice that it is always the first auxiliary that carries tense (and is therefore finite). All the other verbs are nonfinite. As we have seen, finite verb-forms occur either in the present tense or in the past tense. Nonfinite verb-forms come in four types. For the verb *dance* these are given in (70):

(70)   to dance   *to-infinitive*   example: I wanted him *to dance.*
        dance   *bare infinitive*   example: I saw him *dance.*
        dancing   *present participle*   example: He is *dancing.*
        danced   *past participle*   example: He has often *danced.*

The *to*-element of the *to*-infinitive is called the *infinitival particle*. The bare infinitive is not preceded by this particle, hence its name. Be careful not to confuse the past participle with the past tense form: as we have seen, for some verbs the past tense and past participle have the same form and pronunciation. Compare the past tense of *dance* in *They danced until dawn* with the past participle in *He has often danced*. The difference between the past tense and past participle forms is that the past tense is finite, while the past participle is nonfinite. As we briefly saw earlier, in the case of irregular verbs (those whose past tense does not end in *-ed*) the past tense form and past participle form can also be the same, as with the verb *bend*.

Compare *He bent the metal bar* (past tense) with *He has bent the metal bar* (past participle). However, these past tense and past participle forms can also be different, as with *break*. Compare *He broke the bottle* with *He has broken the bottle* (past participle). For a small number of verbs the present tense, past tense and past participle forms are the same, as with *set* and *read*. Compare *They set the standards next year* (present tense) with *They set the standards last year* (past tense), and with *They have set the standards* (past participle). Notice that with *read* the present tense is pronounced differently from the past tense and past participle forms.

Secondly, in (66)–(69) each auxiliary verb determines the form of the verb that follows it. Thus, in (66) the progressive auxiliary *be* determines the *-ing* ending on the passive auxiliary *being*. The passive auxiliary in its turn determines the *-ed* ending on the past participle form of the main verb *taxed*.

Thirdly, notice that there is a strict order of auxiliary verbs. As we can see in (69), the modal auxiliary comes first and is followed by the perfective, progressive and passive auxiliaries, though these need not all be present.

Exercise

Form the negative counterparts of sentences (66)–(69). What conclusion can you draw about the position of *not* in sentences with more than one auxiliary verb?

Your conclusion should be that the negative particle *not* always follows the *first* auxiliary verb.

As with nouns in Noun Phrases and adjectives in Adjective Phrases, we would expect verbs to be able to head a *Verb Phrase (VP)*. And this is indeed the case. However, VPs are a little more complicated than the other phrase types. The reason is that it is not immediately obvious which elements we should allow to be part of the VP of a particular sentence. Let's take a concrete example and try to establish what is its Verb Phrase. Consider (71):

(71)   The library recalled these books.

One possibility would be to say that a Verb Phrase contains only verbs, and this has indeed been suggested by several linguists. Under this approach the VP in (71) would only consist of the verb *recalled*. However, just as NPs may contain elements other than nouns, and APs may contain elements other than adjectives, there would be nothing odd about allowing Verb Phrases to contain elements other than verbs.

Exercise

Try to establish which elements other than verbs we might want to include in the VP. Hint: notice that we cannot say **The library recalled* (cf. also (16) in Chapter 1).

The hint I gave suggests that there is a bond of some sort between *recall* and its Direct Object *these books*. The nature of this bond is such that the verb syntactically requires the presence of a Direct Object in the form of a Noun Phrase. Another way of putting this is to say that the verb *recall* in (71) *subcategorises* for an NP. I will have more to say about subcategorisation in future chapters. For now it will suffice to observe that the existence of the subcategorisation relation between *recall* and its Direct Object is a reason for taking the DO to be part of the Verb Phrase. We can now represent (71) as follows: The library [$_{VP}$ recalled these books]. The VP here contains an NP (*these books*) which functions as DO (cf. also (15) in Chapter 1).

3.5 Prepositions

The word class of prepositions cannot easily be defined by making reference to formal characteristics, in that prepositions do not have typical endings like the parts of speech we discussed above. At most we can say that prepositions tend to be very short, often consisting of only two or three letters. Here are a few examples: *at, behind, beside, by, for, in, like, of, on, through, with, without, under*, etc. Prepositions can be *simple*, i.e. consisting of only one word, as in the list above, or *complex*, i.e. consisting of more than one word as in *by means of, in front of, in spite of*, etc. They often combine with Noun Phrases to form *Prepositional Phrases (PPs)*. Examples: [$_{PP}$ *with* [$_{NP}$ *the dog*]], [$_{PP}$ *on* [$_{NP}$ *her bicycle*]], [$_{PP}$ *through* [$_{NP}$ *the glass*]], etc. The NP in these examples is called a *Prepositional Object* or, equivalently, a *Prepositional Complement*.

From the point of view of meaning, we can say that prepositions often denote a relationship of some sort between two entities. For example, in a simple sentence like *The book is on the table* the preposition signals a spatial relationship between the book and its location, which is denoted in this sentence by the Prepositional Complement. This relationship can also be a metaphorical one as in the sentence *She is in big trouble*.

3.6 Adverbs

Adverbs modify verbs, adjectives or other adverbs. This definition enables us to identify the words *merrily, extremely, very* and *hard* as adverbs in (72)–(74) below:

(72)   Our colleague from Paris *merrily* marks student essays in his bath.

(73)   The teachers are *extremely* unimpressed by his efforts.

(74)   Our new professor works *very hard*.

In (72) *merrily* tells you more about how the marking was performed, namely in a happy way, while in (73) and (74) we are supplied with more specific information about the extent to which the teachers were unimpressed and the new professor works hard. The ending *-ly* which we find tagged onto the adjectives *merry* and *extreme* in (72) and (73) is a typical adverb ending. Caution is in order here, as there are also a number of adjectives that end in *–ly*; for example, *friendly, goodly, lively, masterly, woolly.*

Other adverb endings are *-wards, -wise, -ways* (e.g. *homewards, clockwise, sideways*) and a few others. However, as you can see from (74), not all adverbs are formed with these suffixes, so looking at the suffix alone is not a foolproof test for adverbhood.

Further caution is needed when looking at comparative and superlative forms. As you will remember from our discussion of adjectives, one of the characteristics of this word class is that they form comparative and superlative forms by making use of the suffixes *-er* and *-est*, as in the sequence *clean–cleaner–cleanest*. However, some adverbs also take comparative and superlative forms. Examples are *fast–faster–fastest, soon–sooner–soonest* and *well–better–best*. Notice that *fast* can also be an adjective (*a fast train*).

Let us now turn to some subclasses of adverbs:

Adverb subclasses

Circumstantial adverbs	*often, gleefully, intentionally, reluctantly*
Degree adverbs	*extremely, extraordinarily, less, more, pretty, quite, too, very*
Sentence adverbs	*however, probably, perhaps*

The class of circumstantial adverbs is semantically very heterogeneous: its members can specify a variety of different types of circumstantial information; for example, frequency and manner.

Degree adverbs, as the name suggests, specify the degree to which the adjective they modify applies. For example, in the AP *extremely rude* the adverb *extremely* specifies the extent to which the epithet 'rude' applies.

Sentence adverbs differ from circumstantial and degree adverbs semantically: either they have a linking function, or they modify whole sentences. Here are some examples:

(75)   James's past is not unblemished. *However,* we will disregard this for now.
(76)   *Perhaps* you can sign on the dotted line.
(77)   *Probably,* we will not be able to go on holiday this year.

In (75) *however* links the content of the first sentence to that of the second sentence, while in (76) *perhaps* expresses tentativeness over the following proposition. Finally, in (77) the use of the adverb *probably* indicates that the speaker regards the proposition that follows (*we will not be able to go on holiday this year*) as likely. We say that in (76) and (77) the adverbs have *scope* over a whole sentence.

The three groups of adverbs also differ syntactically: degree adverbs cannot themselves be modified (cf. **very extremely*), while circumstantial and sentence adverbs can (cf. *very often*, *quite intentionally*, *very probably*). Sentence adverbs are syntactically detached from the sentences they modify, unlike circumstantial adverbs and degree adverbs.

Adverbs function as the Heads of *Adverb Phrases (AdvP)*. Many AdvPs consist of a Head only, but, just as in the other phrase types we looked at, the Head can be modified, as in (74).

3.7 Conjunctions

Conjunctions belong to a closed class of words that have a linking function. There are two types of conjunctions: *coordinating conjunctions* (e.g. *and*, *or*, *but*) and *subordinating conjunctions* (e.g. *that*, *if*, *whether*, *for*; *because*, *although*, *when* etc.)

Let us begin by looking at some examples of structures containing coordinating conjunctions. The bracketed portions of the sentences below are coordinated structures. The coordinating conjunction is shown in italics:

(78) (I bought) [$_{NP}$ [$_{NP}$ a computer] *and* [$_{NP}$ a keyboard]]
(79) (These articles were) [$_{AP}$ [$_{AP}$ old] *and* [$_{AP}$ useless]]
(80) (He is) [$_{AP}$ [$_{AP}$ pretty stupid] *but* [$_{AP}$ quite eager]]
(81) (She) [$_{VP}$ [$_{VP}$ likes tea] *but* [$_{VP}$ hates coffee]]
(82) (The books are) [$_{PP}$ [$_{PP}$ on the table] *or* [$_{PP}$ in the cupboard]]
(83) (He killed the fly) [$_{AdvP}$ [wilfully] *and* [$_{AdvP}$ quite mercilessly]]
(84) [$_{S}$ [$_{S}$ They arrived at 10 a.m.] *and* [$_{S}$ they left at 6 p.m.]]
(85) [$_{S}$ [$_{S}$ We will not offer this student a place] *but* [$_{S}$ we can recommend a College that will]]

In (78) the conjunction *and* links two Noun Phrases, while in (79)–(83) we have examples of coordinated APs, VPs, PPs and AdvPs, respectively. In (84) and (85) sentences (S) are linked.

As noted above, *and*, *or* and *but* are referred to as coordinating conjunctions (or simply *coordinators*). The units that are being coordinated we will call *conjoins*. A defining characteristic of conjunctions of this type is that they link units of equal syntactic status; for example, phrases and sentences. We treat coordination as an instance of *parataxis*, a term deriving from the Greek roughly meaning 'syntactic side-by-side arrangement'. Notice that two coordinated phrases form a new phrase of the same type as the two constituent conjoins. The reason why this is so is that the larger phrase functions in the same way as each of the conjoins would do if there had been no coordination. Compare (86) to (87) and (88):

(86) [$_{NP}$ [$_{NP}$ Philosophy] and [$_{NP}$ Linguistics]] are fascinating subjects.
(87) [$_{NP}$ Philosophy] is easy.
(88) [$_{NP}$ Linguistics] is tough.

The string *Philosophy and Linguistics* in (86) occurs in the Subject position before the main verb of the sentence, as do *philosophy* and *linguistics* on their own in (87) and (88). Notice also that the NP in (86) determines the form of the verb *be* in the same way that the singular NPs in (87) and (88) do. Because the conjoined string syntactically behaves in the same way as non-conjoined NPs, we conclude that it is also an NP.

We also speak of coordination in cases where more than two items are being strung together, for example in the sequence *beer, wine and whisky*. Whenever there are two or more items, there is usually only a coordinator between the last two items in the list. All cases of coordination that involve an overt coordinator are referred to as *syndetic coordination*. Where there is no overt coordinator, as in (89), we speak of *asyndetic coordination*.

(89)   Speaker A: What's on your shopping list?
        Speaker B: *Beer, wine, whisky.*

We return to coordination in a later chapter, when we will be discussing the possibility of using it as a test for constituenthood.

Consider now the following sentences:

(90)   He thinks [*that* we will agree]
(91)   I wonder [*if* it will ever change]
(92)   We don't know [*whether* he will come]
(93)   I am hoping [*for* Helen to arrive today]

(94)   She left the course, [*because* she didn't like living in a big city]
(95)   [*Although* they are also very supportive], my teachers are very strict
(96)   They are going to meet her, [*when* she arrives]
(97)   [*In order that* he is cared for properly], he has been moved to hospital.

The italicised elements in (90)–(97) are called subordinating conjunctions, as we have already seen. They are mostly short single words, but there is also a small group of subordinating conjunctions that consist of more than one word; for example, *as if, as long as, in order that, so that*, etc. Subordinating conjunctions (or *subordinators* for short) are elements that introduce *subordinate clauses*, which we define provisionally as sentences within sentences. Notice that, with the exception of the clause introduced by *for*, all the bracketed subordinate clauses in (90)–(97) are finite. I will discuss subordinate clauses in more detail in Chapter 4. Subordinators are quite different from coordinating conjunctions in that they link units of unequal syntactic status. Another way of putting this is to say that subordination is a type of *hypotaxis*, again originally a Greek term that means 'syntactic underneath arrangement'. In (90)–(97) in each case the string of words introduced by the subordinator is syntactically subordinate to what precedes it.

It is important to realise that the nature of the subordination in (90)–(93) is different from that in (94)–(97): in (90) the clause introduced by *that* completes the meaning of the verb *think* and is therefore its Direct Object. The clauses introduced by *if, whether* and *for* are also Direct Object clauses. Because *that, if, whether* and *for* introduce Complement clauses they are called *complementisers*. These elements comprise a subclass of the subordinating conjunctions. In (94)–(97), by contrast, the clauses introduced by *because, although, when* and *in order that* supply circumstantial information about what precedes: they specify a reason, a contrast of some sort, 'time when' and purpose, respectively. These clauses therefore function as Adjuncts. (See Chapter 5, where this issue will be dealt with in detail.) There is no generally accepted label to refer to subordinators that introduce clauses functioning as Adjuncts, so I'll coin the term *adjunctisers* to refer to them.

Schematically, the word class of conjunctions can be represented as follows:

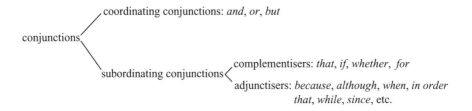

conjunctions
- coordinating conjunctions: *and, or, but*
- subordinating conjunctions
  - complementisers: *that, if, whether, for*
  - adjunctisers: *because, although, when, in order that, while, since,* etc.

We will return to subordination in later chapters, and we will see in Chapter 15 that there are reasons for classifying the adjunctisers as prepositions.

3.8 Interjections

Interjections are expressions of emotion, physical state, agreement, disagreement and such like. Here are a few examples:

ah, erh, hmm, no, oh, ouch, phew, shit, yes, yuck, etc.

They are regarded as a separate word class, but really only in deference to traditional grammarians. If you think about it, they are not really part of the sentences in which they occur, but literally thrown in ('inter-jected').

This concludes our survey of word classes and their associated phrases in English. Remember that Subject, Direct Object, Adjunct, etc. belong to the level of *function*, while nouns and Noun Phrases, adjectives and Adjective Phrases, verbs and Verb Phrases, etc. belong to a level of analysis which we referred to as *form*. In the next chapter we will look at clauses and sentences, two further form notions. Then, in Chapter 5, we will look at ways in which we can relate the levels of function and form.

Key Concepts in this Chapter

word
word class
function and form
noun
determinative
adjective
verb
preposition
adverb
conjunction
   coordinating
   subordinating (complementiser, adjunctiser)
interjection

Exercises

1. Assign word class labels to the words in the sentences below. Be as precise as possible.

    (i)   Did he answer you directly?
    (ii)   James flew to Greece last Wednesday.
    (iii)   It was a sunny day in Balamory.
    (iv)   Sadly, we had problems when we arrived.
    (v)   Why did you say that?

2. Assign a word class label to the italicised elements in the example sentences below. Give syntactic arguments for your answers.

    (i)   Did your *book* arrive yesterday?
    (ii)   Did you *book* that flight yesterday?

3. True or false? In the sentence *All shopping centres in the world look exactly alike*:

    (i)   *all* is a determinative
    (ii)   *in* is an interjection

(iii)   *the* is an adjective
(iv)   *exactly* is a verb
(v)   *alike* is an adjective
(vi)   the Subject of this sentence is *all shopping centres*

4.   Here's a poem by Gerald Manley Hopkins:

   Inversnaid

   This *darksome* burn, horseback brown,
   His rollrock highroad roaring down,
   In *coop* and in *comb* the fleece of his foam
   Flutes and low to the lake falls home.

   A windpuff-bonnet of fáwn-fróth
   Turns and *twindles* over the broth
   Of a pool so pitchblack, *féll-frówning*,
   It rounds and rounds Despair to drowning.

   Degged with dew, dappled with dew
   Are the groins of the *braes* that the brook treads through,
   Wiry heathpacks, *flitches* of fern,
   And the *beadbonny* ash that sits over the burn.

   What would the world be, once bereft
   Of wet and of wildness? Let them be left,
   O let them be left, wildness and wet;
   Long live the weeds and the wilderness yet.

   There are many words in this poem whose meaning we don't know, but, sur-
   prisingly, establishing the word class to which they belong is unproblematic.
   Determine the word class of each of the italicised words in the poem, and
   give reasons for your choices.

5.   Assign the following nouns to one of the categories given in Section 3.2. Take
   care: some of these nouns can be assigned to more than one category!

   taxi, nobody, none, sugar, page, everybody, New York, he, mine, each other

6.   Numerals (*one, two, three*) and ordinals (*first, second, third*) are often assigned to the word class of nouns. This is controversial. How do the data
   below argue either for or against this view?

   (i)   *Thousands* came to see the exhibition.
   (ii)   The *second* train on platform 4 is the 16.43 to Brussels.
   (iii)   The house was bought by the *three* of us.

     (iv)   She was wrong by a factor of *five*.
     (v)   The *first* of these options is not available.
     (vi)   The group divided into *twos* and *threes*.

7.   People sometimes ask 'What is the longest sentence in English?'. Is it possible to answer this question?

8.   Underline the auxiliary verbs in the following sentences and identify the category they belong to (choosing from: modal auxiliary, progressive auxiliary, perfective auxiliary, passive auxiliary or dummy *do*). Give reasons for your answers.

     (i)   We will assign a new tutor to this student.
     (ii)   Seamus is playing in the garden.
     (iii)   She can't have been being interrogated again.
     (iv)   She musn't wait any longer.
     (v)   She may have been abroad.
     (vi)   Janet hasn't done her homework.

9.   The following sentences contain aspectual auxiliaries. Explain in which situations we would use them. Use time lines in your answers.

     (i)   She is laughing.
     (ii)   She was laughing.
     (iii)   He has eaten all the biscuits.
     (iv)   He had eaten all the biscuits.

10.   In the text we distinguished between count and noncount nouns. The noun *sugar* is generally classed as a noncount noun. Is the following example a problem for this view?

     (i)   I take three sugars in my tea.

*11.   You probably agreed that the phrase **a very wooden floor* mentioned in the section on adjectives is not possible in English, but what about *a very wooden performance*? Can you think of any reasons why this is OK?

*12.   Assign word class labels to the italicised items in the phrases below:

     (i)   a *done* deal
     (ii)   the *then* president
     (iii)   a *moving* target
     (iv)   a *moving* film

*13. Consider the following examples, taken from McCawley (1998):

(i) *Blue* is my favorite color.
(ii) The *yellows* in van Gogh's paintings are striking.
(iii) John's necktie was deep *blue*.
(iv) John's shirt is *blue*.
(v) John is wearing the *bluest* shirt that I have ever seen.

Assign word class labels to the italicised words above. Give reasons for your choices. Now do the same for the examples below:

(vi) Ted wore a deep *blue* necktie.
(Notice that **deeply blue necktie* is impossible.)
(vii) In the living room they hung light *green* curtains.
(Notice that **lightly green curtains* is impossible.)

In what way are examples (vi) and (vii) problematic for the answers you gave in the first part of this exercise? How can we solve the problem?

Further Reading

All major reference grammars of English discuss word classes extensively, but see especially Chapters 3 and 9 in Huddleston (1984) and Burton-Roberts (1997). See also Aitchison (2002). A very useful article discussing the problems we face in setting up word classes in English is Crystal (1967).

In line with Huddleston and Pullum et al.'s (2002) *Cambridge Grammar of the English Language* I use the term 'determinative' as a form label for *a, the, this/those*, etc. occurring before nouns, rather than 'determiner', as I did in the second edition of this book. As we will see in Chapter 7, these determinatives function as Specifiers. Many books on grammar use 'determiner' as both a form and a function label, while Quirk et al.'s (1985) *Comprehensive Grammar of the English Language,* and its derivatives, do things the other way round: for them 'determiner' is a form label, while 'determinative' is a function label.

Morphology has not been discussed in any detail in this book. For introductory texts, see Bauer (2004), Katamba and Stonham (2006) and Spencer (1991). Katamba (2005) is a book on English words in general. On word-formation see Adams (1973, 2001) and Plag (2003).

4 More on Form: Clauses and Sentences

In this book our approach to analysing sentences has been to start with the smallest syntactically meaningful units (i.e. words). We then investigated how these words combine into phrases. We referred to an analysis in terms of word classes and phrases as a *formal* analysis. In this chapter we extend the formal analysis of sentences. We will see how phrases combine into clauses, and how clauses in their turn combine into sentences. We can then set up a rank scale accommodating words, phrases, clauses and sentences. We will also establish a typology of sentences in terms of their syntactic characteristics. Finally, we will take a closer look at the way in which we can represent sentences in the form of tree diagrams.

4.1 Clauses and Clause Hierarchies

Consider (1):

(1) Tim thought that Kate believed the story.

We will say that the string of words in (1) collectively forms a *sentence*, which contains two *clauses*: a *matrix clause*, which is coextensive with (i.e. it contains the same elements as) the overall sentence, and a *subordinate clause*, namely *that Kate believed the story*. Clauses consist of a Subject and a Predicate. The element *that* is a complementiser. We can graphically illustrate all this as follows:

(2)   Tim thought that Kate believed the story

    Sentence   ├────────────────────────────┤

    Matrix clause   ├────────────────────────────┤

    Subordinate clause   ├──────────────────┤

Consider next the situation we have in (3):

(3) Tim thought that Kate believed that Greg is a liar.

This sentence contains *three* clauses, as (4) shows:

(4)   Tim thought that Kate believed that Greg is a liar

   Sentence |————————————————————————————————|

   Matrix clause |————————————————————————————————|

   Subordinate clause 1 |——————————————————————————|

   Subordinate clause 2 |——————————|

In this sentence, the matrix clause is superordinate to subordinate clause 1, while in its turn subordinate clause 1 is superordinate to subordinate clause 2. Matrix clauses, by definition, are superordinate clauses which are not themselves subordinate to anything else.

We have seen that in both our examples the matrix clauses are coextensive with the overall sentence. Thus in (1) the matrix clause is *Tim thought that Kate believed the story*, and in (3) the matrix clause is *Tim thought that Kate believed that Greg is a liar*. Within these matrix clauses the *that*-clauses are subordinate clauses. You may find it odd that matrix clauses are coextensive with the sentences that contain them, because this situation entails that the term 'matrix clause' is redundant. Strictly speaking this is true, but it is nevertheless important to be aware of the difference between the labels 'sentence' and 'matrix clause'.

It is important that you realise that in using the terms matrix clause, superordinate clause and subordinate clause, we are only concerned with the hierarchical relations between the clauses. We still need to assign form and function labels to them.

The form of the subordinate clauses in both (1) and (3) is a *that*-clause (named after the first element, the complementiser *that*). Their function in each case is Direct Object. Thus for (1): 'What did Tim think?', answer: 'That Kate believed the story'. And for (3): 'What did Kate believe?', answer: 'That Greg is a liar'. You may be surprised by the fact that Direct Objects can be something other than NPs. Although it is true that DOs are typically NPs, they can be realised in different ways. I will return to this point in the next chapter.

Before moving on, recall that in Chapter 3 we said that verbs can be finite or nonfinite. A finite verb is a verb that carries tense, while a nonfinite verb is tenseless. We now extend this terminology to apply to clauses. We can thus speak of *finite and nonfinite clauses*. Finite clauses, then, are clauses that contain a finite (tensed) main verb, while nonfinite clauses contain a nonfinite (untensed) main verb. Matrix clauses are always finite, though they may of course contain finite or nonfinite subordinate clauses. (2) and (4) are examples of finite matrix clauses which contain finite subordinate clauses. *That*-clauses are a frequently occurring type of finite subordinate clause. *If*-clauses are also always finite:

(5)   I don't know [*if* he is happy or sad]

The bracketed subordinate clause is finite because *is* (the third person singular form of the verb *be*) is a present tense form. We'll come across further instances of finite subordinate clauses as we go along.

We haven't yet seen any instances of nonfinite clauses, so here are some examples. (Recall that the nonfinite forms of the verb are the *to*-infinitive, the bare infinitive, the *-ing* participle and the *-ed* participle.) In each case I've given examples of nonfinite clauses with and without Subjects. The nonfinite clauses are in brackets and the nonfinite verbs are italicised:

     to-*infinitive clause*
(6)   They would hate [Jim *to sell* his boat].   [+Subject]
(7)   He likes [*to be* in Italy in the Spring].   [-Subject]

     bare infinitive clause
(8)   She made [Otto *polish* his shoes]   [+Subject]
(9)   A great thing to do is [*dance* the night away].   [-Subject]

     -ing *participle clause*
(10)   [Billy *discussing* politics] is rather funny.   [+Subject]
(11)   [*Walking* with your lover in the rain] is romantic. [-Subject]

     -ed *participle clause*
(12)   [The song *finished*] he switched off the radio.   [+Subject]
(13)   [*Incensed* by his comments], he stormed out.   [-Subject]

For convenience the terms '*-ing* participle clause' and '*-ed* participle clause' are used, rather than the somewhat clumsy 'present participle clause' and 'past participle clause'. Notice that, like finite subordinate clauses, nonfinite subordinate clauses can also be introduced by a complementiser, as in (14) below:

(14)   I don't know [*whether* to laugh or cry at his jokes].

Whether can, however, also introduce finite subordinate clauses, as in (15):

(15)   She didn't know [*whether* he would come].

We need to add to the list of nonfinite clause types a fifth type which is rather special in that it does not contain a verb. Here are some example sentences:

(16)   Martin considers [Tim a creep].
(17)   Phil deems [Henry foolish].

The bracketed clauses have been called *verbless clauses*, but a more recent term, which we will adopt in this book, is *Small Clause* (SC). Small Clauses are clauses that lack an overt verb, but can be said to contain an implicit verb *be*. We can show that this is the case by paraphrasing (16) and (17) as in (18) and (19):

(18)   Martin considers [Tim *to be* a creep].
(19)   Phil deems [Henry *to be* foolish].

4.2   The Rank Scale

Every sentence can be analysed at four distinct form levels: the word-level, the phrase-level, the clause-level and the sentence-level. (I am disregarding the morphological level.) This is called the *rank scale*. The representation in (20) below uses so-called *labelled bracketings* to show the rank scale of (1). This is a notation method – I've already used it on occasion – where words that belong together in a constituent are enclosed in square brackets. The formal status of the constituent is indicated by attaching a subscript label to the leftmost bracket:

(20)   Tim thought that Kate believed the story

Word level

$[_N$ Tim] $[_V$ thought] $[_{Comp}$ that] $[_N$ Kate] $[_V$ believed] $[_{Det}$ the] $[_N$ story]

Phrase level

$[_{NP}$ $[_N$ Tim]] $[_{VP}$ $[_V$ thought] $[_{Comp}$ that] $[_{NP}$ $[_N$ Kate]] $[_{VP}$ $[_V$ believed] $[_{NP}$ $[_{Det}$ the] $[_N$ story]]]]

Clause level

$[_{MC}$ $[_{NP}$ $[_N$ Tim]] $[_{VP}$ $[_V$ thought] $[_{SubC}$ $[_{Comp}$ that] $[_{NP}$ $[_N$ Kate]] $[_{VP}$ $[_V$ believed] $[_{NP}$ $[_{Det}$ the] $[_N$ story]]]]]]

Sentence level

$[_{S/MC}$ $[_{NP}$ $[_N$ Tim]] $[_{VP}$ $[_V$ thought] $[_{SubC}$ $[_{Comp}$ that] $[_{NP}$ $[_N$ Kate]] $[_{VP}$ $[_V$ believed] $[_{NP}$ $[_{Det}$ the] $[_N$ story]]]]]]

S = Sentence, N(P) = Noun (Phrase), V(P) = Verb (Phrase), A(P) = Adjective (Phrase), Comp = Complementiser (see Section 3.7), MC = Matrix Clause, SubC = Subordinate Clause

Observe that each time lower levels have been included in higher levels. You will no doubt have struggled trying to read the clause and sentence-levels, because of the many details contained in them. It is for this reason that linguists have devised a method of representing syntactic structures in the form of so-called *tree diagrams* (also called *phrase markers*). Using a tree diagram we can obtain a much clearer representation of (1):

(21)

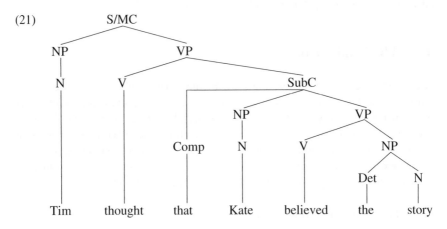

Notice that in (21) the subordinate clause is a constituent of VP for a reason already mentioned: the *that*-clause specifies what it is that Tim thought, and it is therefore the Direct Object of the verb *thought*. Just like other DOs it is positioned inside VP.

The rank scale for (3) is shown in (22):

(22)   Tim thought that Kate believed that Greg is a liar.

Word level

[$_N$ Tim] [$_V$ thought] [$_{Comp}$ that] [$_N$ Kate] [$_V$ believes] [$_{Comp}$ that] [$_N$ Greg] [$_V$ is] [$_{Det}$ a] [$_N$ liar]

Phrase level

[$_{NP}$ [$_N$ Tim]] [$_{VP}$ [$_V$ thought] [$_{Comp}$ that] [$_{NP}$ [$_N$ Kate]] [$_{VP}$ [$_V$ believes] [$_{Comp}$ that] [$_{NP}$ [$_N$ Greg]] [$_{VP}$ [$_V$ is] [$_{NP}$ [$_{Det}$ a] [$_N$ liar]]]]]]

Clause level

[$_{MC}$ [$_{NP}$ [$_N$ Tim]] [$_{VP}$ [$_V$ thought] [$_{SubC}$ [$_{Comp}$ that] [$_{NP}$ [$_N$ Kate]] [$_{VP}$ [$_V$ believes] [$_{SubC}$ [$_{Comp}$ that] [$_{NP}$ [$_N$ Greg]] [$_{VP}$ [$_V$ is] [$_{NP}$ [$_{Det}$ a] [$_N$ liar]]]]]]]]]

Sentence level

[$_{S/MC}$ [$_{NP}$ [$_N$ Tim]] [$_{VP}$ [$_V$ thought] [$_{SubC}$ [$_{Comp}$ that] [$_{NP}$ [$_N$ Kate]] [$_{VP}$ [$_V$ believes] [$_{SubC}$ [$_{Comp}$ that] [$_{NP}$ [$_N$ Greg]] [$_{VP}$ [$_V$ is] [$_{NP}$ [$_{Det}$ a] [$_N$ liar]]]]]]]]]

S = Sentence, N(P) = Noun (Phrase), V(P) = Verb (Phrase), A(P) = Adjective (Phrase), Comp = Complementiser, MC = Matrix Clause, SubC = Subordinate Clause

Again, because of the wealth of details especially in the higher levels of representation, the labelled bracketings are almost impossible to read. A tree diagram provides a better representation of (3):

(23)

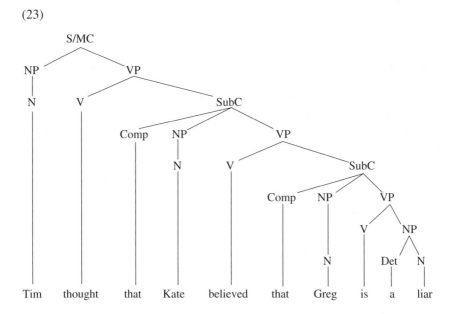

In this tree both subordinate clauses are inside the VP, in a position adjacent to the verb that 'selects' them.

   In Section 4.4 we'll discuss the geometry of tree diagrams in more detail. For now, it will be clear that they are a useful way of representing the hierarchical relations between the various constituent parts of a sentence. In the remainder of the book I will not explicitly label matrix clauses as 'MC' (in the way I did in the second edition of the book).

4.3   Clause Types

Clauses can be classified on the basis of their syntactic properties. We distinguish *declarative, interrogative, imperative* and *exclamative* clauses.

4.3.1   *Declarative Clauses*

Declaratives are the most straightforward clause type. They are syntactic configurations which usually display an *unmarked* (i.e. expected) order of the functional categories Subject, Predicator, Direct Object, etc. This means that the Subject comes first in the sentence, followed by the Predicator, which in turn is followed by an Indirect Object (if there is one) and a Direct Object (again, if present). Non-declarative clauses, by contrast, display *marked* (i.e. in some way out-of-the-ordinary) configurations. Here are two examples of declarative clauses:

(24)   My aunt likes books.
(25)   You haven't closed the door.

You would normally understand (24) and (25) to be making *statements*. However, it is important to realise that declaratives are not always used to make statements. Notice that the context in which (24) and (25) might be uttered affects their interpretation. For example, if I uttered (24) with a rising intonation pattern it would become a *question*: *My aunt likes books?* Similarly (25), while ostensibly a statement about the addressee not having closed the door, could, in a suitable context, be taken to be a *directive* (i.e. an order) to close the door. For example, if the speaker looks sternly from the addressee to the door, and then utters (25), the addressee is likely to interpret this as an order to close the door. Here too tone of voice makes all the difference.

4.3.2   Interrogative Clauses

Interrogative clauses are normally used to ask questions:

(26)   Can you see this?
(27)   Do you agree?
(28)   Will you dance with me?

(29)   What did you eat?
(30)   Why did you leave?
(31)   How did you open the door?

(32)   Do you want lasagne or spaghetti?
(33)   Is it red or is it blue?
(34)   Should I turn left or right?

We will refer to the interrogatives in (26)–(28) as *yes/no interrogatives* because they elicit either 'yes' or 'no' as answers, and to the interrogatives in (29)–(31) as *open interrogatives* or *Wh-interrogatives* because they can potentially elicit an infinite range of answers. Thus, in answer to (26), (27) and (28) we could say 'yes' or 'no' (but not, say, 'Christmas Day'), and in answer to (29) we could say 'bacon and eggs', 'corn flakes', 'toast and jam', etc. (but not 'yes' or 'no'). In answer to

(30) I could give a variety of reasons why I left the party ('because I was tired', 'because I can't stand Tristram', etc.), and in (31) I could give different explanations of how I opened the door. The yes/no interrogatives are syntactically different from the open interrogatives in that they display *inversion* of the Subject with an auxiliary verb (see Section 3.4). The open interrogatives are characterised by the initial question words starting with the letters *wh*. These are called *Wh-words*. Notice that *how* is also considered a Wh-word. In (32), (33) and (34) we have what are called *alternative interrogatives*: the possible answers to such interrogatives are given in the way the question is asked. So, the possible answers to (32) are 'lasagne' and 'spaghetti', to (33) they are 'red' and 'blue', and I can answer 'left' or 'right' to (34).

As with the declaratives, there is no watertight one-to-one relationship between syntactic form and the use this form might be put to. Thus, although the interrogatives in (26)–(30) are difficult to interpret other than as questions, there are situations in which interrogatives are not used to ask questions at all. The clause in (35) is an example of a *rhetorical question*:

(35)   How many times do I have to tell you not to lick your plate!

A parent shouting this at a child would not expect to get the answer 'sixteen times' (and if the child does give that answer it had better cover its ears). Sentence (35) is clearly an enjoiner not to lick plates. Similarly, if someone utters (36), you do not take it to be a question enquiring about your ability to be quiet:

(36)   Can you be quiet?

Instead, you take (36) to be a request (or order) to be quiet. Syntactically, (35) and (36) are interrogative (by virtue of the Subject-auxiliary inversion), but they have the import of directives. (Notice that in (36) we can add *please*, which is common in requests.)

4.3.3   Imperative Clauses

Imperative clauses are sentences that are normally interpreted as directives, i.e. someone is telling someone else to (not) do something:

(37)   Go home.
(38)   Mind your own business.
(39)   Shut up.
(40)   Don't eat that sandwich.

Notice that what syntactically characterises imperative sentences is the fact that they do not normally contain Subjects (an example of an exception is *Don't you start whingeing as well!*), and that their verb is in the base form. As with the declarative and interrogative clause types, sometimes imperatives do not receive the default directive interpretation. Consider the sentence below:

(41)   Take care of yourself.

If someone says this to you, you're hardly likely to interpret it as an order to look after yourself, but rather as a wish of some sort.

4.3.4   Exclamative Clauses

Exclamatives, like the open interrogatives, are formed with an initial Wh-word:

(42)   What a load of nonsense he talks!
(43)   How absolutely disgraceful he looks!

Recall that *how* is standardly also regarded as a Wh-word. Exclamatives differ from interrogatives in that in the former, the Wh-word usually functions as a modifying element inside a phrase (NP and AP respectively in the sentences above), whereas in the latter the Wh-word is an NP, as (29) shows.

There are cases where the Wh-element is a Modifier in interrogative sentences too, but this modifying element then occupies a slightly different syntactic position. Compare (44) and (45):

(44)   What book did he buy?   Interrogative (not **What a book did he buy?*)
(45)   What a book he bought!   Exclamative (not **What book he bought!*)

In (44) there is only one modifying element (*what*), whereas in (45) there are two, namely *what* and the determinative *a*.

Exclamative clauses are used almost exclusively as exclamations. They can, however, also be questions, as B's response in (46) shows:

(46) *A*: What an extraordinary lecturer Kate is!
     B: What an extraordinary lecturer *who* is?

Additionally, we could take A's exclamation to be making a statement.

4.3.5   The Pragmatics of the Clause Types

It is important for you to realise that the terms 'declarative', 'interrogative', 'imperative' and 'exclamative' are *syntactic* labels that refer to clause types that have certain *syntactic* characteristics (e.g., Subject-auxiliary inversion in the case of interrogatives, no Subject in the case of imperatives, etc.). The notions *statement*, *question*, *directive* and *exclamation*, by contrast, are *pragmatic* notions. Pragmatics is the study of the meaning of linguistic expressions in context. In other words, pragmatics is concerned with language *use*. With regard to each of the sentence types discussed above we have observed that they all have a *typical* use. Thus:

Syntax		**Pragmatics**
Declaratives	are *typically* used to make	statements
Interrogatives	are *typically* used to ask	questions
Imperatives	are *typically* used to issue	directives
Exclamatives	are *typically* used to utter	exclamations

I have highlighted the word 'typically' because there is no one-to-one relationship between the clause types and the uses that are made of them.

Let's take a closer look at questions. Be aware of the fact that this notion is used in its technical linguistic sense here. Questions need not always be syntactically interrogative. As we saw above, if we add a rising intonation contour to a declarative sentence a question results, as has happened in (47), the question version of (25):

(47) You haven't closed the door?

This last example we refer to as a *yes/no question*. A yes/no question is an utterance that has the force of a question and elicits a 'yes' or 'no' response. Its syntactic form can, but need not be, interrogative. (47), then, is an example of a declarative clause with the force, not of a statement, but that of a question. Be careful to distinguish yes/no questions from yes/no interrogatives. The former need not be syntactically interrogative; the latter, by definition, always are.

We also have *open questions*. These are utterances that have the force of questions which elicit a potentially infinite variety of answers. An example is (48), which might be uttered in disbelief at someone else having just said (24).

(48) My aunt likes WHAT?

Notice that (48) is syntactically declarative, but pragmatically an open question.

Finally, there are also *alternative questions*:

(49) You want beer or kir?

This clause is syntactically declarative (compare the alternative interrogative *Do you want beer or kir?*). It could be used in a situation in which a person hasn't quite heard what another person has said. For example speaker A might utter (50) a to which speaker B might respond with (50)b.

(50) *A*: I would like some kir.
  B: Sorry, I didn't catch that. *You want beer or kir?*

Again, (49) is syntactically declarative, as we have just seen, but pragmatically it is a question.

4.4   More on Tree Diagrams

In this section I will discuss in more detail the ways in which we can represent syntactic structures. We've already come across the concept of *tree diagrams*. We now need some terminology to talk about them in a more precise way.

As we have seen, tree diagrams are visual representations of hierarchical linguistic structures. (51) is the tree diagram for the sentence *Tim thought that Kate believed the story.*

(51)

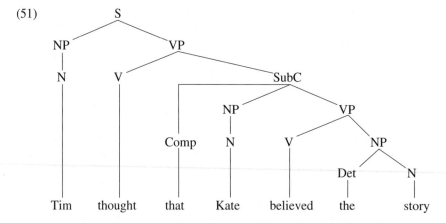

Moving away now from representations of particular structures like (51), we turn to a discussion of the relationships between the elements in trees. Consider (52) below:

(52)

In this abstract tree we call X, Y and Z *nodes*. We will say that X *dominates* Y and Z. What this means is that we can draw a line from the higher position X in the tree to the lower positions Y and Z. Furthermore, Y *precedes* Z. This means simply that Y occurs to the left of Z in the tree structure. Consider next the tree in (53):

(53)

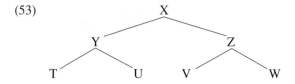

The relationships between X, Y and Z are the same, except that we can be a little more precise. In (53) X still dominates Y and Z, but it also dominates T, U, V and W. To distinguish the dominance relation between X and Y/Z from that between X and T/U/V/W let us draw a distinction between dominance and *immediate dominance*: X dominates all the nodes below it, but immediately dominates only Y and Z. Using family terminology, we say that X is the *mother* of Y and Z, and, conversely, that Y and Z are the *daughters* of X. Furthermore, Y and Z are *sisters* of each other. Analogous to the terminology concerning dominance, we say T *immediately precedes* U, but only precedes V and W.

The new terminology allows us to be more precise about the notion constituent. We defined constituents in Chapter 1 as strings of one or more words that syntactically and semantically behave as a unit. Formally we now define a constituent as follows:

Constituent
Y is a constituent of X if and only if X dominates Y.

Thus in (53) all of Y, Z, T, U, V and W are constituents of X. Notice in addition that the nodes T and U make up the constituent Y, and that V and W make up the constituent Z. We define immediate constituents as follows:

Immediate constituent
Y is an immediate constituent of X if and only if X immediately dominates Y.

Thus Y and Z are immediate constituents of X, T and U are immediate constituents of Y, and V and W are immediate constituents of Z.

In addition, consider the structure below:

(54)

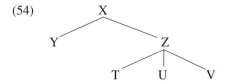

Here T, U and V together form the constituent Z, but T and U do not form a constituent. The reason for this is that:

A set of nodes A forms a constituent B, if B dominates *all and only* the nodes of A.

I will discuss the notion of constituency in much greater detail in Chapters 11 and 12.

Exercise

Answer the following questions with either *yes* or *no* using the tree diagram in
(53). Explain your answers.

(i)   Does T dominate U?
(ii)   Does Z dominate U?
(iii)   Does Z dominate W?
(iv)   Does Z immediately dominate W?
(v)   Does T precede W?
(vi)   Does T precede Y?
(vii)   Is U a sister of T?
(viii)   Is V a sister of T?
(ix)   Is V a daughter of X?
(x)   Is V a daughter of Z?
(xi)   Do T and U form a constituent?
(xii)   Do U and V form a constituent?
(xiii)   Do T, U, V, W form a constituent?
(xiv)   In (54), do Y and T form a constituent?

Tree diagrams are a very clear way of representing syntactic structure graphically.
They have a major disadvantage, though, and that is that they take up a lot of space on
the printed page. One way of getting round this is to use triangles (sometimes called
clothes-hangers). We use these when we are not interested in the structure of a particular constituent. Using triangles we can also represent (51) as in (55), or as in (56):

(55)

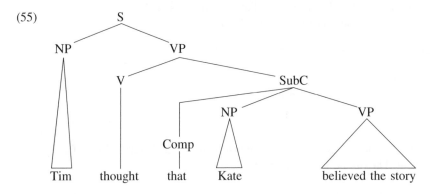

(56)

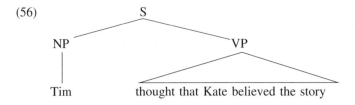

The tree in (55) only takes up marginally less space than the one in (51), however. Another, more effective, way of saving space in representing syntactic structure is by using labelled bracketings, which were introduced in Section 4.1. These, however, suffer from the disadvantage that they can be difficult to read. It is important for you to realise that labelled bracketings are a different way of representing syntactic structure, but they are otherwise equivalent to phrase markers.

Exercise

'Translate' the following labelled bracketings into phrase markers (cc = coordinating conjunction).

(57)   [$_{AP}$ [$_{AP}$ old] [$_{cc}$ *and*] [$_{AP}$ useless]]
(58)   [$_{NP}$ [$_{NP}$ a computer] [$_{cc}$ *and*] [$_{NP}$ a keyboard]]
(59)   [$_{AP}$ [$_{AP}$ pretty stupid] [$_{cc}$ *and*] [$_{AP}$ quite eager]]
(60)   [$_{VP}$ [$_{VP}$ likes tea] [$_{cc}$ *and*] [$_{VP}$ hates coffee]]
(61)   [$_{PP}$ [$_{PP}$ on the table] [$_{cc}$ *and*] [$_{PP}$ in the cupboard]]
(62)   [$_{AdvP}$ [$_{AdvP}$ wilfully] [$_{cc}$ *and*] [$_{AdvP}$ mercilessly]]
(63)   [$_{S}$ [$_{S}$ They arrived at 10 a.m.] [$_{cc}$ *and*] [$_{S}$ they left at 6 p.m.]]
(64)   [$_{S}$ [$_{S}$ we will not offer this student a place] [$_{cc}$ *and*] [$_{S}$ we can recommend a College that will]]

To round off this section I will briefly discuss the question how the grammatical functions (GFs) of constituents in sentences are represented in tree diagrams. You may already have noticed that they aren't. We will assume that functions can be 'read off' tree diagrams by looking at the structural configuration of the constituents. The GF of Subject can then be defined as the NP immediately dominated by the S-node, notated as [NP, S], whereas the GF of Direct Object is an NP immediately dominated by VP, notated [NP, VP]:

(65)

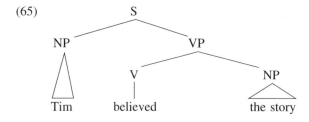

Let us now take a step back and see what we have achieved so far. In the last two chapters we took a preliminary look at the elements that make up sentences in English (words, phrases, clauses and sentences) and at the way these elements function. In this chapter the nature of these building blocks has been scrutinised in more depth. We also took a closer look at the way in which we can represent sentences in tree diagrams. The subject matter of the next chapter is to relate the function and form levels in a more systematic way than has been done so far.

Key Concepts in this Chapter

clause
matrix clause
subordinate clause
finite clause, nonfinite clause
the rank scale
tree diagram
clause types and their typical uses
    declarative clause/statement
    interrogative clause/question
    imperative clause/directive
    exclamative clause/exclamation
node
    mother node
    sister node
(immediate) dominance
(immediate) precedence
(immediate) constituent

Exercises

1. Consider the following sentence: *I suggest that we have some lunch now.*
    True or false?

    (i)   This sentence contains only one clause.
    (ii)   This sentence contains two VPs.
    (iii) The DO of *suggest* is an NP.
    (iv) The matrix clause is nonfinite.

2. Produce labelled bracketings for the trees below. Underline the Heads.

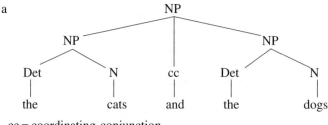

cc = coordinating conjunction

b

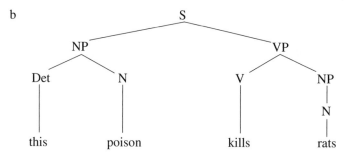

3. Identify the matrix clause and the subordinate clause(s) in the sentences below. Are the subordinate clauses finite or nonfinite?

(i)   She believes that he is devious.
(ii) I made her laugh.
(iii) Sara concluded that Jamie heard that the story was untrue.
(iv) She wanted me to sell my bike.

4. Using labelled bracketings, analyse the following sentences at the word, phrase, clause and sentence levels, as in Section 4.2. Then produce tree diagrams.

(i)   The giraffe ducked.
(ii) Television destroys relationships.
(ii) Freddy sent the doctor a postcard.
(iii) I believe that Geri adores gherkins.
(iv) I know that Krum likes New York.

5. Assign the following sentences to one of the clause types. Can they be used in situations other than the ones they are typically used for? Explain your answer.

(i)   You may leave.
(ii) Could you be quiet, please?
(iii) Enjoy your meal!
(iv) This is a pavement! (imagine a pedestrian saying this to a cyclist using the pavement)
(v)   Who likes right-wing dictators?
(vi) It's so hot in here.

*6. Identify the correct tree diagram for the sentence in (i). What's wrong with the other trees?

(i)   Doctors cure patients.

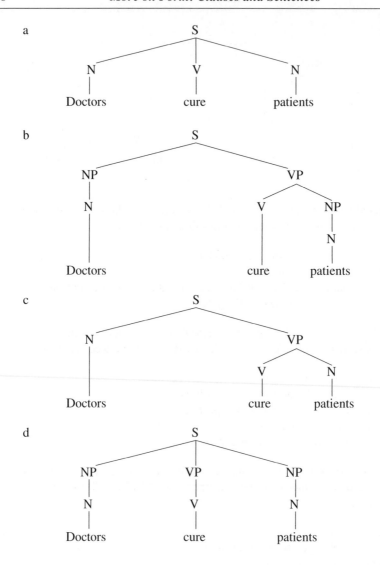

Further Reading

Clause types are sometimes also called *sentence types*, a term I used in the first and second editions of this book. However, as Huddleston (1984), Chapter 11, makes clear, the system of classification really applies to clauses, both superordinate and subordinate. See also Levinson (1983). Tree diagrams are found mostly in more theoretically oriented approaches to language. For further discussion in a somewhat different framework, see Radford (1988), Chapter 3.

5 The Function–Form Interface

In the last three chapters we looked at the various components that make up sentences in English. We were concerned with two levels of analysis: first we examined the *functions* of the constituent parts of sentences. Then we investigated *form*, i.e. how the different elements in sentences combine into larger units. Remember that 'function' refers to Subjects, Direct Objects, Adjuncts, etc., and 'form' refers to words, word classes (noun, adjective, verb, etc.), phrases (NP, AP, VP, etc.), clauses (matrix clause, subordinate clause) or sentences. Because I dealt with function and form in separate chapters, you may have gained the impression that these levels of analysis are quite distinct and unrelated. Quite the contrary! The interrelationships between function and form are of immense importance in the study of syntax, and a good understanding of the issues involved is essential to a proper understanding of sentence structure. Because the function–form interface is so important, I will devote an entire chapter to a detailed discussion of how we can link these two levels more systematically than we have done so far.

5.1 Function–Form Relationships

Before turning to a discussion of the linguistic notions of function and form, let's first consider the general notion 'function' in connection with ordinary three-dimensional objects. Rather superficially, an observation we can make is that most objects perform a certain practical function. Consider, for example, a pencil. What is its function? Depending on the person you are, your circumstances, your interests, your profession, etc. you may give a variety of answers to this question. For example 'writing' (if you're a student), 'drawing' (if you're an artist), or perhaps 'designing' (if you're an architect). Or take a rather more complex object, a personal computer. Again we might ask: what is its function? There is no uniform answer. We can use a computer for word processing, for making calculations, for sending e-mail messages, etc. Notice that as regards objects and the functions we can carry out with them, the reverse situation also holds: for most functions that we may want to perform a variety of objects can be used. For example, the function 'transportation' can be performed by a car, a train, a bus, a boat, a bicycle, etc. The point is that there is no one-to-one relationship between a particular function (writing, drawing, word processing, etc.) and the object used (pencil, computer) to carry out that function. Having said that, of course it is true that there is often a salient function for any one object. For example, the salient function of buses is 'transportation'.

For present purposes it is important for you to see that in language too there is a lack of a one-to-one relationship between the various forms we encounter and the functions they perform. The converse also holds: a particular function may be performed by different forms. This is why we need to distinguish between function and form.

It is time now to become a little more concrete and see what exactly is meant when we say that there is no unique relationship between form and function in language. In the remainder of this chapter I will discuss the several ways in which each grammatical function can be *realised*.

5.2   Realisations of the Subject

Recall that we can identify the Subject of a sentence by asking 'Who or what carried out the action denoted by the verb?' and 'Who or what is this sentence about?' So, in a simple sentence like *Fred eats his breakfast in bed* we can identify the expression *Fred* as the Subject, because this NP refers to the individual who is doing the eating, and because the sentence can be said to be about him. We saw in Chapter 2 that this semantic characterisation of the notion Subject was not enough, and we therefore also characterised Subjects in terms of the kinds of syntactic structures they occur in. In most cases, however, asking the two simple questions above leads to a correct identification of the Subject.

In this section we will concern ourselves with the following question: which are the particular forms that Subjects can assume? When we discussed Subjects in Chapter 2 we saw that they are typically Noun Phrases:

NPs functioning as Subject

(1) $[_{NP}$ *The hedgehog]* ate the cream cake.
(2) $[_{NP}$ *A rat]* bit my toe.
(3) $[_{NP}$ *This shoe]* hurts me.
(4) $[_{NP}$ *Academics]* never lie.

However, Subjects can also be realised by other phrase types. Take the set of sentences in (5)–(8) where the Subjects are realised as Prepositional Phrases:

PPs functioning as Subject

(5) $[_{PP}$ *Under the stairs]* was a safe area to be during the war.
(6) $[_{PP}$ *Outside the fridge]* is not a good place to keep milk.
(7) $[_{PP}$ *After Saturday]* would be a good time to go away for a few days.
(8) $[_{PP}$ *Between eleven and midnight]* suits me alright.

There are some restrictions on PPs as Subjects in English. Firstly, they are usually phrases that specify a location, as in (5) and (6), or time interval, as in (7) and (8). Secondly, the main verb of the sentence is often, though not exclusively (cf. (8)), a form of the verb *be*.

Consider next some examples of APs and AdvPs functioning as Subjects.

AP functioning as Subject

(9)   [*AP Restless*] is what I would call him.

AdvP functioning as Subject

(10)   [*AdvP Cautiously*] is how I would suggest you do it.

More common than PPs, APs or AdvPs as Subjects are clausal Subjects. Here are some examples of sentences with finite clauses as Subject.

Finite clauses functioning as Subject

(11)   *[That he will go to New York soon]* is obvious.
(12)   *[Because he is generous]* doesn't mean that he is rich.
(13)   *[What the terrorists said]* puzzled the police.
(14)   *[Why she consented]* remains a mystery.

The bracketed Subject clauses in (11) and (12) are introduced by a conjunction, while those in (13)–(14) are introduced by a *Wh-word*, i.e. a word that begins with the letters *wh*; for example, *who, what, where, why*, etc. (see Section 4.3.2) These clauses are called *Wh-clauses*. The syntax of Wh-clauses needs special attention, and we'll therefore return to them in Chapter 8.

Nonfinite clauses too can perform the function of Subject. Recall from Chapter 4 that such clauses can be of five types: we have *to*-infinitive clauses, bare infinitive clauses, *-ing* participle clauses, *-ed* participle clauses and Small Clauses. Four of these types of clauses can perform the function of Subject: *to*-infinitive clauses ((15)–(26)), bare infinitive clauses ((27)), *-ing* participle clauses ((28)-(35)), and Small Clauses ((36)).

In (15)–(18) the *to*-infinitive clauses take a Subject of their own. This Subject is always preceded by *for*. In (19)–(22) the Subject clauses do not have their own Subject. *To*-infinitive clauses without a Subject can be of two types: they are either not introduced at all, as in (19)–(22), or they are introduced by a Wh-word, as in (23)–(26), in the same way as in (13) and (14), except that this time we are dealing with verbs that do not carry tense.

Nonfinite clauses functioning as Subject

To-infinitive clauses functioning as Subject

with a Subject of their own:

(15)   *[For Judith to buy that house]* would spell disaster.
(16)   *[For us to understand the issues]* requires a major mental effort.
(17)   *[For Janet to go to College]* would be a good idea.
(18)   *[For Karl to visit art galleries]* would not be desirable.

without a Subject of their own:

(19)   *[To be a good teacher]* is more difficult than people think.
(20)   *[To see her]* is to love her.
(21)   *[To surrender our arms]* will seem cowardly.
(22)   *[To break down this fence]* could lead to a conflict with the neighbours.

without a Subject of their own, introduced by a Wh-word:

(23)   *[What to read during the holidays]* is the question all students are asking.
(24)   *[Who to ask for permission]* seems quite clear.
(25)   *[Where to sleep in this town]* will not be an easy problem to solve.
(26)   *[Whether to teach grammar or not to schoolchildren]* is a hotly debated issue.

Notice that where the Subject clause has no Subject of its own, one is usually implied and can easily be inferred. For example, in (19) the implied Subject of the bracketed clause is *someone*: *For someone to be a good teacher is more difficult than people think.*

Sentence (27) is an example of a sentence that contains a bare infinitive clause as Subject. These are quite rare, used informally and perhaps not acceptable to all speakers. (28)–(35) instantiate Subject clauses in the form of *-ing* participle clauses, both with a Subject (in (28)–(31)), and without a Subject (in (32)–(35)):

Bare infinitive clauses functioning as Subject

(27)   ?*[Party the night away]* is a nice thing to do.

-ing participle clauses functioning as Subject

with a Subject of their own:

(28)   *[Pete breaking the rules]* is unacceptable.
(29)   *[Students walking on the roof]* poses a safety risk.

(30)   *[Damien fooling around]* embarrasses his friends.

(31)   *[George buying all those books]* will cost his father a fortune.

without a Subject of their own:

(32)   *[Going on holiday]* always creates tensions.

(33)   *[Running a business]* is hard work.

(34)   *[Swimming in this lake]* will make you ill.

(35)   *[Refusing to help the needy]* is selfish.

As with the *to*-infinitive clauses, if there is no Subject, it can be inferred from the context or from one's knowledge of the world.

We now turn to Small Clauses (SCs) functioning as Subject. You will remember from Chapter 4 that SCs are clauses without an overt verb, but in which the verb *be* is implied. SC Subject clauses are rare. They always have a Subject of their own, as the following example shows:

Small Clauses functioning as Subject

(36)   *[The kitchen free of cockroaches]* is a welcome prospect.

5.3   Realisation of the Predicate and Predicator

Recall that the Predicate in a sentence consists of everything but the Subject. Thus, in (37) *Eric* is the Subject and *lost his keys yesterday* is the Predicate. Inside the Predicate we distinguish the Predicator (the verb *lose*), the Direct Object (the NP *his keys*) and an Adjunct (the Noun Phrase *yesterday*):

(37)   Eric lost his keys yesterday.

Predicates are Verb Phrases, and Predicators are always main verbs. There is little variability as regards the realisation of Predicates and Predicators, but there is some, which we will deal with in Part IV of this book.

5.4   Realisations of the Direct Object

Direct Objects are usually constituents which refer to an entity that can be said to undergo the action denoted by the verb. The way we put it in Chapter 2 was to say that Direct Objects typically have the semantic role of Patient. A simple way of determining what is the Direct Object in a particular sentence is to ask 'Who or what is affected by the action denoted by the verb?' For example, in (37) if we ask 'What is affected by the process of losing?' the answer is *his keys*. This NP is therefore the DO of the sentence. Now we must address the question how DOs can be realised syntactically.

Direct Objects can be realised by the following range of phrases and clauses: Noun Phrases, Prepositional Phrases, finite clauses and nonfinite clauses. Let's start with some simple examples of NPs as Direct Objects:

NPs functioning as Direct Object

(38)   Monica admires *[NP the President]*.
(39)   Ralph enjoys *[NP her company]*.
(40)   William lit *[NP the barbecue]*.
(41)   Nina described *[NP the event]*.

Prepositional Phrases as DO are even rarer than Prepositional Phrases as Subject, but some possible structures are shown in (42) and (43):

PPs functioning as Direct Object

(42)   Speaker A: Where will the new discotheque be built?
       Speaker B: I don't know, but the council rejected *[PP behind the church]*.
(43)   Speaker A: Are you going on holiday before or after Easter?
       Speaker B: I prefer *[PP before Easter]*.

Like PPs as Subjects, PPs as Direct Objects tend to be locative phrases or phrases specifying a time span.

Let us now turn to examples of Direct Objects in the form of clauses. First I will give some examples of finite DO clauses. In (44)–(47) we have *that*-clauses as Direct Objects, and in (48)–(51) we have Wh-clauses:

Finite clauses functioning as Direct Object

That-clauses functioning as Direct Object

(44)   The government believes *[that the voters are stupid]*.
(45)   She admits *[that she ignored the red light]*.
(46)   Maggie doubts *[that her boyfriend will ever change]*.
(47)   We regret [*that we appointed you*].

Finite Wh-clauses functioning as Direct Object

(48)   He knows *[what she means]*.
(49)   He explained *[who would be in charge of the investigation]*.
(50)   I don't remember *[why Paul said that]*.
(51)   They finally decided *[where they will send their child to school]*.

Nonfinite Direct Object clauses can be realised by all five types of nonfinite clause: *to*-infinitive clauses, bare infinitive clauses, *-ing* participle clauses, *-ed* participle clauses and Small Clauses.

We'll start with examples of *to*-infinitive clauses as Direct Objects, both with a Subject of their own, as in (52)–(55), and without a Subject of their own, as in (56)–(63). *To*-infinitive DO clauses without a Subject of their own can be of two types: either they are not introduced at all, as in (56)–(59), or they are introduced by a Wh-word, as in (60)–(63):

Nonfinite clauses functioning as Direct Object

To-infinitive clauses functioning as Direct Object

with a Subject of their own:

(52)   Ann considers *[Helen to be an excellent director]*.
(53)   They believe *[the tabloid newspapers to contain nothing but smut]*.
(54)   The company expects *[its employees to dress smartly]*.
(55)   She imagined *[the others to want promotion also]*.

without a Subject of their own:

(56)   Gary wants *[to leave]*.
(57)   We hope *[to see you soon]*.
(58)   They expect *[to leave the country within twenty-four hours]*.
(59)   She proposed *[to open a restaurant in London]*.

without a Subject of their own, introduced by a Wh-word:

(60)   He forgot *[what to say to the examiners]*.
(61)   The dentist couldn't decide *[who to see next]*.
(62)   They told their family *[when to come over]*.
(63)   You should know *[how to do arithmetic without a calculator]*.

You will remember from the previous section, when we were looking at nonfinite Subject clauses without a Subject of their own, that a Subject was nevertheless recoverable from the context, or from our knowledge of the world. For example, in (21), repeated here

(64)   *[To surrender our arms]* will seem cowardly.

the understood Subject of the subordinate clause is 'us': 'for us to surrender our arms will seem cowardly'. We are faced with a similar situation in the case of nonfinite Direct Object clauses without a Subject, except that now a Subject is recoverable from the matrix clause. For example, the implied Subject of each of the subordinate clauses in (56)–(63) is the Subject of the matrix clause. To illustrate this, consider (56): here it is clear that *Gary* is the Subject both of the 'wanting' and of the 'leaving'.

Let us turn now to bare infinitive clauses as Direct Objects. You will recall that such clauses contain an infinitive without the particle *to*. Bare infinitive clauses as DO always contain a Subject:

Bare infinitive clauses functioning as Direct Object

(65)   We saw *[the sun rise]*.
(66)   Rick could hear *[his tutor rage with anger]*.
(67)   She made *[her boyfriend cry]*.
(68)   I let *[the situation pass]*.

The verbs that take bare infinitive clauses as DO are mostly verbs of perception (*see, hear*) and so-called *causative verbs*, i.e. verbs that denote a process of causation (*make, let*).

There are three remaining types of Direct Object clause: *-ing* participle clauses, *-ed* participle clauses and Small Clauses.

Like *to*-infinitive clauses, Direct Object *-ing* participle clauses can occur both with and without a Subject of their own. Where the subordinate clause has no Subject, it is interpreted as being the same as the matrix clause Subject.

-ing participle clauses functioning as Direct Object

with a Subject of their own:

(69)   I heard *[Jamie singing in the bath]*.
(70)   The witness saw *[someone running away]*.
(71)   They remember *[the cast rehearsing for days]*.
(72)   We could smell *[something burning]*.

without a Subject of their own:

(73)   She abhors *[eating meat]*.
(74)   Willy intended *[registering for the exams]*.
(75)   Ray regrets *[buying a sports car]*.
(76)   I can't imagine *[travelling to Moscow]*.

Direct Object clauses can also come in the form of an *-ed* participle clause. Like bare infinitive DO clauses, *-ed* participle clauses always take a Subject:

-ed participle clauses functioning as Direct Object

(77)   We had *[the prisoners jailed]*.
(78)   She watched *[the ship moored]*.

(79)   I need *[my watch repaired]*.

(80)   They found *[the front door locked]*.

Finally, here are some examples of SCs functioning as Direct Object:

Small Clauses functioning as Direct Object

(81)   Martin considers *[Tim a creep]*. (= (16) of Chapter 4)

(82)   Larry judges *[the Head of Department a genius]*.

(83)   Phil deems *[Henry foolish]*. (= (17) of Chapter 4)

(84)   Katie thinks *[us clever]*.

5.5   Realisations of the Indirect Object

The function of Indirect Object was characterised in Chapter 2 as the Goal/ Receiver or Beneficiary of the activity denoted by the verb. Thus, in *The boss paid Roland a lot of money* the NP *Roland* is the Indirect Object because it is the Goal/Receiver of the paying activity.

Indirect Objects are very restricted in their realisation. More often than not they are Noun Phrases. Occasionally they are Wh-clauses.

Noun Phrases functioning as Indirect Object

(85)   She told *[$_{NP}$ her brother]* a lie.

(86)   Gertrude gave *[$_{NP}$ her friend]* a birthday present.

(87)   We sent *[$_{NP}$ the committee]* an angry letter.

(88)   The curator of the museum showed *[$_{NP}$ the party]* some rare paintings.

Wh-clauses functioning as Indirect Object

(89)   Sean told *whoever wanted to hear it* his story.

5.6   Realisations of Adjuncts

From Chapter 2 you will remember that Adjuncts are constituents that tell you more about the *how, when, where* or *why* of the activity or situation expressed by the sentences they occur in. For example, in *I left London on Saturday* the PP *on Saturday* is an Adjunct, because it tells you *when* I left London.

Let's now take a look at the ways in which Adjuncts can be realised. There are no fewer than six ways. Adjuncts can be Adverb Phrases, Prepositional Phrases, Noun Phrases, finite clauses, nonfinite clauses and Small Clauses.

Let's start with some examples of Adjuncts realised as Adverb Phrases.

AdvPs functioning as Adjunct

(90)   He cleaned the house *[AdvP quite cheerfully]*.
(91)   The company *[AdvP officially]* denied all responsibility.
(92)   He *[AdvP urgently]* needed to see a doctor.
(93)   *[AdvP Repeatedly]* they had their car stolen.

Adjuncts realised as AdvPs can express a variety of meanings: in (90) *quite cheerfully* communicates the *manner* in which the cleaning of the house was carried out, while the AdvPs in (91)–(93) express *viewpoint, degree* and *frequency*. Notice the various positions the Adjuncts can occupy.

PPs functioning as Adjunct

(94)   Otto cooked his evening meal *[PP in a rush]*.
(95)   We met *[PP outside Paris]*.
(96)   *[PP With a penknife]* Frank cut the bread.
(97)   They always drink sherry *[PP before dinner]*.

Adjunct-PPs can also express a multiplicity of semantic notions: *manner* (94), *location* (95), *instrument* (96) and *time* (97), among others.

NPs functioning as Adjunct

(98)   Helen discovered the Italian restaurant *[NP yesterday]*.
(99)   The crisis began *[NP last year]*.
(100)   He resigned *[NP the month before last]*.
(101)   He wants me to do it *[NP this second]*.

NPs as Adjunct usually specify 'time when'.
    We now turn to clauses that function as Adjuncts, starting with finite clauses introduced by a subordinator (see Section 3.7 if you've forgotten what a subordinator is). Again, as with AdvPs, PPs and NPs functioning as Adjuncts, there is a wide variety of meanings that such clauses can express. The most important of these are *time* (introduced by *as soon as, before, since, till, until, when, whenever, while, whilst*, among others), *reason* (introduced by *because, as* or *since*), *condition* (introduced by *if, even if* or *unless*), *result* (introduced by *so* or *so that*), and *purpose* (introduced by *so that* or *in order that*). Here are some examples. (Notice that the Adjunct clause can be in sentence-initial or sentence-final position.)

Finite clauses functioning as Adjunct

(102)   They will be cooking the meal, *[when we arrive]*.
(103)   *[While Francis was watching TV]*, Paul was peeling the potatoes.
(104)   Gay doesn't like Mark, *[because he gives her the creeps]*.

(105)   *[Since he never used his card]*, the library cancelled his membership.
(106)   We'll go to Paris, *[if you promise not to smoke]*.
(107)   *[Unless you object]*, I'll smoke a cigar.
(108)   Tell Nelly to hurry up, *[so that we can go out]*.
(109)   *[So she doesn't have to carry around her spectacles]*, Emily wears contact lenses,
(110)   She'll give the money to a charity, *[in order that they will spend it on a good cause]*.
(111)   *[In order that his son might take over the shop]*, Jack retired.

Exercise

Classify the bracketed Adjunct clauses above in terms of the semantic notions of 'time', 'reason', 'result', 'purpose' or 'condition'.

Some subordinators can introduce Adjunct clauses of more than one semantic type. Consider the sentences below, both of which contain an Adjunct clause introduced by *since*:

(112)   Charlie has never been back, *[since he last visited us in the spring]*.
(113)   We didn't ask Neil to come, *[since nobody likes him]*.

Exercise

Determine which semantic type of Adjunct clause we are dealing with in (112) and (113).

In (112) the clause introduced by *since* is a temporal Adjunct clause. It tells us that Henry hasn't been back since the time of the occasion on which he visited us in the spring. In (113), by contrast, the *since*-clause gives the reason why Neil wasn't asked to come.

We turn now to nonfinite Adjunct clauses. All types of nonfinite clause can function as Adjunct: *to*-infinitive clauses, bare infinitive clauses, *-ing* participle clauses, *-ed* participle clauses and Small Clauses. They can express the same range of meanings as their finite counterparts: time, reason, purpose, etc. Examples are given below.

Nonfinite clauses functioning as Adjunct

To-infinitive clauses functioning as Adjunct

with a Subject of their own:

(114)   We need some music *[for us to enjoy the evening]*.
(115)   *[For Marie to pass her driving test]* she will need to take many more lessons.

(116)   Catherine will need to work harder *[for her to reach her life's ambition]*.

(117)   *[For Rick and Rachel to appreciate oysters]* they will need to overcome their revulsion for eating raw fish.

without a Subject of their own:

(118)   Alex replaced the lock on the door *[in order to make the house more secure]*.

(119)   *[So as to move about more easily]*, Robert bought himself a car.

(120)   You will need to travel to the United States *[to hear him lecture]*.

(121)   *[To produce an essay every two weeks]* you will have to work very hard.

Notice that in (118)–(121) the Subjects of the Adjunct clauses are interpreted as being the same as the Subjects of the matrix clauses.

Bare infinitive clauses functioning as Adjunct

These are very rare. Only bare infinitive clauses introduced by *rather than* and *sooner than* can function as Adjuncts. They have no Subject.

(122)   *[Rather than sell the painting]* Ike preferred to destroy it.

(123)   Ray wants to travel by train *[sooner than fly]*.

-ing participle clauses functioning as Adjunct

with a Subject of their own:

(124)   *[The streets being completely empty]*, Jackie preferred to take a cab.

(125)   Sally stared out of the window, *[her thoughts drifting away dreamily]*.

(126)   *[His dog scampering beside him]*, Leonard walked home.

(127)   Henry will send the manuscript of his novel to a publisher, *[his wife persuading him that it was a good piece of work]*.

without a Subject of their own:

(128)   *[Working on his essay late]*, Tom was quickly becoming tired.

(129)   Bob talked to his girlfriend on the phone, *[watching TV at the same time]*.

(130)   *[Standing on a table]*, Dawn addressed the crowd.

(131)   Gus got off the train, *[buttoning up his coat]*.

The Subjects of the Adjunct clauses are understood as being the same as the Subjects of the matrix clauses.

-ed participle clauses functioning as Adjunct

with a Subject of their own:

(132) *[The attack averted]*, the people of the town could come out of hiding.
(133) We were all excited, *[the plan accepted by the government]*.
(134) *[The trees chopped down]*, the park looked miserable.
(135) She went home, *[all the work completed]*.

without a Subject of their own:

(136) *[Disgusted by what he had witnessed]*, Frank left the party.
(137) Meg joined Amnesty International, *[convinced that this would benefit political prisoners]*.
(138) *[Formulated clearly]*, this form will cause no problems.
(139) She died in her car, *[suffocated by exhaust fumes]*.

Small Clauses functioning as Adjunct

(140) He is from a wealthy background, *[his father a businessman]*.
(141) *[The doctor ill]*, we had no-one to look after my sister.
(142) She went back to her homeland, *[her mind free of hate]*.
(143) *[The police unrepentant]*, we took them to court.

For each of the example sentences in this chapter I have indicated a particular analysis, using labelled bracketings. What I have *not* done so far is justify why a particular analysis was chosen in preference to another. For example, take sentence (52), repeated here for convenience:

(144) Ann considers *[Helen to be an excellent director]*.

The analysis of constructions like this is controversial. In (144) I take the string *Helen to be an excellent director* to be the Direct Object of the verb *consider*, and *Helen* to be the Subject of the DO clause. You may have wondered why I haven't analysed *Helen* as the DO instead. There are linguists who would argue that such an analysis is to be preferred (see the Further Reading section at the end of the chapter). However, there are a number of reasons for rejecting the view that *Helen* is a Direct Object, and in favour of adopting the analysis indicated in (144). Part IV of this book will cover the area of verb complementation extensively, and we will discuss the justification for analyses like (144) in detail. Anticipating that discussion, let us here take a brief look at one of the arguments in favour of the bracketing in (144).

Remember that one way of finding out what is the Direct Object of a sentence is to ask 'Who or what was affected by the action denoted by the verb?'. Thus, if we have the simple sentence *Joe kicked the stone*, and we ask 'Who or what was affected by the kicking?' the answer is *the stone*.

Exercise

Think for a moment about the question who or what is affected by the 'considering' that Ann is engaged in. In other words, what is the answer to the question 'Who or what is Ann considering?'

The answer is not *Helen*: Ann is not considering Helen as such, she is considering a *proposition*, namely the proposition 'that Helen is an excellent director'. This means that the DO of (144) is the nonfinite *to*-infinitive clause.

Consider next (145):

(145)   Larry considers *[my brother a genius]*.

The analysis of sentences like (145) is also controversial because linguists do not agree about the functional status of the NP *my brother* that follows the verb. Some grammarians would argue that it is a Direct Object, while others would say that it is the Subject of a Small Clause, as in (146):

(146)   Larry considers *[Small Clause my brother a genius]*.

The analysis of (145) as in (146) may seem novel to you, but if you think for a moment what (145) actually means, then perhaps the reason for this analysis will become clear. In (145) Larry is not considering a person (*my brother*); what he is considering is a proposition, namely the proposition 'that my brother is a genius'. For this reason (147), which contains a finite *that*-clause as Direct Object, is a perfect paraphrase of (145):

(147)   Larry considers *[Clause that my brother is a genius]*.

Because Larry is not considering a person in (145), but a proposition, the DO of the verb *consider* is not the NP *my brother* but the (verbless) small clause *my brother a genius*. In further support of the analysis in (146), observe that, in addition to (147), we can paraphrase (145) as in (148):

(148)   Larry considers *[Clause my brother **to be** a genius]*.

The analyses proposed in this chapter will require a more detailed justification. This will be provided in Part IV of the book.

To end this chapter there follows below a table summarising the main function-form relationships (the functions Predicate and Predicator have been left out):

Table 5.1 Form–Function Relationships

Form	Function			
	Subject	Direct Object	Indirect Object	Adjunct
Noun Phrase	✓	✓	✓	✓
Adjective Phrase *	✓	–	–	–*
Prepositional Phrase	✓	✓	–	✓
Adverb Phrase	✓	–	–	✓
Finite Clauses				
That-clause	✓	✓	–	–
Wh-clause	✓	✓	✓	✓
Clauses introduced by *because, while*, etc.	✓	–	–	✓
Nonfinite Clauses				
to-infinitive clause	✓	✓	–	✓
bare infinitive clause	✓	✓	–	✓
-ing participle clause	✓	✓	–	✓
-ed participle clause	–	✓	–	✓
Small Clause	✓	✓	–	✓

* Though see Chapter 7, where I will argue that APs that modify nouns are also Adjuncts.

The central concern of this chapter has been to demonstrate the fact that there exists no one-to-one relationship between function and form in language, and this is why the two notions need to be kept apart. With the exception of Predicators, all grammatical functions can be performed by different form classes, and most form classes can perform a variety of grammatical functions, as the table above shows.

Key Concepts in this Chapter

function and form
the syntactic realisation of the functions
   Subject
   Predicate and Predicator
   Direct Object
   Indirect Object
   Adjunct
the lack of a one-to-one relationship between function and form

Exercises

1. Identify the grammatical functions of the italicised constituents in the following sentences, and then specify how they are syntactically realised:

    (i)   *The doctor* uses *a bicycle* to get to work.
    (ii)   *What to do at this point* is a big mystery.
    (iii)   They sold *the headmaster* faulty computers.
    (iv)   We deem *her very competent*.
    (v)   *Gleefully*, Henry ran out of the house.
    (vi)   *Jake* left *because he was angry*.
    (vii)   He *left* his car *in front of the cinema*
    (viii) *She* doesn't understand *what she wants*.
    (ix)   I would hate *to see you cry*.
    (x)   *The policeman* made *me pay the fine*.

2. Think of *two* examples of each of the following:

    A sentence with its Subject realised as a clause.
    A sentence with its Direct Object realised as a clause.
    A sentence with its IO realised as a clause.
    A sentence with an Adjunct realised as a clause.

3. With regard to the sentence in (i) below, are the statements in (ii)–(v) true or false?

    (i)   The monks regularly brew beer on their premises.
    (ii)   Sentence (i) contains two Adjuncts.
    (iii)   The Prepositional Phrase *on their premises* functions as Direct Object.
    (iv)   The Subject of (i) is *monks*.
    (v)   The Direct Object of (i) is *beer on their premises*.

4. And again, with regard to (i) below, are the statements in (ii)-(v) true or false?

    (i)   After seeing the film we had a meal in a restaurant.
    (ii)   The VP of this sentence is *had*.
    (iii)   *After seeing the film* is the matrix clause.
    (iv)   *in a restaurant* is a PP.
    (v)   *A meal in a restaurant* is a DO.
    (vi)   *The film* is a DO.

5. Identify the clauses in the following examples (don't forget the matrix clause). Then assign grammatical function labels to all the subordinate

clauses (Subject, Direct Object, etc.) and give them a form label (e.g. finite *that*-clause, nonfinite *to*-infinitive clause, etc.):

(i)   We all think that Dan is a bore.
(ii)   She hates to go to the beach.
(iii) Having dressed herself, Rachel thought that she would be late for work.
(iv)   When he was young, Pete liked to go to the movies.
(v)   I consider him dim.

*6.   Draw trees for the following sentences:

(i)   He claims that he knows the answer.
(ii)   They believe that she thinks that he eats meat.

*7.   The table at the end of this chapter suggests that Indirect Objects cannot be realised as PPs. But what about the PP *to Phil* in (i) below?

(i)   Gerry gave the book to Phil.

Further Reading

The function-form interface is dealt with extensively in Aarts and Aarts (1982), see especially Chapter 8. Clauses which perform a grammatical function in sentence structure (other than Adjunct) are arguably NPs. This is particularly true for strings like *whoever wanted to hear it* in *Sean told **whoever wanted to hear it** his story* (= (89)), or *what she wants* in *She doesn't understand **what she wants*** (= (viii) of exercise 1 above), which are called *free relatives* or *fused relatives*. See Huddleston (1984: 402–4) and Huddleston and Pullum et al. (2002) for discussion. The analysis in which the NP following *consider* in (144) is regarded as a DO can be found in Quirk et al. (1985) and Huddleston and Pullum et al. (2002). On Small Clauses, see Aarts (1992).

Part II
Elaboration

6 Predicates, Arguments and Thematic Roles

In this chapter we will be concerned with an area of grammar where syntax interacts with semantics.

6.1 Predicates and Arguments

Up to now, we have described each sentence of English in two separate ways: functionally and formally. Consider (1) below:

(1)   The crocodile devoured a doughnut.

This sentence consists of a Subject (*the crocodile*), a Predicator (*devoured*) and a Direct Object (*a doughnut*). Both the Subject and Direct Object are realised by Noun Phrases, whereas the Predicator is realised by a verb.

Let us now consider (1) from a different angle. Notice that the verb *devour* cannot form a sentence on its own: it requires the presence of other elements to form a meaningful proposition. As will be clear from (2) and (3) below, *devour* requires that it be specified who was engaged in the act of devouring something, and what it was that was being devoured:

(2)   *Devoured a doughnut.
(3)   *The crocodile devoured.

In (2) there is no Subject, whereas (3) lacks a Direct Object. Both situations lead to ungrammaticality. We will refer to elements that require the specification of the participants in the proposition expressed as *predicates* (e.g. *devour*), and we will refer to the participants themselves as *arguments* (*the crocodile, a doughnut*).

Below you will find some further examples of sentences containing argument-taking predicates. Each time the predicates are in bold type and the arguments are in italics:

(4)   *Henry* **smiled**.
(5)   *The police* **investigated** *the allegation*.
(6)   *Sara* **gave** [*Pete*] [*a parcel*].
(7)   *Melany* **bet** [*Brian*] [*a pound*] [*that he would lose the game of squash*].

Sentence (4) has a predicate that takes only one argument. We will call such predicates *one-place predicates* (or *monadic predicates*). (5) is like (1) above: the predicate *investigate* requires the presence of two arguments. It is a *two-place predicate* (or *dyadic predicate*). In (6) the verb *give* takes three arguments, and is called a *three-place predicate* (or *triadic predicate*). Sentences like (7) are very exceptional in English; a verb like *bet* can be said to take four arguments: three Noun Phrase arguments (*Melany, Brian, a pound*), and one clausal argument (*that he would lose the game of squash*). In each of the cases above we refer to the arguments inside VP (i.e. following the verb) as *internal arguments*, and to the Subject argument as the *external argument*. It is important to see that the *semantic notions* one-place predicate, two-place predicate and three-place predicate correspond to the *syntactic notions* intransitive verb, transitive verb and ditransitive verb.

Two caveats are in order at this point. Firstly, you may remember that we already used the term *Predicate* in Chapter 2. We said that we can subdivide sentences into Subjects and Predicates. Subject and Predicate in the sense of Chapter 2 are functional labels; the term Predicate refers to everything in a sentence except the Subject, i.e. the verb together with its Complements (if present) and Adjuncts (if present). This is a syntactic use of the term Predicate. In this chapter the term 'predicate' is used in a semantic sense. It would have been better if we had two different terms for the syntactic and semantic notions, but unfortunately this is not the case. Notice that when I use Predicate as a functional term it is written with a capital letter 'p'. When I use it as a semantic term it is written with a lower-case letter 'p'. Secondly, do not confuse the terms *predicate* and *Predicator*: the first is a semantic label, as we have just seen, while the second is again a functional label. Review Chapter 2 if you've forgotten about the earlier notions of Predicate and Predicator.

We can represent predicates and their arguments in a formal notation, used in a branch of philosophy called *predicate logic*. The sentences in (1) and (4)–(7) can be represented as follows:

(8)   D (c, d)
(9)   S (h)
(10)   I (p, a)
(11)   G (s, p, p)
(12)   B (m, b, p, c) (c = clause)

Semantic predicates are represented by a single capital letter, corresponding to the first letter of the verb in (1) and (4)–(7). Arguments are represented by lower-case letters. They indicate the first letter of the associated argument(s). They are enclosed in brackets. Thus, (8) can be read as follows: **D**evour (**c**rocodile, **d**oughnut).

Notice that this notation enables us to represent only predicates and their associated arguments. We have no way of making clear the categorial status of the arguments. For this reason representations like (8)–(12) are inadequate for syntactic purposes. What we would like to be able to do is to make more informative statements about the argument-taking properties of particular predicates.

In linguistics an alternative way of representing predicates and their arguments has been developed. Each predicate is associated with a unique *argument structure* which specifies the number of arguments a predicate takes and their categorial status. The predicates in (1) and (4)–(7) can be represented as follows:

(13) *devour* (verb)
      [1 <NP>, 2 <NP>]

(14) *smile* (verb)
      [1 <NP>]

(15) *investigate* (verb)
      [1 <NP>, 2 <NP>]

(16) *give* (verb)
      [1 <NP>, (2 <NP>), 3 <NP>]

(17) *bet* (verb)
      [1 <NP>, 2 <NP>, 3 <NP>, 4 <Clause>]

These argument structures indicate not only the number of arguments each predicate takes, but also their categorial status. In addition, in each case the external argument is underlined. Notice that in (16) the second argument is in round brackets. This is because with the verb *give* it is possible to leave the Indirect Object argument implicit, as in B's response below to A's statement:

(18)A Ivan gave me a book for Christmas.
    B Ivan is so boring: he always gives books!

The implicit Indirect Object can be interpreted here as 'his friends' or 'people'.

It is important to realise that not only verbs can be predicates. Nouns, adjectives and prepositions can too, as (19)–(21) make clear:

(19) *Paul's* **study** *of art history.*
(20) *Freddy is* **fond** *of his sister.*
(21) *The bird is* **inside** *the house.*

In (19) the noun *study* requires the specification of a Subject expression, i.e. it requires the specification of a 'studier', in this case *Paul*. It also requires the specification of an internal argument, i.e. what is being studied, namely *art history*. Compare (19) to the sentence *Paul studies art history*. In (20) and (21) the Subject expressions are *Freddy* and *the bird*, respectively, while *of his sister* and *the house* correspond to the internal arguments we find in VPs. The semantic content of the verb *be* in (20) and (21) is empty; the verb only serves as a carrier of the present tense inflection.

6.2   Thematic Roles

Arguments are participants in what one linguist has called 'the little drama' that a proposition expresses. To be a participant in a drama you must be playing a role. What sort of roles are we talking about here? We have already alluded to the notion of participant roles in an earlier chapter. We talked there about *Agents* and *Patients*, and we saw that these roles are typically fulfilled by Subjects and Objects, respectively. We now elaborate on this, and say that each argument carries at most one *thematic role* (as we will call participant roles from now on). Apart from Agents and Patients, there are a number of other roles. Linguists don't agree exactly how many there are, nor do they agree exactly which roles we should recognise. However, the following thematic roles are widely accepted:

Thematic roles (also known as *theta roles* or *θ-roles*)

Agent	The 'doer' or instigator of the action denoted by the predicate.
Patient	The 'undergoer' of the action or event denoted by the predicate.
Theme	The entity that is moved by the action or event denoted by the predicate.
Experiencer	The living entity that experiences the action or event denoted by the predicate.
Goal	The location or entity in the direction of which something moves.
Benefactive	The entity that benefits from the action or event denoted by the predicate.
Source	The location or entity from which something moves.
Instrument	The medium by which the action or event denoted by the predicate is carried out.
Locative	The specification of the place where the action or event denoted by the predicate is situated.
Proposition	The specification of a state of affairs.

Exercise

Consider the sentences below and determine which thematic roles the bracketed phrases can be said to carry.

(i)   [His mother] sent [David] [a letter].
(ii)   [David] smelled [the freshly baked bread].
(iii)   [We] put [the cheese] [in the fridge].
(iv)   [Frank] threw [himself] [onto the sofa].
(v)   [Greg] comes [from Wales].

In (i) the Subject Noun Phrase carries the role of Agent, as do the Subjects in (iii) and (iv). The role of *David* in (ii) is that of Experiencer. Sentence (v) illustrates that it is by no means always easy to determine the thematic role of a particular phrase: which θ-role do we assign to the NP *Greg*? None of the roles on our list is quite appropriate. We can adopt two possible solutions to this problem. Either we say that *Greg* carries one of the θ-roles on our list, though marginally so, say Theme, or we invent a new role altogether, say Topic. The first solution has the advantage that we keep our list of thematic roles short; the second solution allows us to make finer distinctions. In this book we won't worry too much about such problems, and we will use the list as given above. What's important is to know which elements bear a thematic role in a particular sentence.

We have yet to discuss the roles of the non-Subject phrases in the exercise. In (i) *David* is the Goal of the act of sending. The NPs *a letter* in (ii), *the cheese* in (iii) and *himself* in (iv) are Themes. They could also be said to be Patients, and it is for exactly this reason that you will often find the Theme and Patient θ-roles lumped together in textbooks. *In the fridge* and *onto the sofa* are Goals (or perhaps Locative in the case of *in the fridge*), while *from Wales* in (v) clearly carries the role of Source. There only remains one case, and that is the NP *the freshly baked bread* in (ii). Again, it is not entirely clear which thematic role we are dealing with here. Is it a Patient, or some other role? We won't rack our brains too much, and settle for Patient. Once again, the important thing is to be aware that this NP carries a thematic role.

We can add the thematic information about predicates, which we will refer to as their *thematic structure*, i.e. the number and types of thematic roles they assign, to their argument structures. If we do this for the predicates in (13)–(17), we derive the following results:

(22) *devour* (verb)
      [1 <NP, Agent>, 2 <NP, Patient>]

(23) *smile* (verb)
      [1 <NP, Agent>]

(24) *investigate* (verb)
      [1 <NP, Agent>, 2 <NP, Patient>]

(25) *give* (verb)
      [1 <NP, Agent>, (2 <NP, Benefactive>), 3 <NP, Theme>]

(26) *bet* (verb)
      [1 <NP, Agent>, 2 <NP, Goal>, 3 <NP, Patient>, 4 <Clause, Proposition>]

What we have now in (22)–(26), in the angled brackets following the numbered arguments, are combinations of the argument structures of the predicates in question with their thematic structures. Frames like this can be hypothesised to be the kind of specifications that are attached to lexical items listed in our mental *lexicon* (dictionary).

Let us now turn to elements in sentences that do not receive thematic roles. Above we defined arguments as participants in a propositional drama. From this it follows that an element in a sentence that does not refer to a participant is not an argument. Instead, we could say that such an element is merely part of the scenery. What type of expression would qualify for non-participant status? In Chapter 2 we discussed sentences like (27) and (28):

(27)   It always rains in London.
(28)   There were six policemen on the bus.

The grammatical Subjects in these sentences are *it* and *there* respectively. We called *it* in (27) weather *it*, because it often occurs in sentences that tell you about the weather, and we called *there* in (28) existential *there*, because it is used in propositions about existence. Notice that unlike referential *it* and locative *there* in (29) and (30) below, the Subjects in (27) and (28) do not refer to entities in the outside world. They are purely Subject slot fillers.

(29)   I hate the number 31 bus, *it* is always packed!
(30)   I'll put your coffee over *there*.

Other non-arguments are expressions in sentences that furnish only circumstantial, non-participant, information. In English these are typically phrases or clauses that function as Adjunct. If we modified sentence (1) above as in (31), then the italicised phrases would not be arguments:

(31)   *Last night*, the crocodile *greedily* devoured a doughnut.

Neither of the phrases *last night* and *greedily* can be said to participate in the mini-scene enacted by the crocodile and the doughnut. They merely tell us *when* it took place and *how*. In the formal notation we developed in this chapter Adjuncts are ignored, and (31) receives the same notation as (1), namely (22). Adjuncts are never arguments, and it follows that not all grammatical functions are linked to argument positions. The reverse, however, *does* hold true: each argument realises a grammatical function.

6.3   Grammatical Functions and Thematic Roles

Why do we need thematic roles? To answer this question, consider (32)–(35) below, all of which contain the verb *smash*:

(32)   David smashed the window.
(33)   The window was smashed by David.

(34)   A brick smashed the window.
(35)   David used a brick to smash the window.

Exercise

Before reading on, first underline the argument expressions in these sentences, and then determine which thematic role they carry.

Notice that although the grammatical functions of the argument expressions *David, the window* and *a brick* can be different in each of the sentences in which they appear, their thematic roles are the same. For example, the NP *David* carries the role of Agent in each case, despite the fact that it has two different syntactic functions, namely Subject in (32) and (35), and Complement of a preposition in (33). Similarly, in all sentences the NP *the window* is a Patient, regardless of the grammatical function it carries (Direct Object in (32), (34) and (35); Subject in (33)). Finally, the NP *the brick* carries the role of Instrument, and appears in two different functional slots: Subject and Direct Object. What these examples clearly show, then, is that there is no one-to-one relationship between grammatical functions and thematic roles, and we therefore need to distinguish these notions. Remember that grammatical function is primarily a syntactic notion, whereas thematic roles are first and foremost semantic in nature.

6.4   Selectional Restrictions

Consider the sentences below:

(36)   The keyboard designed some clothes.
(37)   The stapler took a break.
(38)   My colleague broke his feelings.

You will agree that in the world we live in there is something odd about these sentences: keyboards are not in the habit of designing clothes, staplers don't take breaks, and feelings aren't entities that can be broken. We refer to the restrictions imposed by the predicates of the sentences above on their arguments as *selectional restrictions*. Linguists have suggested that one way of dealing with selectional restrictions is to assign *features* to predicates and their arguments. For example, we might say that the verb *design* carries a feature [+animate] and that its Subject must also carry this feature. If it doesn't, the resulting sentence is deviant. Clearly, in (36) the Subject expression *the keyboard* is not an animate entity and the sentence is odd as a result. (37) is strange for the same reason. (38) can also be handled in terms of features: we might say that the verb *break* carries the feature [+concrete] which must be matched by a Direct Object that carries the same feature. In (38) the DO is an abstract NP, and this accounts for its peculiarity.

This way of handling selectional restrictions is a syntactic one: we require particular elements to be properly matched in terms of the features they carry.

In recent years the perspective on selectional restrictions has changed. It is now felt that they can be handled in a way that does not require a complicated array of features. An alternative way of dealing with selectional restrictions is to regard them as being a semantic, rather than a syntactic, phenomenon. This would account for the fact that (36)–(38) are syntactically well-formed, though odd meaningwise. It could be argued that selectional restrictions can be handled in terms of thematic roles. We have already seen that the grammar specifies, in its thematic structure, which thematic roles a predicate assigns. One possible avenue of research is to see whether we can *predict* which selectional restrictions a predicate imposes on its arguments, simply by looking at the thematic roles the arguments carry. Consider again sentence (36) above. We have seen that the verb *design* in (36) requires a Subject with an Agent role. We might now reasonably make the general observation that Agents are typically animate entities. If we do this, then there is no need to stipulate separately for each verb which particular selectional features it carries. (36) above is deviant simply because a general rule has been broken, namely the rule that says that Agents are typically animate entities. The advantage of handling selectional restrictions in this way is that there is no longer a reason to set up a separate mechanism in the grammar that handles them, and the result is that the grammar becomes more streamlined. Henceforth, then, we will assume that selectional restrictions are restrictions on thematic roles.

6.5   Three Levels of Description

I started this chapter with the observation that sentences can be described in two ways: by assigning functions to constituents, and then by assigning categorial labels to them. These are the by now familiar levels of function and form. In this chapter we saw that sentences can be described at a *third* level, namely the level of thematic roles. A sentence like (32) can be represented as follows at the three levels of description:

(39)		*David*	*smashed*	*the window*
Syntax	Function level	Subject	Predicator	Direct Object
	Form level	[$_S$ [$_{NP}$ N]	[$_{VP}$ V	[$_{NP}$ Det N]]]
Semantics	Thematic level	Agent	**predicate**	Patient

Remember that function and form are syntactic notions, while the thematic level of representation is semantic in nature.

Key Concepts in this Chapter

predicate
   one-place predicate
   two-place predicate
   three-place predicate
argument
   internal argument
   external argument
argument structure
thematic structure
thematic roles
   Agent
   Patient
   Theme, etc.
selectional restrictions

Exercises

1. In Section 6.1 we looked at one-place predicates, two-place predicates, three-place predicates and, exceptionally, four-place predicates. Consider now the sentences below.

   (i)   it rained
   (ii) it snowed

   Can weather verbs like rain and snow be classified into one of the predicate types mentioned above? If your answer is 'yes', which type is it? If your answer is 'no', why not?

2. The following constructions have been called *activo-passives*. Why is this an appropriate label? In answering this question pay particular attention to the thematic role of the Subjects. In which situations would we use such constructions? Can you think of other verbs that can occur in this type of construction?

   (i)   This book reads well.
   (ii) This car steers poorly.

3. In Section 6.2 we listed Locative as being one of the thematic roles. Would you assign this role to the italicised phrase in the sentence below? Why (not)?

   (i)   Kids love to swim *in the sea*.

4. Describe the following sentences as in (39). You may ignore the internal structure of subordinate clauses.

    (i)   Jane saw a UFO last night.
    (ii)   Bill used a penknife when he cut the bread.
    (iii)   The President stumbled.
    (iv)   Penny put the bread on the table.
    (v)   I believed him.
    (vi)   I thought that he was wrong.

5. Produce representations like those in (22)–(26) to show the combined argument structure and thematic structure of the verbs in Exercise 4. Use curly brackets ({ ... }) if an argument can be syntactically realised in more than one way.

*6. Frawley (1992: 201ff.) contrasts the thematic role of Agent with that of *Author*: 'whereas the agent is the direct doer, the author is simply the enabler, or the indirect cause' (1992: 205). He claims that distinguishing these roles allows us to account for the differences between (i) and (ii) below.

    (i)   Bill floated down the river.
    (ii)   The canoe floated down the river.

    From the point of view of thematic roles, which differences can you detect between the Subject expressions of these sentences? Do you feel that adding a new θ-role of Author to the list in the text is justified?

*7. Both of the following are possible sentences of English. They have the same meaning.

    (i)   The Government faces a difficult debate.
    (ii)   A difficult debate faces the Government.

    First analyse these sentences functionally, then discuss the thematic properties of the verb *face*. Can you think of any other verbs that behave like *face*?

*8. In the text we saw that there is no agreement among linguists about which thematic roles we should recognise, or indeed how many. Consider the following query which appeared on the LINGUIST list, an Internet discussion group (for more details, see the Further Reading section below):

    Q: If *John* is an Agent in *John opened the door*, and *John* is an Experiencer in *John saw the movie*, what is *John* in *John weighs 200 pounds*?

Try to answer this question, and then see below which answers some linguists have given to this question.

> According to Jackendoff (1972: 44)(*Semantic Interpretation in Generative Grammar*, 1972, MIT Press), the theta-role of *John* in the above sentence is theme. Jackendoff follows Gruber (*Studies in Lexical Relations*, MIT dissertation 1965 and other work) in assuming the following definition for theme: Theme is defined as either an NP which undergoes physical motion, or as the NP whose location is being asserted (Jackendoff 1972: 29–30). The use of *John* in the above sentence falls under the latter definition. Jackendoff says that the above sentence corresponds with the following sentence: *John weighs in at 200 pounds*. Hence, *John* is a theme by virtue of the fact that its location is being asserted, the location being 200 pounds on the scale. One final note is that elsewhere in the literature theme and patient are often used interchangeably. However, Jackendoff (1987: 394–5, 'The status of thematic relations in linguistic theory', *Linguistic Inquiry* 18: 369–411) makes a distinction between these two theta-roles. He defines patient as the 'object affected', and he reserves theme only to refer to NPs undergoing movement or whose location is being asserted.   (L. Kaiser)

> I suggest that *John* in your sentence *John weighs 200 lb.* is a patient, which these days is more usually called theme.   (L. Connolly)

> In *John weighs two hundred pounds* [the NP] *John* bears no special thematic role, *John* is merely the subject of a predicate. That is, *John* bears the same role or nonrole that he bears in *John is male, John is a mason, John is good at cross-word puzzles*. Consider that: *John weighs two hundred pounds* is rather close to the purely copular/predicative construction: *John is two hundred pounds in weight*.   (B. Ulicny)

> Overweight.   (A. Marantz)

> (Answers compiled from *LINGUIST* Vol. 5, 1076)

This should give you quite a good idea of the extent of the disagreement between linguists about the assignment of thematic roles. The disagreement is quite considerable, and even the last facetious comment is telling, in that it indicates that some linguists (syntacticians!) simply don't worry much about thematic roles.

Further Reading

On predicates and arguments, see Hurford, Heasley and Smith (2007). This book also deals with thematic roles (which are called *participant roles*). For a slightly more advanced treatment, see Allwood, Andersson and Dahl (1977). The classical references for thematic roles are Fillmore (1968), who refers to them under the heading of 'case' and Gruber (1976). An excellent and very accessible discussion of the grammatical function of Direct Object, and why it is difficult to associate it with a particular thematic role, can be found in Schlesinger (1995). The syntactic feature-based treatment of selectional restrictions was proposed in Chomsky 1965. For later treatments see e.g. Horrocks (1987: 35–6), and Radford (1988: 369f., 388–9).

In Exercise 8 above I mentioned the LINGUIST list. This is an electronic discussion forum on the Internet which deals with all branches of linguistics. You need an e-mail account to use this service. You can subscribe free by visiting www.linguistlist.org; then go to the section 'Join LINGUIST'.

7 Cross-Categorial Generalisations: X-Bar Syntax

In our discussion of English syntax in the preceding chapters we've learnt how to parse sentences at the functional, formal and thematic levels. What we haven't done in any great depth so far is look *inside* the various constituents that sentences are composed of to see how they are structured. The internal structure of the phrase types is the topic of this chapter.

7.1 Heads, Complements and Specifiers

In Chapter 3 we saw that all phrases have something in common, namely the fact that they must minimally contain a Head. In the bracketed phrases in the sentences below the Heads are shown in bold type:

(1) The defendants denied the charge: they claim that they did [$_{VP}$ not **destroy** the garden]
(2) She proposed [$_{NP}$ an **analysis** of the sentence]
(3) Jack is [$_{AP}$ so **fond** of coffee]
(4) They are [$_{PP}$ quite **in** agreement]
(5) My sister cycles [$_{AvP}$ much **faster** than me]

Notice that apart from the obligatory presence of the Heads, there are further similarities between these phrases. First of all, there appears to be a strong bond between the Head and the constituent that follows it in each case. Thus, in (1) the verb *destroy* requires the presence of a Noun Phrase that refers to an entity that is destroyable. Similarly, in (2) the PP *of the sentence* complements the noun *analysis* in that it specifies what is being analysed. Notice that in this case the noun *analysis* with its associated Complement *of the sentence* can be contrasted with a verb + Complement sequence: *analyse the sentence*. Compare (2) with (6):

(6) She proposed to *analyse the sentence.*

In (3)–(5) something analogous to (1) and (2) is going on: in each case the constituent that follows the Head is required to complete the sense of the Head. In Chapter 2 we briefly introduced the notion *Complement* as a general term to denote any constituent whose presence is required by another element. We now see that all the major syntactic categories can take a Complement. This is an important generalisation captured by the notion of *subcategorisation*, which we introduced in Chapter 2, and to which we will return in Section 7.4 below. How can we represent the close bond between a Head and its Complement in a tree diagram? One way of doing this is to assume that the two together share a node (i.e. they are sisters), as in (7) below:

(7)

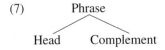

Of course, this can only be a partial representation of the structure of phrases like those in (1)–(4). What about the elements that immediately precede the Heads, such as *not, an, so, quite* and *much* in (1)–(4)? Unlike Complements, these seem to relate not so much to the Head, but to the Head and Complement taken together. For example, in (1) we could say that *not* adds something to the sequence *destroy the garden*: it negates it. We can ask the question 'what did the defendants *not* do?', and the answer would be 'destroy the garden'. In (2) the determinative *an* relates to the sequence *analysis of the sentence*, not just to the Head. And in (3)–(5) the adverbs *so, quite* and *much* intensify the strings *fond of coffee, in agreement* and *faster than me*, respectively. We will say that the elements that precede the Head in (1)–(5) *specify* the Head + Complement sequence and we will accordingly refer to them as *Specifiers* (abbreviated as 'Spec'). We can now expand our partial tree in (7) as follows for each of the phrases in (1)–(5):

(8)

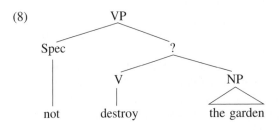

(9)

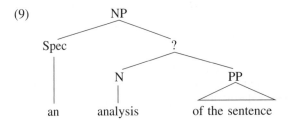

(10)

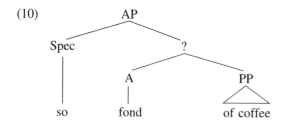

(11)

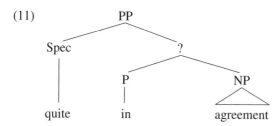

(12)

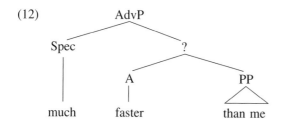

Notice that there is a generalisation to be made here. In each case the configuration of the various phrasal components is identical. The generalised structure for each of the phrases above is as follows:

(13)

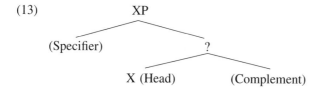

In this tree 'XP' is a phrase headed by X, where X stands for V, N, A, P or Adv. The Specifier is a sister of the node that dominates the Head + Complement sequence, indicated by '?'. In (13) we now have an unlabelled category, namely the category that dominates the Head + Complement string. What is the nature of this node? It doesn't seem to have the status of something we have come across before. From the tree in (13) it appears that '?' is at a level that is intermediate between the phrase XP and the Head X. Let us call this level *X'* (read: X-bar).

We can now present a full representation of the bracketed phrases in (1)–(5):

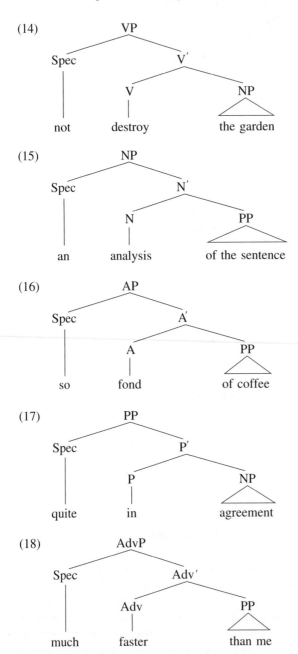

(14)

(15)

(16)

(17)

(18)

There are two important points to make at this juncture. Firstly, notice that in the tree in (14) the auxiliary verb *did* is not part of the VP. I will return to this issue in due course. Secondly, following standard practice I have included Specifier nodes in the trees above. Strictly speaking this is inappropriate, because the notion Specifier is a functional one, and we saw in Chapter 4 that functional labels do not appear in trees.

Exercise

Why would a 'flat' representation like (i) below for the NP *an analysis of the sentence* not be a satisfactory way of showing the relationships between the various components of this phrase?

(i)

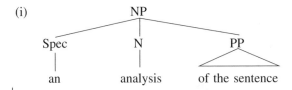

The reason why flat representations are unsatisfactory is that they do not account for the fact that phrases are structured *hierarchically*, i.e. the relationships between the various elements that make up a phrase are not the same. In the NP *an analysis of the sentence* we want to account for the fact that the determinative *an* bears a relationship to the Head noun and PP *taken together*. Structure (15) is able to account for this, whereas (i) in the exercise above is not. I will return to 'flat' structures below.

Observe that the trees in (14)–(18) the Specifiers are different types of elements. The Specifier position of VP is the subject of much current research which we can't go into here. In this book we will assume that in VPs negative elements such as *not* and *never* are in Spec-of-VP. In NPs determinatives are Specifiers, and in the remaining phrasal categories the Specifier position contains intensifying elements.

You will have noticed that both the Specifier and Complement positions in (13) are in brackets. This indicates that they are optional. Specifiers appear only if the meaning of the phrase requires it. Thus, for example, in the case of VPs, a Specifier *not* appears only if we want to express a negative VP. The Specifier position is left empty if the VP does not contain *not*. Similarly, in the case of NPs without determinatives (e.g. *trains* in *Trains are slow*), we will assume that the Specifier position of NP remains empty. As for Complements, these appear only if the Head of a phrase requires their presence. What exactly is meant by 'requires their presence' will be clarified in Section 7.4.

In (13) we regard each of the levels XP, X' and X as *projections* of the Head. To be more precise, XP is the *maximal projection* of the Head (also called a *double-bar projection*, sometimes written as X''), while the X'-level is a *single bar projection*. The Head itself is a *zero bar projection* (or *lexical projection*). Every phrase, then, has three levels of structure: X'', X' and X.

Exercise

Assign tree structures to the bracketed phrases below:

(i)   [the destruction of Carthage]
(ii)   He is [so envious of his sister]
(iii)   We are [citizens of the world]
(iv)   She [travelled to Rome]
(v)   He walked [straight through the door]

Your answers should look like this:

(19)

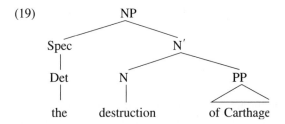

(20)

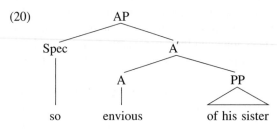

(21)

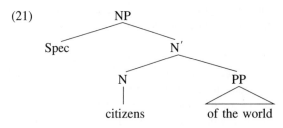

(22)

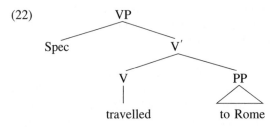

(23)

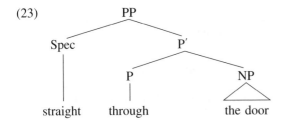

We end this section with two tables showing typical Specifiers and Complements for the different phrase types.

Table 7.1   Typical Specifiers for the Major Phrase Types NP, VP, AP and PP

Phrase	Specifier	Example(s)
NP	determinatives	[*the* examination] [*this* book] [*those* bicycles] [*many* answers]
VP	negative elements	He does [*not* like planes] She [*never* eats meat]
AP	degree adverbs	[*how* nice] They are [*so* eager to please] He isn't [*that/this* fat] [*too* bad] That's [*rather/quite* disgusting] She is [*as* rich as the Queen]
PP	adverbs	The supermarket is [*right* up your street] My office is [*quite* in disarray] The office is [*just* to your left]

Table 7.2   Typical Complements for the Major Phrase Types NP, VP, AP and PP

Phrase	Head	Complement	Example(s)
NP	N	PP	his *insistence* [PP on the arrangement] (cf. He *insists* on the arrangement.) their *specialisation* [PP in wines] (cf. They *specialise* in wines.)
		clause	their *realisation* [*that*-clause that all is lost] (cf. They *realise* that all is lost.) her *consideration* [*whether*-clause whether the expense was worth it] (cf. She *considered* whether the expense was worth it.)

Continued

Table 7.2 Continued

Phrase	Head	Complement	Example(s)
			her *requirement* [$_{for\text{-}clause}$ for all candidates to comply with the rules] (cf. She *requires* all candidates to comply with the rules.)
		NP	a *literature* teacher (cf. He *teaches* literature/a teacher of literature)

Note: Complement-taking nominal heads often have a verbal counterpart (cf. (2) and (6) above).

Phrase	Head	Complement	Example(s)
VP	V	NP	She *placed* [$_{NP}$ an advertisement].
		Clause	They *know* [$_{that\text{-}clause}$ that the sun will shine tomorrow]
		PP	He *looked* [$_{PP}$ at the picture]
		AP	He *is* [$_{AP}$ very healthy]

Note: for many more examples of verbal Complements, see Chapter 4.

Phrase	Head	Complement	Example(s)
AP	A	PP	*glad* [$_{PP}$ about your decision] *pleased* [$_{PP}$ with the result] *dependent* [$_{PP}$ on his brother]
		clause	I am so *eager* [$_{to\text{-}infinitive\ clause}$ to work with you] He's *engaged* [$_{-ing\ clause}$ teaching the students] She's *unsure* [$_{Wh\text{-}clause}$ what we should do next]
PP	P	NP	*in/under/behind* [$_{NP}$ the car]
		PP	*out* [$_{PP}$ of love] *from* [$_{PP}$ behind the bookcase] *down* [$_{PP}$ by the sea]
		Clause	He is uncertain *about* [$_{wh\text{-}clause}$ what you said to me]

Complements in the form of a clause will be discussed in more detail in Chapter 8.

7.2 Adjuncts

The phrases we have looked at so far contained only a Specifier, a Head and a Complement. Phrases can, however, be structurally more complicated. Consider first the bracketed VP below:

(24) The defendants denied the charge: they claim that they did [$_{VP}$ not destroy the garden deliberately]

In this sentence the AdvP *deliberately* modifies the sequence *destroy the garden*, and is positioned after the Head *destroy* and its Complement *the garden*. This AdvP functions as an Adjunct in that it tells us *how* the defendants destroyed the garden (or rather, in this particular case, how they didn't destroy the garden). Disregarding the AdvP for a moment, the structure of the VP in (24) is as in (25) below (= (14)):

(25)

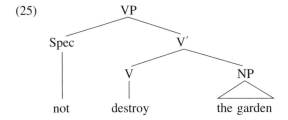

How can we now add the Adjunct?

One way of doing this is simply to have a third branch coming from V' for the AdvP, as in (26):

(26)

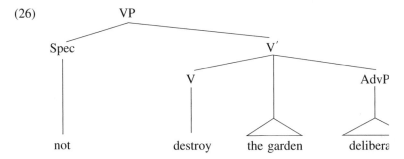

However, this representation cannot account for the fact that *deliberately* modifies *destroy* and *the garden* taken together: 'what did the defendants not do deliberately?' Answer: 'destroy the garden'.

Another way of positioning Adjuncts in VPs is to *adjoin* them to V'. This is done as follows:

(27)

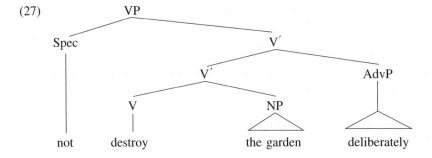

What we have done here is *repeat* the V′-node, and add the AdvP as its daughter. This process is called *adjunction* and is defined as follows:

Adjunction

Category B is adjoined to category A by:

- by making B a sister of A, and
- by making A and B daughters of a copy of the original node A

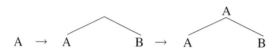

We can have adjunction to the right, as in (27), shown schematically in the definition above, but also adjunction to the left, as in (28) below, where *deliberately* is left-adjoined to the lower V′:

(28)

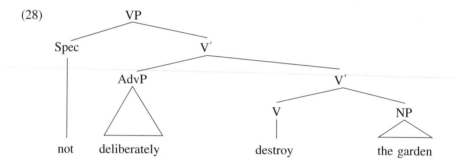

In this case the Adjunct is positioned between the Specifier and the Head. Notice that in both (27) and (28) the Complement *the garden* is closer to the Head *destroy* than the Adjunct *deliberately*: the Complement is a sister of V, whereas the Adjunct is a sister of the V′ that immediately dominates V. This situation is exactly what we want: *deliberately* is not an argument of *destroy* and hence more peripheral to it than *the garden*, which *is* an argument of the verb.

Up to now we have used the term Adjunct in a somewhat restricted sense to refer to the grammatical function of a constituent that specifies the 'how', 'when', 'where' or 'why' of the situation expressed by a sentence. Under this definition the AdvP *deliberately* in (24) clearly qualifies as an Adjunct. We will now widen the notion of Adjunct, in such a way that not only VPs can contain them, but other phrase types as well. Consider the strings below:

(29)   [NP an analysis of the sentence *with tree diagrams*]
(30)   [AP so fond of coffee *after dinner*]

(31) [_PP_ quite in agreement *about this*]
(32) [_AdvP_ much faster than me *by far*]

The italicised strings in the bracketed phrases above, like *deliberately* in (27) and (28), have a modifying function, and we will therefore analyse them as Adjuncts. Like Adjuncts in VP, they are adjoined to a bar-level category in tree structures, as follows:

(33)

(34)

(35)

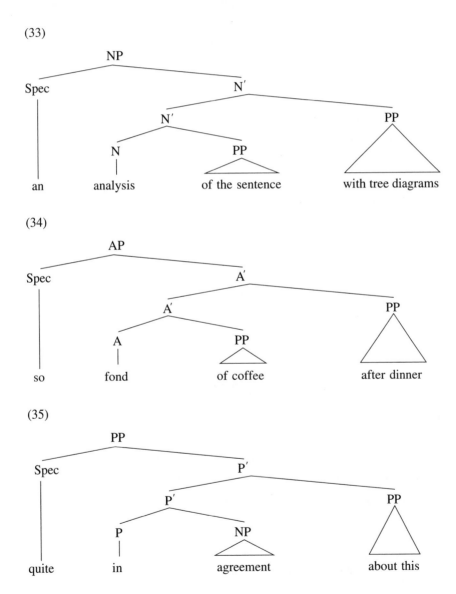

(36)

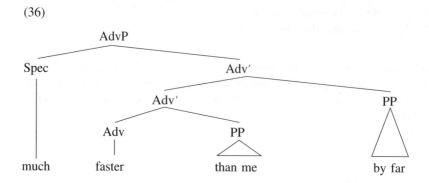

Consider next (37)–(39):

(37) [NP a *silly* analysis of the sentence]
(38) [AP so *terribly* fond of coffee]
(39) [PP quite *unhesitatingly* in agreement]
(40) [AdvP *clearly* faster than me]

In these cases we have Adjuncts that are positioned *before* the Head (compare the VP in (27)). (41)–(44) are the tree structure representations for these phrases:

(41)

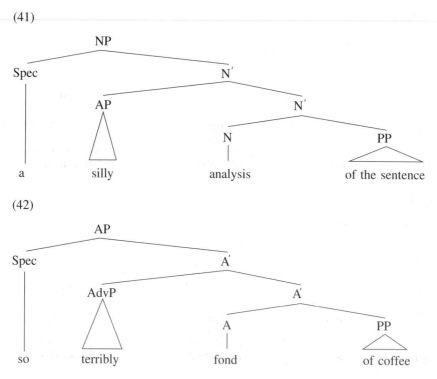

(43)

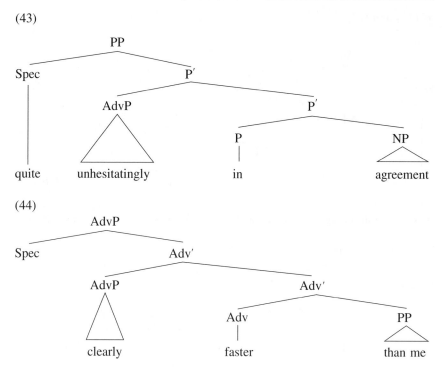

(44)

In all of these cases, just as in (28), the Adjuncts are left-adjoined to a bar-level category. Notice that Adjuncts are often Adverb Phrases, but can be of any category.

We can now make a generalisation and say that Adjuncts are always sisters of bar-level categories in phrases. They are adjoined either to the right or to the left of single-bar categories, and have a modifying function. Complements, as we have seen, are always sisters of Heads.

There are a number of important points to bear in mind about Adjuncts. First, they can be *stacked*. In other words, several of them can appear in any one phrase. Here are two examples of phrases containing multiple pre-Head Adjuncts:

(45)   The defendants denied the charge: they claim that they did [_{VP} not *unthinkingly, deliberately* destroy the garden]
(46)   [_{NP} a *silly, preposterous* analysis of the sentence]

In (47) and (48) we have phrases that contain both a pre-Head and a post-Head Adjunct:

(47)   [_{AP} so *terribly* fond of coffee *after dinner*]
(48)   [_{PP} quite *unhesitatingly* in agreement *with each other*]

The structure of such phrases is simple: all we need to do is add more single-bar levels. Below I give the trees for the bracketed portions of (45) and (47):

(49)

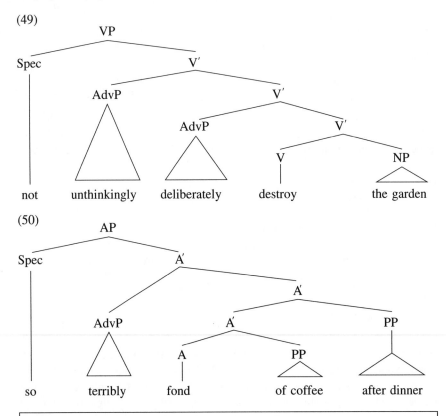

(50)

(51)

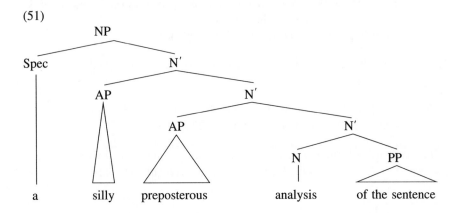

Your answers should look like this:

Exercise

Draw the trees for (46) and (48). You may use triangles for the PPs.

---

(52)

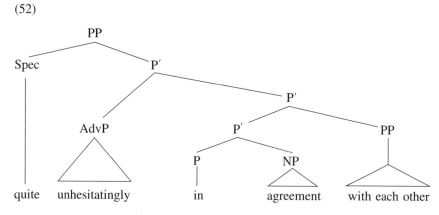

The property of being stackable differentiates Adjuncts on the one hand from Complements and from Specifiers on the other: while phrases can in principle contain an unlimited number of Adjuncts (though they can become stylistically clumsy), lexical Heads, for example, verbs, are restricted in the number of Complements they can take (rarely more than three), while Specifiers are generally not recursive (cf. *The my dog*).

A second point to observe about Adjuncts, already mentioned in connection with Verb Phrases, is that the bond between them and their associated Heads is less close than that between a Head and its Complements. This fact is reflected in tree diagrams: as we have seen, Complements are sisters of their Head, while Adjuncts are sisters of the single-bar level above the Head. We can demonstrate the closer bond between Heads and their Complements by reversing the order of Complements and post-Head Adjuncts, as has been done below:

(53) *...they did [$_{VP}$ not destroy deliberately the garden]
(54) *[$_{NP}$ an analysis with tree diagrams of the sentence]
(55) *[$_{AP}$ so fond in the morning of coffee]
(56) *[$_{PP}$ quite with each other in agreement]
(57) ?*[$_{AdvP}$ much faster by far than me]

The results of reversing the order of Complements and Adjuncts are clearly ungrammatical or of dubious acceptability in most of these cases, and this is because Complements must be adjacent to their Heads.

To end this section here is a table showing typical Adjuncts for the different phrase types.

Table 7.3 Typical Adjuncts for the Major Phrase Types NP, VP, AP and PP

Phrase	Head	Adjunct	Examples
NP	N	AP	The *warm* summer
		NP	The *woman* busdriver
		PP	The tiles *on the floor*

Continued

Table 7.3   Continued

Phrase	Head	Adjunct	Examples
		clause	My youngest sister, *who lives in Italy* The information *that you supplied*
VP	V	AdvP	He *quickly* absconded. She read the prospectus *eagerly*.
		PP	We came here *in the summer*.
		clauses	She phoned *because she likes you*.
AP	A	PP	He was abusive *to the extreme*.
		AdvP	We were *unconsolably* disappointed.
PP	P	AdvP	I was *totally* over the moon. She was in doubt *entirely*.
		PP	They designed the museum in tandem *with an Italian architect*.

Adjuncts in the form of a clause will be discussed in more detail in Chapters 8 and 15.

7.3   Cross-Categorial Generalisations

Let us now return to our schematic tree in (13), modified as in (58) below:

(58)

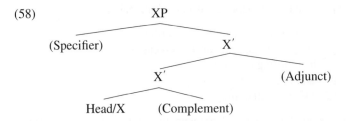

This tree embodies what has been called a *cross-categorial generalisation* which is part of *X'-syntax* (read: X-bar syntax). X'-syntax is a theory of syntax which stipulates that all the major phrase types are structured in the same way, namely as in (58).

Notice that the labels Specifier, Adjunct, Head and Complement are functional notions, and that of these four only the Head is always obligatory. I have positioned the optional Adjunct to the right of the lower X' in (58), but bear in mind that Adjuncts can also be left-hand sisters of X' (see e.g. (41)–(44) in the preceding section). The existence of the single-bar level in phrases was posited largely on intuitive grounds, but we will obviously need to justify its existence on syntactic grounds as well. For now, we will simply assume that this intermediate category exists, and in Chapter 10 we will present syntactic evidence for it.

The phrase structure that X'-syntax posits is a major improvement on so-called 'flat' structures, i.e. structures where all the elements are on the same level. To see this, consider the NP in (59):

(59)   a silly analysis of the sentence with tree diagrams

From what has been said so far it will be clear that the words in this phrase bear different relationships to each other. The most important element is the Head *analysis*, and there are various additional words that relate in different ways to this Head: some have a modifying function (e.g. *silly, with tree diagrams*), others have a complementing function (e.g. *of the sentence*). In other words, (59) is *structured*. Moreover, it is structured *hierarchically*, as becomes clear when we compare two different representations of (59):

(60)

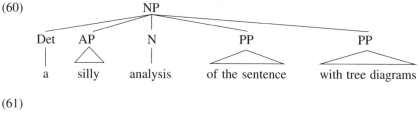

(61)

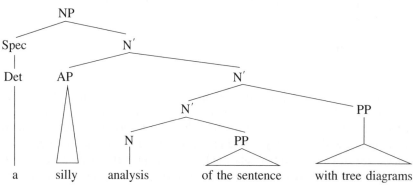

(60) is a flat structure, where all the elements are positioned at the same level, whereas (61) is a hierarchical structure which conforms to X'-syntax. Looking at (59) from left to right, we first come across the determinative *a*. This element has the function of adding indefiniteness to the rest of the phrase. In (61) this is brought out by making it the sister of the N'-constituent *silly analysis of the sentence with tree diagrams*. In (60) all we have is a linear sequence of words which all seem to have the same relationship to each other. (Recall that Spec is the

functional label associated with the word class of determinative. Exceptionally, it is the only functional label that appears in trees, as we have seen.) Turning now to the words following the determinative, we have already seen that the relationship between the Head *analysis* and the Complement *of the sentence* is closer than that between the Head and the Adjunct *with tree diagrams*. The first tree does not bear out this fact, but the second one does: here the Complement is analysed as a sister of the Head, whereas the Adjunct is analysed as a sister of the N′ that dominates the Head. What is clear, then, is that representations in the X′-format enable us to graphically represent the hierarchical relationships that hold between the various elements of phrases. What's more, these kinds of relationships are identical for all the phrase types, and this is why we can use 'XP', as in (58) above, when we talk about syntactic structure in general.

7.4   Subcategorisation

In this section we will take a closer look at the tight bond that exists between Heads and their Complements. In Section 7.1 we saw that this bond is so strong that a Complement must always be adjacent to its Head, and that an Adjunct may not intervene. Another way of claiming that there is a strong connection between Heads and Complements is to say that Heads *subcategorise for* (i.e. syntactically require the presence of) their Complements. Different Heads subcategorise for different Complements, and we can use so-called *subcategorisation frames* to specify exactly which Complements a Head takes. Here's the subcategorisation frame for the verb *destroy*:

> *destroy* (verb)
> [– , NP]

This frame contains two parts: on the top line we have the element that is sub-categorised, with a word class label. On the bottom line, inside square brackets, we have a dash, indicating the position of the subcategorised element, followed by a comma and the category whose presence is required by the subcategorised element. *Destroy* is a verb that takes only one Complement. A ditransitive verb like *send* in the sentence *He sent her some details of the plan* takes the following frame:

> *send* (verb)
> [– , NP NP]

This frame indicates that *send* takes two Objects as its Complements: an Indirect Object (*her*) and a Direct Object (*some details of the plan*). However, *send* does not always require two Complements. For example, we can say the following: *Martin didn't come to the party, but he sent his sister*, where the verb takes only one Complement. We revise the subcategorisation frame for *send* as follows:

> *send* (verb)
> [– , (NP) NP]

Here the first NP is placed inside brackets to indicate its optionality.

Of course, some Heads do not take Complements at all, and this will be indicated in the subcategorisation frame by the zero symbol (Ø). The frame for *blush* looks like this:

> *blush* (verb)
> [– , Ø]

For some verbs there is a choice of Complements. As an example, consider the sentences below which contain the verb *believe*:

(62)   I believed the allegations.
(63)   I believed that the allegations were true.
(64)   I believed the allegations to be true.

The subcategorisation frame for *believe* is as follows:

> *believe* (verb)
>
> $[-, \left\{ \begin{array}{l} \text{NP} \\ \textit{that}\text{-clause} \\ \textit{to}\text{-infinitive clause} \end{array} \right\}]$

The curly brackets indicate that a choice should be made from one of the items inside them.

Verbs are not the only word classes that can be subcategorised. Nouns, adjectives, prepositions and adverbs also occur in subcategorisation frames. However, as we have already seen, the extent to which these word classes take Complements varies enormously. Here are some examples:

> *fact* (noun)
> [– , (*that*-clause)]
> e.g. She hates the **fact** that he is a genius.

> *appreciative* (adjective)
> [– , *of*-NP]
> e.g. She is **appreciative** *of classical music.*

> *behind* (preposition)
> [– , NP]
> e.g. The bike is **behind** *the shed.*

fortunately (adverb)
[– , (*for*-NP)]
e.g. **Fortunately** *for me* the train departed late.

Exercise

Produce subcategorisation frames for *hit, put, idea* and *smile*. You will need to think of sentences or phrases containing these lexical items. Alternatively, consult a dictionary which gives information about complementation patterns, for example, the *Oxford Advanced Learner's Dictionary.*

Your answers should look like this:

hit (verb)
[– , NP]
e.g. You should never **hit** *animals*.

put (verb)
[– , NP PP]
e.g. He **put** *the glasses on the table.*

idea (noun)
[– , (*that*-clause)]
e.g. The **idea** *that we will all go to heaven* is absurd.

smile (verb)
[– , Ø]
e.g. She **smiled**.

7.4.1   *Subcategorisation versus Argument/Thematic Structure*

You will have noticed that the subcategorisation frames we introduced in the previous section are reminiscent of the frames we used to represent the argument/ thematic structure of predicates. What exactly is the difference between these two kinds of frames?

Let's start with subcategorisation. What does this term actually mean? The point about subcategorisation is that by assigning an element to a particular subcategorisation frame, we create a *subcategory* for the word class that this element belongs to. For example, by assigning a verb like *destroy* to the frame [–, NP] we create a subcategory for the word class of verbs, namely a subcategory that takes an NP Complement. This subcategory we have called the class of transitive verbs. Similarly, by assigning a verb like *smile* to the frame [– , Ø], we create a subcategory of intransitive verbs. It's important to remember that subcategorisation concerns only the *internal* arguments, i.e. the Complements, of the element that is being subcategorised. The reason for this is that only internal arguments are capable of creating subcategories. You will have noticed that external arguments, i.e. Subjects, are conspicuously absent from subcategorisation frames. The reason for this is that if an element, for example a verb, takes a Subject expression, no subcategory of verbs is established for it. For example, the fact that the verb *drive* must have a Subject in any sentence in which it occurs does not create a special class of 'Subject-taking verbs'. This is because all verbs take Subjects.

Unlike in subcategorisation frames, external arguments *do* appear in the frames that specify the argument/thematic structure of lexical items (cf. (22)–(26) of the previous chapter). In these frames *all* arguments are listed, together with the thematic roles that are assigned to them.

Key Concepts in this Chapter

Head
Complement
Specifier
projections
lexical projection: X
bar-level projection: X′
maximal projection: XP
adjunction
cross-categorial generalisations
subcategorisation

Exercises

1. Explain how X-bar theory can account for the parallel interpretation of the italicised phrases below.

   (i)   (He) *appreciates good wine.*
   (ii)   (He is) *appreciative of good wine.*
   (iii) His *appreciation of good wine.*

   Draw the tree for each of the italicised phrases.

2. Draw the tree for the sentence *Geri completely adores pickled vegetables*. Then decide whether the statements below are true or false.

   (i)   the NP *pickled vegetables* is a sister of a lexical category
   (ii)   *pickled* is adjoined to the N *vegetables*
   (iii) *vegetables* is an N′ and an N at the same time
   (iv)   *adores pickled vegetables* is a V′

3. We have seen that Adjuncts are optional in sentences, and that they are excluded from subcategorisation frames. How does the sentence below pose a problem for this claim?

   (i)   Jimmy treats his cat badly.

4. Consider the following exchange from a TV sitcom.

Alan:	I am so happy!
Ben:	Happy?
Alan:	Yes, you remember happy?

   On the basis of Alan's last contribution to this mini-exchange we might want to say that the verb *remember* can subcategorise for an Adjective Phrase. Why would such a claim be dubious? If *remember* does *not* subcategorise for an AP, how do we explain the fact that *happy* can occur after this verb in the exchange above?

5. Here's another exchange, from a James Bond movie.

   Marceau: You'd never kill me, you'd miss me.

   Bond shoots her dead and says:

   Bond: I never miss.

   Explain the joke, making reference to subcategorisation frames.

6. In the text I gave the subcategorisation frame in (i) for *behind*. Should the sentence in (ii) lead us to revise this frame?

   (i)   *behind* (preposition)
          [– , NP]
   (ii)   We are hopelessly *behind*.

*7. The verb *locate* in English is transitive, and usually takes a Direct Object that denotes a three-dimensional entity, as in the example below:

   (i)   The police located the driver.

The meaning of locate is 'find the position, location of something'. Give the subcategorisation frame for the verb *locate*. We can also have (ii):

(ii)   The police located the driver in the High Street.

Does *locate* in (ii) involve the same verb *locate* as in (i), or do we need a different subcategorisation frame for this verb?

*8.   Although X'-syntax is a neat way of capturing similarities in phrase structure, it is not always obvious whether we should treat a particular string of words in a phrase as a Complement or as an Adjunct. In VPs the situation is usually fairly clear, in that Complements are obligatory, while Adjuncts are not. Thus, using the omissibility criterion we can safely say that the NP in (i) below is a Complement, because it cannot be left out, as (ii) shows.

(i)   Pete encouraged his sister.
(ii)   *Pete encouraged.

In phrases other than VPs, the situation is often more complex. In Sections 7.1 and 7.2 above I listed typical Complements and Adjuncts for the different phrase types. Very often it is hard, if not impossible, to decide whether a particular string of elements functions as an Adjunct or as a Complement. The omissibility criterion sometimes works, as with the AP in (iii) below, where clearly the PP must be a Complement, because it cannot be left out. But sometimes it doesn't, as with the NP in (iv), where the PP *of biology* can be left out, but is nevertheless analysed as a Complement, because of the analogy with the verb *study*, which takes an NP Complement (cf. *He studies biology*).

(iii)   He is [$_{AP}$ keen *on hot buns*] (cf. *He is keen.)
(iv)   He is [$_{NP}$ a student *of biology*] (cf. He is a student.)

Discuss the functional status (Adjunct or Complement?) of the italicised words in the following phrases:

(v)   I was assisted by [$_{NP}$ a man *in a dark suit*].
(vi)   They are [$_{NP}$ a family *of four*].
(vii)   I am [$_{AP}$ glad *that you are well*].
(viii) He is [$_{AP}$ extremely delighted *about that*].

*9.   English is a *Head-first language*. What this means is that Heads occur before Complements (cf. *bake a cake/*a cake bake*). Other languages are *Head-final*, e.g. Japanese and Korean (**bake a cake/a cake bake*). This means that Complements (e.g. Direct Objects) occur *before*, rather than after, the verb. However, as linguists have pointed out, the Head-first/Head-final distinction is not an absolute one. Consider the following data, taken from Radford

(1988). The NP in (i) involves a regular post-Head Complement (cf. *She studies physics.*), while the NP in (ii) involves a pre-Head Complement.

(i)   a student of physics
(ii)   a physics student

Assuming that both *of physics* in (i) and *physics* in (ii) are indeed Complements, draw the trees for these phrases.

*10.   In the text I wrote 'Specifiers are generally not recursive'. You will have spotted the hedge by my use of the word *generally*. The following are examples of Noun Phrases that contain stacked Specifiers. Can you think of ways of dealing with them in the X-bar framework?

(i)   all my problems
(ii)   his many virtues

*11.   Consider the sentence in (i) below. Arguably it is ambiguous between the following readings: 'Bob reviewed the book competently, and did so eagerly' or 'Bob reviewed the book eagerly, and did so competently'. Draw the trees that correspond to these meanings.

(i)   Bob eagerly reviewed the book competently.

Further Reading

X'-syntax was first introduced in Chomsky (1970), and refined in Jackendoff (1977).

Adverbs and Adverb Phrases are somewhat problematic for X'-theory. Some textbooks on theoretical syntax mention them only in passing, while others ignore them altogether. The reason for their special status is that they do not fit into the X'-mould very comfortably. For example, it is very hard to think of adverbs that can take Complements. Jackendoff (1977: 78) gives only one example of a Complement-taking adverb, namely *unfortunately for our hero*, but observes that '[o]n the whole, adverbs take no complement' (ibid.). In my own example, *faster than me*, it isn't entirely obvious whether *than me* is a Complement or an Adjunct of *faster*.

Specifiers are sometimes also hard to slot in. Consider, for example, (44) above, where I have had to leave the Specifier position empty, simply because I couldn't think of an element that can occupy that position if an Adjunct and Complement are also present in the AdvP. Some linguists have argued that adverbs are not a problem at all. They would claim that they are really a special type of adjective (see, e.g., Radford 1988: 138–41 for discussion). On the whole, though, it seems that we are forced to recognise a word class of adverbs, and that they are an embarrassment for X′-theory.

My claim that the Specifier position of VP is filled by negative elements (if they are present) is unusual. Other linguists have proposed that aspectual auxiliaries are positioned here (cf. e.g. Radford 1988: 230f.), or that Subjects of sentences originate from Spec-of-VP (cf. Haegeman 1994 and Adger 2003 for discussion).

8 More on Clauses

The notion of clause was introduced in Chapter 4. In this chapter we will take a closer look at the internal structure of clauses and their tree structure representations. Specifically, we will see how we can add a new node to our existing set of nodes. Then we will discuss a variety of different types of clauses.

8.1 The I-Node

So far in this book we have dealt with simple straightforward sentences. In this section we'll be homing in on the finer details of sentential analysis. To begin, let us briefly review the analysis of sentences in terms of tree diagrams that we have arrived at so far. We analysed a simple sentence like (1) as in (2):

(1)   My brother baked a cake.

(2)

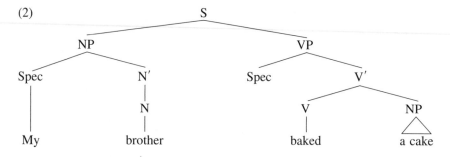

In this tree the S-node branches into NP and VP, and each of these phrases is structured in accordance with the principles of X′-syntax. We have said that VP contains the Direct Object of a sentence, if it is present, the reason for this being the strong bond that obtains between the verb and the DO: using the terminology introduced in Chapter 7, we say that the verb subcategorises for an NP. Notice that, because (2) is not a negative sentence, the Spec-of-VP position remains empty.

What we have been tacitly glossing over is the question how verbs acquire their inflectional endings. More concretely, how does the verb *bake* in (2) obtain its past tense *-ed* ending? We could of course simply assume, as we have in fact so far been doing, that tensed verbs are simply attached underneath the appropriate V-node. However, this idea is unattractive. The reason is the following: assuming that word-level elements in trees are taken directly from a list of words we have in our heads, i.e. from a *mental lexicon*, we would then have to say that the lexicon lists inflected words. If that is indeed the case, the lexicon would be enormously large, containing not only uninflected words but also all their inflected variants. For example, it would contain not only the base-form of the verb *bake*, but also the forms *bakes, baked* and *baking*. It would make more sense to suppose that the lexicon is constrained, and contains only what we have called *lexemes* (see Chapter 2), and that some sort of mechanism makes sure that verb-lexemes that are inserted into trees end up being either finite, i.e. inflected for tense, or remain nonfinite, i.e. uninflected for tense.

What sort of mechanism could we make use of for these purposes? In line with recent work in linguistics we will assume that sentences contain a node labelled 'I' (short for 'inflection'), which is immediately dominated by S. This node is responsible for two things. One of them is making sure that verbs acquire tense, the other is taking care of the *agreement* that obtains between Subjects and verbs (e.g. the *-s* ending on *bakes* in *he bakes a cake*).

The I-node looks like this:

(3)

$$
\begin{array}{cc}
& \mathrm{I} \\
\overbrace{\hspace{4cm}} \\
[\pm\mathrm{Tense}] & [\pm\mathrm{Agr}] \\
[\pm\mathrm{Present}] &
\end{array}
$$

As you can see, 'I' contains a number of components, which we will refer to as *features*. One is the abstract feature [Tense], which can have either a positive or a negative value, i.e. it can be [+Tense] or [–Tense] (indicated by the symbol '±'). If it has a positive value, we have a further choice between [+present] or [–present], as follows: [+Tense, +present] or [+Tense, –present]. The other abstract feature in 'I' is [Agr], which is short for 'Agreement'. Again, this feature can have either a positive or a negative value: [+Agr] or [–Agr]. English makes use of only three combinations of features, namely:

[+Tense, +present][+Agr]
[+Tense, –present][+Agr]
[–Tense][–Agr]

Other combinations are attested in other languages, but it would take us too far afield to discuss them further.

We assume that a finite clause, i.e. a tensed clause, will have an I-node with a positive value for the features [Tense] and [Agr], and that a nonfinite clause will have negative values for these features. We can now revise the analysis of (2) as in (4) below:

(4)

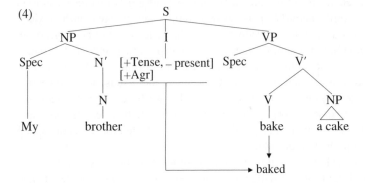

Notice that in this tree the verb *bake* has been inserted in its base-form, i.e. in an uninflected form. We now need to find a way of establishing a link between the I-node and the main verb inside VP. Let's assume that the tense and agreement features are *lowered* from the I-node onto the verb inside VP (a process that is sometimes called *affix hopping*), and that they are *spelled out* as an inflectional ending on the verb. In the case of a sentence with a third person singular Subject this ending can be either the present tense suffix *-s* or the past tense suffix *-ed*. In the case of present tense Subjects other than third person singular, an abstract null ending is lowered from the I-node onto the verb, while in the past tense we again have *-ed*.

What about nonfinite clauses? For them the I-node is marked [–Tense] and [–Agr]. In the following example the matrix clause is finite, but the bracketed subordinate clause, which functions as the Direct Object of the verb *want*, is nonfinite:

(5)   She wanted [her brother to bake a cake].

Here is the tree diagram for (5):

(6)

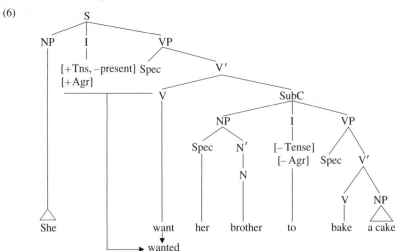

In the case of the matrix clause we again say that the features [+Tense, –present] and [+Agr] are lowered onto the main verb *want*, which is then spelled out as *wanted*. If a subordinate clause contains the features [–Tense] and [–Agr] and the element *to* (often called an *infinitival marker* in descriptive grammars, in contrast to the preposition *to*), then this element is positioned under the I-node. *To* is therefore regarded as an inflectional element.

Apart from inflection features and agreement features, the I-node is also relevant to auxiliary verbs. You'll remember from Chapter 3 that auxiliary verbs are 'helping' verbs that precede main verbs. Recall that we distinguished four subcategories of auxiliaries: the modal auxiliaries (a.k.a. the modals), the aspectual auxiliaries (a.k.a. the aspectuals), the passive auxiliary *be* and the dummy auxiliary *do*. So far we haven't discussed in any detail the structure of sentences that contain auxiliaries. Here we'll be concentrating on the modals, turning to aspectuals and other auxiliaries in the next chapter.

Consider the following sentence:

(7)   My brother will bake a cake.

This sentence contains the modal auxiliary *will*. We might now ask where in a tree diagram this auxiliary is positioned. As *will* is a verb, it would be reasonable to assume that it is positioned inside VP. It would then need to be placed in front of the main verb, i.e. before *bake*. It would also need to be placed in front of the negative element *not* when it is present, as the sentence below shows:

(8)   My brother will not bake a cake.

However, we know that the element *not* occupies the Specifier position inside VP (see Section 7.1), and we also know that there are no further positions to the left of the Specifier. We are therefore led to conclude that modals like *will* are *not* inside VP. But if they're not inside VP, what do we do with them? A plausible option would be to place modal auxiliaries under the I-node. Sentence (7) would then be analysed as follows:

(9)

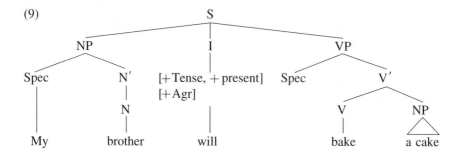

What motivation do we have for this analysis? Well, one reason is that modals are always tensed, as we saw in Chapter 3. This fact can be accounted for if we place them under 'I', the node that contains the tense feature. Another reason for placing the modals under 'I' is that this analysis is compatible with the behaviour of so-called *sentence adverbs* (see Section 3.6). Sentence adverbs, as their name implies, modify complete sentences. Examples are *however, frankly, perhaps, probably*, etc. These adverbs can occur in a variety of positions in sentences, as (10) below makes clear:

(10)a. *Perhaps* my brother will not bake a cake.
    b. My brother *perhaps* will not bake a cake.
    c. My brother will *perhaps* not bake a cake.
    d. My brother will not bake a cake *perhaps*.

In a tree diagram *perhaps* can appear in the positions indicated by the symbol '▾':

(11)

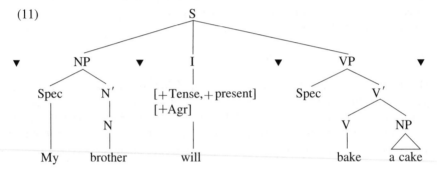

Now, given the fact that *perhaps* is a sentence adverb, i.e. immediately dominated by S in a tree diagram, and given also the fact that it can occur between a modal verb and the Specifier of VP, a reasonable assumption would be to place the modal under 'I'. We will discuss further evidence that modal auxiliaries are positioned in 'I' in Chapter 11.

Summarising this section: we've seen that, apart from an NP and a VP, clauses also contain an I-node which accommodates tense and agreement features. Finite clauses contain the combination [+Tense, ±present][+Agr], while nonfinite clauses contain [−Tense][−Agr]. If a clause contains a modal verb or the infinitival marker *to*, these elements are positioned under 'I'. Notice that the modals and *to* cannot co-occur (e.g. *He will to sleep*), and this can be seen as further evidence that they fill the same slot in a tree diagram.

8.2   Subordinate Clauses

8.2.1   *Clauses Functioning as Direct Object, Subject and Adjunct*

Earlier in this book we discussed the sentences in (12) and (13) and their associated tree diagrams in (14) and (15), which now include the new

I-node:

(12) Tim thought that Kate believed the story.

(13) She wanted her brother to bake a cake. (= (5) above)

(14)

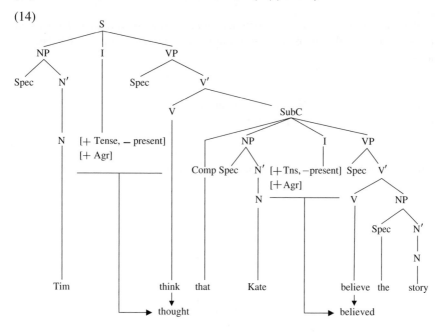

(15)

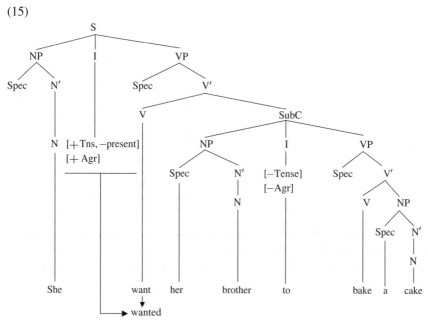

Both sentences contain subordinate clauses which function as Direct Objects of the verbs *believe* and *want*, respectively. Note that the subordinate clause in (14) is finite and is introduced by the complementiser *that* (cf. Section 3.7), while the subordinate clause in (15) is nonfinite and not introduced by a subordinating conjunction.

We haven't so far discussed sentences that contain subordinate clauses that have a function other than DO, for example, Subject or Adjunct (cf. Chapter 5), as in (16) and (17):

(16)   [That Ken adores Nadia] annoys Jenny.
(17)   I will repair it [when I return].

(16) can be represented as follows in a tree diagram:

(18)

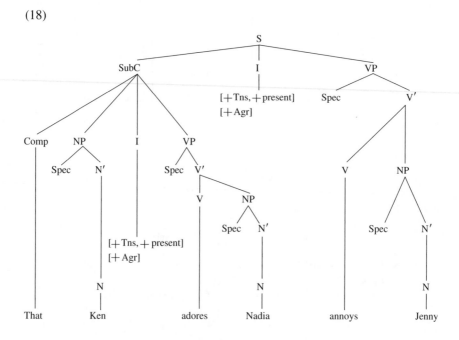

As for (17), notice that the subordinate clause is positioned *after* the Direct Object, and that its function is Adjunct (cf. Section 5.6). Because the *when*-clause is not a Complement of the verb *repair*, it cannot be analysed as its sister in a tree diagram. Instead, it must be adjoined as a sister to the V' *repair it*:

(19)

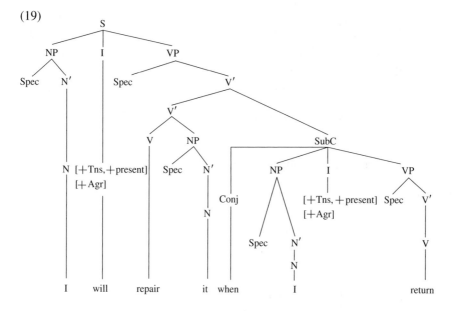

8.2.2 Clauses Functioning as Complements within Phrases

In Chapter 7 we saw that not only verbs can take clausal Complements, other lexical Heads can too. Consider the bracketed phrases in the examples below, taken from Table 7.2:

(20) The article was about [$_{NP}$ their **realisation** *that all is lost*]
(21) I am [$_{AP}$ so **eager** *to work with you*]
(22) He is uncertain [$_{PP}$ **about** *what you said to me*]

The Heads in each case are in bold, the Complements are in italics. The clausal Complements in each case are subordinate clauses. In the NP and AP they give more information about the content of their associated Head. In the PP the clause identifies the nature of the uncertainty mentioned in the sentence.

Exercise

Draw the trees for the phrases in (20)–(22). Use triangles for the clausal Complements.

Your answers should look like this:

(23)

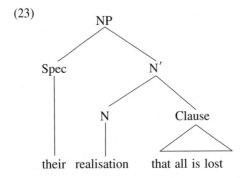

(24)

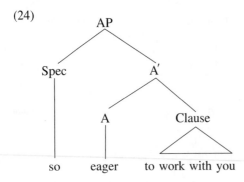

(25)

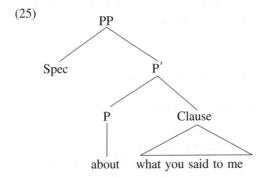

Because the clauses in each case are Complements, they are represented as sisters of their Heads.

8.2.3   *Clauses Functioning as Adjuncts within NPs*

Apart from inside VPs (see Section 7.2 above) clausal Adjuncts are also found in NPs. Here they have a special name: they are called *relative clauses*, and can be introduced by a Wh-word or by *that*. There are two examples in Table 7.3 of the previous chapter. Here are some further examples:

(26) Do you remember *[NP that summer, which was so sunny]*?
(27) Do you remember *[NP that summer which was so sunny]*?
(28) I'm worried about *[NP the watch that was stolen]*, not the one on the table.

Imagine (26) being uttered in a situation where the interlocutors know which particular summer is being referred to, say last year's summer. In this case the relative clause does not add further information that contributes to identifying the summer in question. We call it a *nonrestrictive relative clause*. Notice the comma, which marks the relative clause off intonationally, i.e. there is a pause after the word *summer*. (Read the sentence out aloud to see what I mean.) Consider now (27). It looks exactly the same as (26), except that this time there is no comma, which signals that there is no pause after *summer*. When uttered in this way the relative clause *does* single out a particular summer for the interlocutors, for example a hot summer in a series of wet ones. (Again, read the sentence out aloud.) We call such a clause a *restrictive relative clause*. In (28) the clause *that was stolen* is a further example of a restrictive relative clause, because it uniquely identifies a particular watch. Should we distinguish structurally between restrictive and nonrestrictive relative clauses? Because the distinction between them is arguably a semantic one, and because relative clauses often depend for their interpretation on a particular context of utterance, we will not structurally distinguish the way they are positioned relative to their associated Heads: we will treat both restrictive and nonrestrictive relative clauses functionally as Adjuncts (i.e. they are adjoined to N'). Thus, (29) represents the NP in both (26) and (27), while (30) represents the NP in (28):

(29)

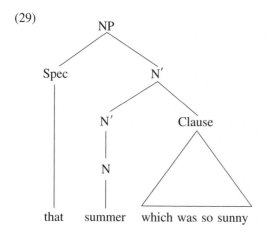

(30)

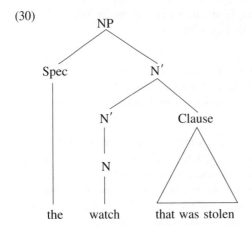

Key Concepts in this Chapter

The I-node
subordinate clauses
    functioning as Direct Object, Subject and Adjunct
    clauses functioning as Complements or Adjuncts within phrases
    relative clauses (restrictive, nonrestrictive)

Exercises

1.   Draw the tree for the sentence *Linda can arrange the event*. Then answer the following question: true or false?

    (i)   *can* takes the VP *arrange the event* as its Complement
    (ii)   *can* has moved from inside the VP to the I-node
    (iii) *can* is a finite verb
    (iv) *can* is a present tense aspectual auxiliary verb

2.   In accordance with X-bar theory, draw complete trees (i.e. include all the Specifiers and all the I-nodes with the relevant features) of the following phrases/sentences. Treat *be* in (x) as a main verb.

    (i)   I will go.
    (ii)   She rode her bicycle slowly.
    (iii) Seamus can speak Chinese.
    (iv) Elaine should not enrol.

(v)   [That we will succeed] will surprise nobody.
(vi)   I prefer you to stay in London.
(vii)   She phoned because she likes you.
(viii) I thought that she was a student of law.
(xi)   We will have a picnic, when Frank arrives.
(x)   He is grumpy, but he is kind.
(xi)   We will not budge.
(xii)   She wrote the story very quickly

3. How can the following utterance be taken as evidence to support our claim that modal auxiliary verbs are positioned in 'I'?

(i)   He might, and I stress might, pass his exams.

4. The following sentence is ambiguous:

(i)   John decided that they would move after Easter.

Explain the ambiguity, then draw the trees that correspond to the two meanings.

*5. Draw trees for the italicised phrases below. Use triangles for the subordinate clauses.

(i)   *Her father, who was arrested,* protested his innocence.
(ii)   I am *so happy to leave England.*

*6. Consider (i) and (ii) below. Is there a grammatical difference between the *that*-clauses? Draw the full tree diagrams (so no triangles!) for the italicised phrases.

(i)   He denied *the fact that she is clever.*
(ii)   *The fact that she is clever* is important.

*7. Draw the tree for *I told you not to do it.*

Further Reading

The I-node contains a different sort of Head than we have come across so far. It is a *functional category*, as opposed to a *lexical category* (such as N, V, A and P). Chomsky (1986) proposed that the I-node be given its own maximal projection, namely *Inflection Phrase* (IP). In the same way complementisers head *Complementiser Phrases* (CP). See Radford (1988), Haegeman (1994), Ouhalla (1999) and Adger (2003) for further details. It has furthermore been proposed that a number of additional functional categories, for example, tense, agreement and aspect, also head their own maximal projections, so that we can also speak of *Tense Phrases* (TP), *Agreement Phrases* (AgrP) and *Aspect Phrases* (AspP), among others. See Webelhuth (1995) for an historical overview of developments in X'-theory.

On relative clauses, see Quirk et al. (1985: 1244–60). On nonrestrictive relative clauses, see Fabb (1990) and Burton-Roberts (1999).

9 Movement

This chapter will look at four different ways in which elements, or strings of elements, can be *moved* in a sentence. I will first discuss verb movement and NP-movement, then movement in interrogative sentences, and finally Wh-movement. I will finish the chapter with a section on the structure of sentences containing sequences of auxiliaries.

9.1 Verb Movement: Aspectual Auxiliaries

In the previous chapter we argued that modal auxiliaries are not positioned in VP, but in 'I', and we used the sentences in (1) and (2) to demonstrate this.

(1) My brother will *not* bake a cake.
(2) My brother will *perhaps* not bake a cake.

In (1) the modal auxiliary *will* is positioned before the negative element *not*, which we argued to be in the Specifier position of VP. As there are no further slots to the left of the Specifier in VP, we concluded that the modal must be outside VP. In (2) the sentence adverb *perhaps* is positioned between the modal *will* and *not*. On the assumption that sentence adverbs are directly dominated by S, the conclusion must again be that the modal cannot be inside VP. Furthermore, we observed that modals are always finite, and that the 'I'-node is therefore a natural location for them, given the fact that it contains the tense feature (see Section 8.1).

But what about the aspectual auxiliaries *have* and *be* in sentences like (3) and (4)? Where are they positioned?

(3) He *has* broken the mirror.
(4) I *am* dreaming.

Let's look at these sentences more closely. In (3) the last two constituents are the verb *broken* (a nonfinite past participle form of the main verb *break*) and the Noun Phrase *the mirror*, which functions as a Direct Object. Now, we know that a main verb + DO form a V-bar (V′), and that this V′ is a sister of a Specifier. We

also know that the Specifier node and V′ are dominated by VP, so we assign the
structure in (5) to the sequence *broken the mirror*:

(5)
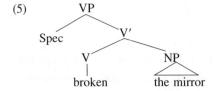

We still need to account for the finite aspectual auxiliary *has*. We will assume
that this verb takes the VP *broken the mirror* as its Complement. In a tree diagram this VP should therefore be represented as the sister of *have*, as in (6), the
representation of (3) (the Specifier position of the lower VP has been left out to
make the tree visually easier to interpret):

(6)
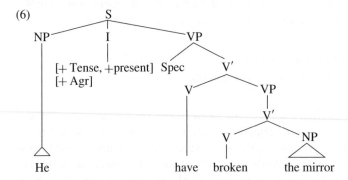

Notice that in this tree the aspectual auxiliary *have* is inserted in its base form,
which raises the question how it ends up in its finite form *has*. The answer is that
the aspectual auxiliary acquires its inflectional present tense ending by *moving*
from the VP that dominates it into the I-node, as indicated below:

(7)
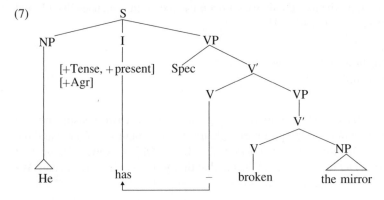

This process we refer to as *verb movement*.

What would be the structure of sentence (4)? Assuming that the aspectual auxiliary moves from VP into 'I', draw the tree diagram for (4). Indicate the movement with an arrow, as above. You may omit irrelevant nodes, such as the Specifier position of the lowest VP.

The tree diagram for (4) is as in (8):

(8)

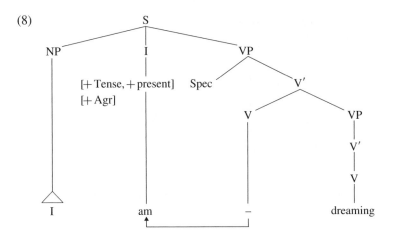

Here too the aspectual auxiliary moves from the position in VP marked '–' to 'I' in order for the verb to acquire its present tense form. Notice that as the verb *dream* is an intransitive verb, there are no further Complements present in the lowest VP.

You may well be wondering why we are positing movement of aspectual auxiliaries into 'I'. Why don't we simply assume that the inflectional features are lowered from 'I' into the VP, exactly in the same way as was suggested in Chapter 8 for main verbs in simple sentences like (9)?

(9)   Ted opened the window.

Well, there is evidence that we need to posit movement for the aspectuals, and this evidence concerns sentences involving negative elements, sentence adverbs or modals, or a combination of these. Consider the following examples:

(10)   He has not broken the mirror.
(11)   I am not dreaming.

Notice that both sentences contain *not*. As we have seen, this element is positioned in the Specifier of the higher VP (the lower VP may also contain *not*, as in *he has not not broken the window*). This being so, and there being no further slots inside the higher VP to the left of the Specifier, the most obvious position for the aspectuals is inside 'I'. But if *have* and *be* are inside VP in trees like (6), but in 'I' in (10) and (11), then we need to account for this difference in position. One way of doing so is by positing movement of the aspectuals from VP to 'I'. This would then also explain how they end up in their finite forms (cf. **He have not broken the mirror./*I be not dreaming.*). Here is the tree for (10):

(12)

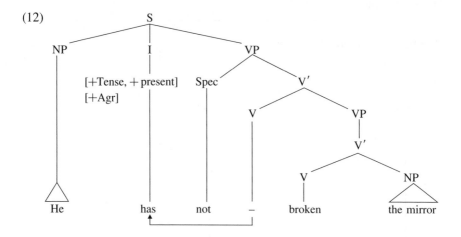

We will assume that the past participle *broken* is inserted in the tree in its inflected form.

Exercise

Now draw the tree for (11). Use an arrow to show the movement of the aspectual auxiliary. As before, you may leave out irrelevant nodes such as the Specifier position of the lowest VP.

You should have drawn your tree like this:

(13)

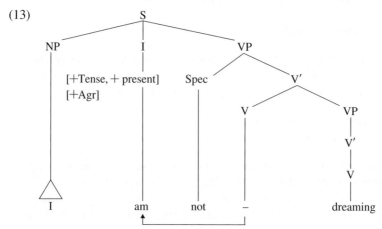

Further evidence that finite aspectual auxiliaries are in 'I' comes from the following pair of sentences, which contain the sentence adverb *probably*:

(14)   He has probably broken the mirror.
(15)   I am probably dreaming.

The reasoning here is as follows: because the sentence adverb *probably* is immediately dominated by S (cf. (11) of the previous chapter), and the aspectual auxiliaries *has* and *am* occur to the left of this adverb, we cannot assume that the latter are inside VP. As they are in their finite forms (cf. **He have probably broken the window/*I be probably dreaming*), it is reasonable to assume that they are in 'I'. But if they are, we will need to say that they moved from inside the Verb Phrase, because we have been assuming that aspectuals 'start out' in VP. We can use the sentences in (16) and (17), which contain *both* sentence adverbs *and* negative elements, to make the same point.

(16)   He has probably not broken the mirror.
(17)   I am probably not dreaming.

(Note: other adverbs can occur in the position occupied by *probably* in (14)–(17), e.g. *intentionally* or *unwittingly*, but these can be shown to be positioned inside VP. See the exercise section at the end of the chapter.)

Exercise

Draw the trees for (16) and (17). Use arrows to show movement. You may omit irrelevant nodes.

Your answers should look like this:

(18)

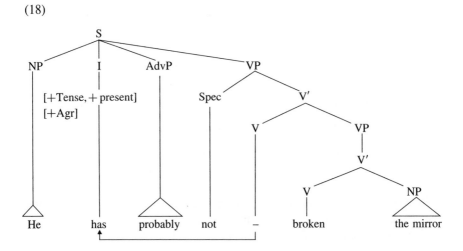

(19)

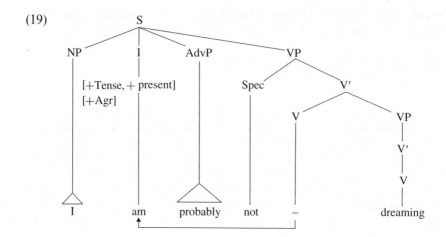

Now, at this point I may have convinced you that aspectual auxiliaries should some-how be related to the I-position, but you may well have noticed that all the evidence that has been put forward so far is also compatible with an analysis in which the aspectuals are always positioned in 'I', and never part of VP, as in for example (6). In other words, why not take the structure of (3) and (4) to be as in (20) and in (21), where the aspectual auxiliaries are treated like the modal auxiliaries?

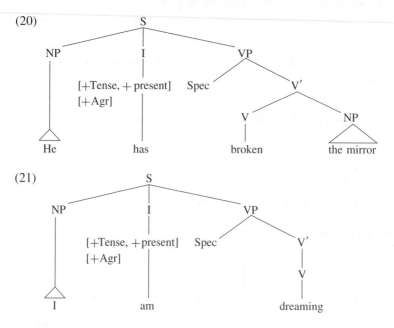

Why do we want to insist that aspectual auxiliaries originate inside VP, and that they are different from modal auxiliaries, which I have claimed to be positioned in 'I', without being moved from inside VP?

The structures above would be possible if it wasn't for the fact that in English we can have combinations of modal auxiliaries with aspectual auxiliaries, as in (22):

(22)   He will not have broken the mirror.

Here, as before, the modal *will* is positioned in 'I', where it originates, while the aspectual auxiliary turns up to the right of the negative element *not*. (Cf. also *He will probably not have broken the mirror*, where there is also a sentence adverb present.) In (22) the aspectual must therefore be inside VP, to the right of the Specifier *not*.

Exercise

Draw the tree for (22). You may leave out irrelevant nodes, such as the Specifier position of the lowest VP.

The tree for (22) looks like this:

(23)

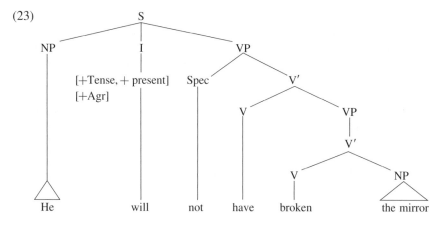

The situation we're faced with, then, is that we have evidence that aspectuals can be positioned *inside* VP, namely when there is also a modal in the sentence (cf. (22)), but we also have evidence that aspectuals can be positioned *outside* VP, namely when there is a sentence adverb and/or negative element present, but no modal verb (cf. (10)–(17)). In order to account for this situation we posit movement of aspectual auxiliary verbs from VP to 'I', but *only* if there is not already a modal verb present in 'I' to block it.

9.2   NP-Movement: Passive

Consider the active sentence in (24), and its passive counterpart in (25):

(24)   These lorries produce filthy fumes.
(25)   Filthy fumes are produced by these lorries.

We saw in Chapter 3 that the active-passive alternation is quite a common one, and that, in contrast with active sentences, passive sentences contain the passive auxiliary *be*, a past participle and an optional PP introduced by *by*.

If we consider (24) and (25) from the point of view of thematic roles, we observe that the NP *these lorries* carries an agentive role both in (24) and (25). The NP *filthy fumes* carries the role of Patient (or Theme if you prefer) in both sentences.

Linguists have suggested that in order to capture the strong thematic affinities between active and passive sentences we might view passive sentences as being the result of movement, in such a way that the Subject of a passive sentence derives from the position immediately following the main verb. We can indicate the position that the Subject of (25) derives from with a '—':

(26)   Filthy fumes are produced — by these lorries

Such an account would explain how a phrase with a Patient thematic role ends up in Subject position, while its canonical position is after the main verb. Movement of this type in passive sentences is an instantiation of *NP-movement*.

We might wonder where the passive auxiliary *be* should be located in a tree diagram. Before dealing with this problem, it might be a good idea to reiterate two points that I made in Chapter 3 regarding the syntactic behaviour of auxiliary verbs (both modals and aspectuals). The first point is that if there is a sequence of auxiliaries in a sentence, each auxiliary determines the form of a following one. The second point is that the various types of auxiliaries that English possesses always occur in the same order. I will illustrate these points with a few examples. Consider first (27)–(30):

(27)   This student *must write* two essays.
(28)   This student *has written* two essays.
(29)   This student *is writing* two essays.
(30)   Two essays *were written* by this student.

In (27) the main verb is preceded by the modal verb *must*. In (28) and (29) it is preceded by an aspectual auxiliary (*have* and *be*, respectively), while in (30) (the passive version of *This student wrote two essays*), the main verb is preceded by the plural past tense form of the passive auxiliary *be*. Notice that in each case the form of the main verb is determined by the auxiliary that precedes it. Thus, in (27) the modal *must* is followed by the base form of the verb *write*. In (28) and (30) the main verb is in the form of the past participle *written*, while in (29) the verb-form *writing* is determined by the progressive auxiliary *be*.

Combinations of auxiliaries are also possible (we have seen some examples of this already):

(31)   This student *must have written* two essays.
       modal auxiliary + perfective auxiliary + main verb

(32)   This student *must be writing* two essays.
        modal auxiliary + progressive auxiliary + main verb
(33)   This student *has been writing* two essays.
        perfective auxiliary + progressive auxiliary + main verb
(34)   Two essays *must have been being written* by this student.
        modal auxiliary + perfective auxiliary + progressive auxiliary + passive
        auxiliary + main verb

While sentences (31)–(33) are perfectly acceptable in English, (34) is unusual, but nevertheless possible.

Exercise

Other combinations of auxiliaries are possible in English. Try to construct sentences with additional possibilities.

The auxiliary + main verb sequence always occurs in the following order:

(35)   (modal) (perfective) (progressive) (passive) main verb

The main verb is always obligatory. The auxiliaries are optional. Notice that if we do have a sequence of auxiliaries, it is possible to 'skip' one of the bracketed auxiliary slots shown in (35), as (32) shows. Here we have a modal auxiliary immediately followed by a progressive auxiliary. There is no perfective auxiliary. In (34) all auxiliary slots given in (35) are filled. We can only select one auxiliary of a particular type, so it is not possible for a Standard English sentence to contain two modal verbs, or two progressive auxiliaries.

You may have noticed that auxiliaries share a property with transitive and ditransitive verbs: like these main verbs they too determine what follows them. As we have seen, a transitive verb requires a following Direct Object, while a ditransitive verb requires an IO and a DO. Using the terminology introduced in Chapter 7, transitive verbs subcategorise for a DO, and ditransitive verbs subcategorise for an IO and a DO. In the same way auxiliary verbs subcategorise for VPs. To see this, take another look at (27)–(30) above. The modal in (27) subcategorises for a VP headed by a verb in the base form (*write two essays*), the perfective and passive auxiliaries in (28) and (30) are followed by a VP headed by a participle (*written two essays* and *written by this student*), while the progressive auxiliary in (29) subcategorises for a VP headed by an *-ing* form (*writing two essays*). We will see in a moment how to draw the trees for these sentences.

Let's now return to the question we asked ourselves earlier: where in a tree diagram do we position the passive auxiliary *be*? We will try to answer this question by reasoning our way through a number of sentences. First, we already know where modal verbs, aspectual auxiliaries and negative elements are located. The way we will proceed is to analyse sentences which contain a combination of these elements, and then see how passive *be* fits in. So, let's produce a number of test sentences containing different auxiliary verbs and negative elements:

(36)   Filthy fumes are not produced by these lorries.
(37)   Filthy fumes have not been produced by these lorries.
(38)   Filthy fumes are not being produced by these lorries.
(39)   Filthy fumes may not have been produced by these lorries.
(40)   Filthy fumes may not be being produced by these lorries.
(41)   Filthy fumes may not have been being produced by these lorries.

(36) is the negative counterpart of (25): here the passive auxiliary *be* combines with the negative element *not*. As we have seen, *not* is located in the leftmost position in VP, namely Spec-of-VP, and this suggests that the passive auxiliary should be positioned *outside* VP. Because it is tensed, a suitable location would be the 'I'-node. We should now use other data to test this hypothesis. In (37) the passive auxiliary (this time in the form of the past participle *been*) is preceded not only by *not*, but also by the perfective aspectual auxiliary *have*. Contrary to our initial hypothesis, this leads us to conclude that the passive auxiliary is *inside* VP, the reason being that it is preceded by *not*, which, as before, is located in the leftmost position of VP.

Let's turn to some further examples and see if we can resolve this contradiction. Consider (38). This sentence is structurally similar to (37), except that it contains the progressive auxiliary *be*, rather than perfective *have*. In (39) and (40), in both cases we have a combination of a modal verb (*may*) with an aspectual auxiliary (*have* in (39), *be* in (40)) and the passive auxiliary (in the form of *been* in (39), *being* in (40)). These sentences show that this time the modal is outside VP, whereas the aspectual and passive auxiliaries are inside VP. Finally, in (41) we have the modal *may*, the negative marker *not*, the perfective auxiliary *have*, the progressive auxiliary *been*, and the passive auxiliary *being*. Only the modal is outside VP, all the elements to the right of *not* are inside VP.

So what do we make of these, at times conflicting, data? If you look carefully at (36)–(41) again, you will see that in each case the first auxiliary verb in the sequence is finite, and precedes the negative marker *not*. Now, bearing in mind that modal auxiliaries are positioned in 'I', the picture that emerges is really quite straightforward: if the sentence you are analysing contains a modal verb, then it is positioned in 'I', any other verbs then being located in VP. If there are only non-modal auxiliaries in the sentence, then again the first of these is in 'I', the other verbs being positioned in VP. If there is only a main verb, then it is inside VP, functioning as the VP-Head.

Returning now to our passive sentence in (26), we can conclude that its tree looks like this:

(42)

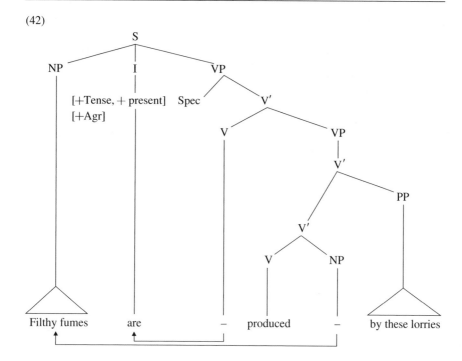

Notice that we have *two* movements here: the passive auxiliary *be* has moved to 'I' under verb movement, while the Direct Object has moved from a position following the main verb to the Subject position of the sentence under NP Movement.

Exercise

Draw the tree for (27)–(30). As before, you may use triangles for NPs and leave out the Specifier positions of lower VPs.

Your answers should look like this:

(43)

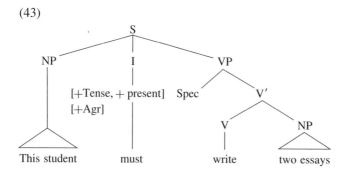

(44)

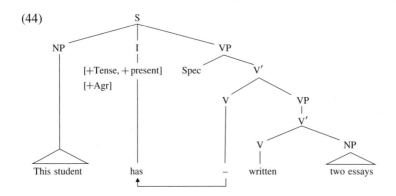

(45)

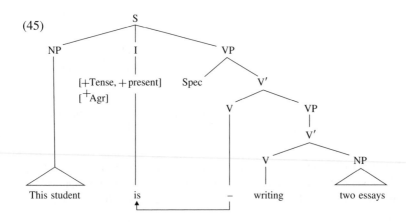

(46)

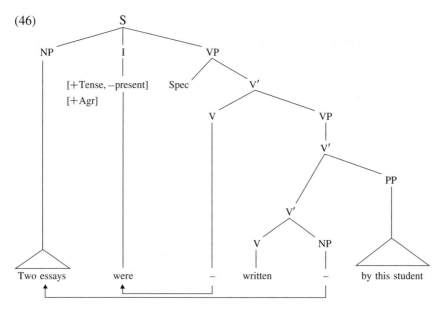

I will return to the analysis of sentences containing sequences of auxiliary verbs in Section 9.6.

9.3   NP-Movement: Subject-to-Subject Raising

There is a further type of NP-movement in English which we will only discuss very briefly. Consider the sentences below:

(47)   Danny seems to be working.
(48)   Phil appears to be singing.

As we saw in Chapter 3, *seem* and *appear* are linking verbs. In (47) and (48) they link the Subjects *Danny* and *Phil* to the strings *to be working* and *to be singing*, respectively.

   If we now think about (47) and (48) from the point of view of meaning, observe that we can paraphrase them as follows:

(49)   It seems that Danny is working.
(50)   It appears that Phil is singing.

Notice the appearance of the dummy pronoun *it* in these sentences. We have already seen in Chapter 6 that this pronoun is never assigned a thematic role, and the very fact that it can appear as a Subject immediately before a linking verb suggests that linking verbs do not assign thematic roles to their Subjects. In fact, it would be hard to determine what kind of thematic role verbs like *seem* and *appear* would assign to their Subjects in (47) and (48). It is, however, less difficult to think of a thematic role that *(to be) working* and *(to be) singing* might assign. This would clearly be an Agent role. Linguists have suggested that sentences like (47) and (48) involve two clauses, and that *Danny* and *Phil* receive their thematic role from *(to be) working* and *(to be) singing* in a subordinate clause, before being moved to the matrix clause Subject position. We can now represent (47) and (48) as follows:

(51)   [MC Danny seems [SubC — to be working]]

(52)   [MC Phil appears [SubC — to be singing]]

This type of displacement, along with the movement discussed in the previous section, is an instance of NP-movement. It is also sometimes referred to as *Subject-to-Subject raising*. The reason for this is that the NP Subjects move from the Subject position of the subordinate clause to the Subject position of the matrix clause.

In a tree this movement can be represented as follows:

(53)

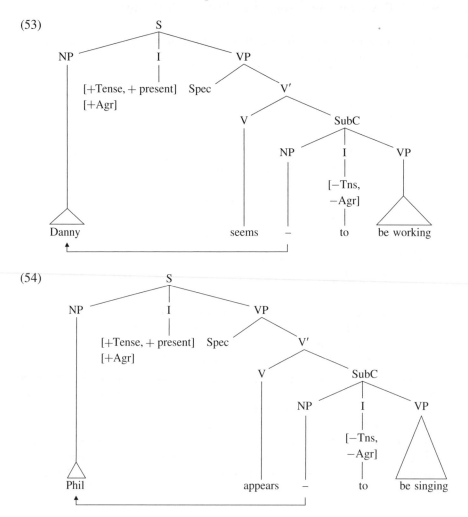

The upshot of all this is that linking verbs are one-place predicates that take clausal arguments. Thus, *seem* takes the clause *Danny to be working* as its argument, while *appear* takes *Phil to be singing* as its argument. The combined argument structure and thematic structure representations of *seem* and *appear* are as in (55) and (56):

(55)   *seem* (verb)
        [1 <Clause, Proposition>]

(56)   *appear* (verb)
       [1 <Clause, Proposition>

The way we should read this is as follows: *seem* and *appear* take one argument
in the form of a clause, and this clause is assigned a propositional thematic role.
If we compare (47)/(48) with (49)/(50), we see that the clausal arguments specified in (55) and (56) can take the form of a nonfinite *to*-infinitive clause or a finite
that-clause. However, only in the case of *to*-infinitive clauses does the Subject get
displaced under NP-movement. Remember that *it* in (49) and (50) is not an argument of the linking verb and does not get a thematic role. For this reason it does
not appear in the frames in (55) and (56).

9.4   Movement in Interrogative Sentences: Subject–Auxiliary Inversion

We saw in Chapter 3 that one of the characteristics of auxiliary verbs (be they
modals, aspectuals, passive *be* or dummy *do*) is that they invert with the Subject
in interrogative sentences. This process of *Subject–auxiliary inversion* is illustrated by the sentences below:

(57)   Saul can play the piano.
(58)   Can Saul play the piano?

(59)   Neil is playing squash.
(60)   Is Neil playing squash?

(61)   Simon hates game shows.
(62)   Does Simon hate game shows?

If a sentence already contains an auxiliary verb, then this verb inverts with the
Subject, as in (58) and (60). If the original sentence does not contain an auxiliary,
then *do* is added, as in (62), a process we have been calling *do*-support.

   Let us now see where auxiliaries end up in a tree diagram after Subject–auxiliary
inversion. We will assume that the moved verb is adjoined to S at the leftmost
periphery of the sentence, as is shown below for (63):

(63)

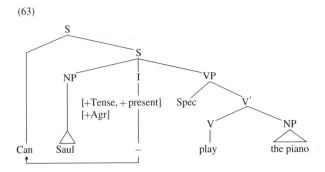

Exercise

Draw the tree for (60). Indicate movement with arrows, as has been done above. (Remember that the aspectual auxiliary *be* moves twice: once to acquire Tense and Agreement, and a second time under Subject–auxiliary inversion!)

The tree for (60) looks like this:

(64)

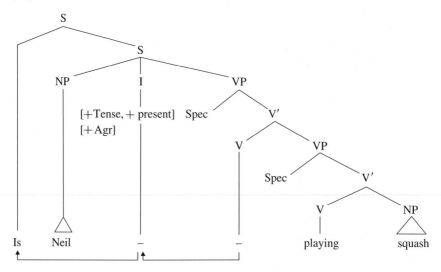

We now return to the dummy auxiliary *do*. As you know, this auxiliary is exceptional in that it is only inserted when it is required in negative or interrogative sentences that do not already have an auxiliary (cf. (61)/(62)), or if emphasis is required (e.g. *He DID see it!*). We might wonder whether dummy *do* is also subject to movement. In other words, do we assume that it is moved from the I-node in the same way as modal verbs, as in (63), or that it is first moved from inside VP to 'I', and then on to a sentence-initial position, as in (64)? To put this question differently: as far as its syntactic behaviour is concerned, do we group dummy *do* with the modal verbs (as being always tensed and originating in 'I'), or with the other auxiliaries (originating in VP and moving to 'I' to acquire tense)? The answer to this question is not straightforward. The reason is that in some ways dummy *do* behaves like the modal auxiliaries, in other respects it behaves like the aspectual auxiliaries.

Recall that modal verbs display three characteristics, in addition to the NICE properties:

1. They are always finite.
2. They are followed by a verb in the form of a bare infinitive.
3. They do not take third person endings.

Dummy *do* resembles the modals in that it conforms to two of these characteristics, namely the first two. However, it resembles non-modal auxiliaries in that it can take a third person singular ending (*does*). Furthermore, a difference between the modals and the aspectuals on the one hand, and dummy *do* on the other, is that the former can be followed by other auxiliaries, whereas dummy *do* cannot. It is a 'lone auxiliary', in that it cannot be preceded or followed by other auxiliaries. Thus, none of the following are possible in English:

(65)   *He must do like wine.
(66)   *He did have spoken in public.
(67)   *He did be walking fast.

From the point of view of meaning, dummy *do* behaves neither like the modals, nor like the aspectuals (nor like the passive auxiliary for that matter). In fact, it is often said to be meaningless, and solely to perform the function of tense-bearer in interrogative, negative and emphatic sentences, hence the name.

Exercise

Why is (i) below *not* a counterexample to the claim that dummy *do* does not co-occur with other auxiliaries?

(i)   Leo must do his exercises.

The reason is that in this sentence the verb *do* is a main verb, not an auxiliary: unlike auxiliary *do*, it can occur on its own (e.g. *He did his homework this morning.*).

What comes out of the discussion of dummy *do* is that it is a hybrid auxiliary: it resembles the modal auxiliaries in two respects, and the aspectual auxiliaries in another. What we will do here is take criteria 1 and 2 above for modal auxiliaries to be decisive in saying that dummy *do*, when present, is positioned in 'I'.

9.5   Wh-Movement

Consider the following sentence:

(68)   What will you buy?

This is a simple interrogative structure which displays three notable features: one is that there is a Wh-element placed at the beginning of the sentence, the second is the occurrence of Subject–auxiliary inversion, and third, the verb *buy* appears apparently without a Direct Object.

Let's turn our attention first to the verb *buy*. This is a transitive verb whose subcategorisation frame specifies that a Direct Object must be present in a sentence in which it occurs. Notice, however, that in (68) *buy* is *not* followed by a DO, but the sentence is nevertheless grammatical. We would expect ungrammaticality to result if a verb's subcategorisation requirements are not met (cf. *They bought*). How can we explain that (68) is a good sentence? Well, one way of doing so is to say that despite appearances, there *is* a Direct Object in (68), but that it is not in its normal place. Which element in (68) would qualify for DO status? Clearly, *what* is the most likely candidate. If this is correct, we need to account for the fact that it is not in its normal position.

We will assume that in (68) the Wh-element is moved from the DO position following the main verb to the beginning of the sentence. This type of movement is called *Wh-movement*, for obvious reasons. We can easily show that *what* in (68) is associated with the DO position by constructing a sentence in which it occurs in that location, for example (69):

(69)   You will buy WHAT?

This sentence (which we might imagine ourselves uttering after a friend has just announced that he will buy himself something outlandish) is syntactically declarative, but has the force of a question (see Chapter 4). Notice that the Wh-element is heavily stressed.

The important point about (69) is that the Wh-element occurs *after* the verb. This shows that it functions as DO. It is now natural to say that in relating (69) to (68) we move the Wh-element to the beginning of the sentence. In the process the Subject is inverted with the auxiliary.

An obvious question to ask at this point is where in a tree diagram a fronted Wh-element is positioned. If you look at (68) again, you will see that the moved Wh-element is placed before the inverted auxiliary. Inverted auxiliaries are adjoined to S, cf. (63) and (64), and we will simply assume that Wh-elements are adjoined to them on their left. The tree for (68) then looks like this:

(70)

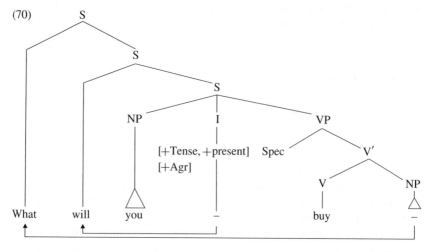

We have so far been talking somewhat loosely about Wh-*elements*. This is because in the example we examined above a single word was moved. However, we should really be speaking of Wh-*phrases*. In (68) we moved a Wh-NP, and the same has happened in (71):

(71)   Which book did you read — ?

Notice that in this sentence *which* is a determinative (see Section 3.2).

Exercise

Draw the tree for (71).

Your answer should look like this:

(72)

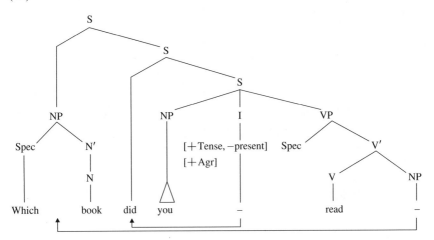

In (73) and (74) a Wh-AP and a Wh-PP, respectively, have been fronted:

(73)   *How old* are you – ?
(74)   *In which house* do you live – ?

Recall from Chapter 3 that *how* is also a Wh-word.

    We can also express the meaning of (74) by fronting only the Wh-NP *which house*. The resulting sentence is (75):

(75)   *Which house* do you live in – ?

This is called preposition stranding.

Exercise

Draw trees for the following sentences:

(i)   Who did you see?
(ii)   What did Sally give James?
(iii)   Which film did you like?

Your answers should look like this:

(76)

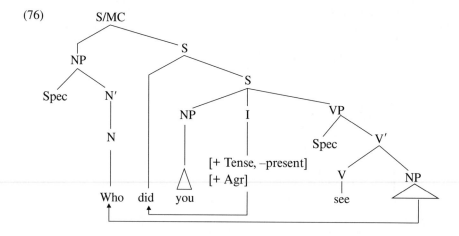

(77)

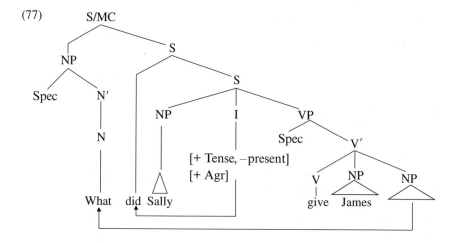

(78)

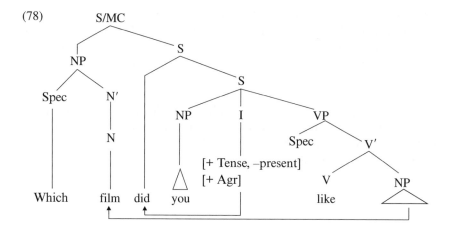

9.6 The Structure of Sentences Containing One or More Auxiliaries

In Section 9.2 above we saw that auxiliaries, like all other verbs (except intransitive ones), are subcategorised to take Complements. More specifically, auxiliary verbs take VP-Complements. Furthermore, auxiliaries determine the form of the verb that heads the VP-Complement. Thus, perfective and passive auxiliaries are always followed by a VP headed by an *-ed* form (*-en* for some verbs, e.g. *eat–ate–eaten*). Modal auxiliaries are always followed by a VP headed by a verb in the base form, and progressive auxiliaries are always followed by a VP headed by an *-ing* form. The sentences in (79)–(82) illustrate this:

(79) This artist *has painted two portraits.*
  perfective auxiliary + a VP headed by a main verb in *-ed.*
  (The main verb is a past participle.)

(80) This artist *will have painted two portraits.*
  modal auxiliary + a VP headed by a perfective auxiliary in the base form
  + a VP headed by a main verb in *-ed.*
  (The main verb is a past participle.)

(81) This artist *will have been painting two portraits.*
  modal auxiliary + a VP headed by a perfective auxiliary in the base form
  + a VP headed by a progressive auxiliary in *-ed (-en)* + a VP headed by a
  main verb in *-ing.*
  (The main verb is a present participle.)

(82)   Two portraits *will have been being painted by this artist.*
        modal auxiliary + a VP headed by a perfective auxiliary in the base form
        + a VP headed by a progressive auxiliary *-ed* (*-en*) + a VP headed by a pas-
        sive auxiliary in *-ing* + a VP headed by a main verb in *-ed.*
        (The main verb is a past participle.)

Assuming in each case that the first auxiliary is positioned in 'I', and that the
following auxiliaries subcategorise for a VP Complement (cf. also (6) above), we
derive the following tree structures for (79)–(82). (In order to make the trees more
readable the Specifier positions of the VPs have been left out):

(83)

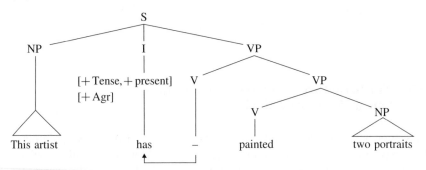

(84)

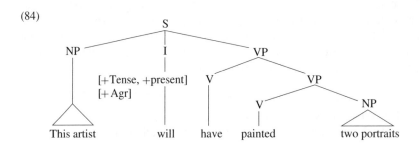

(85)

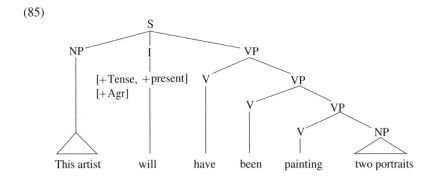

(86)

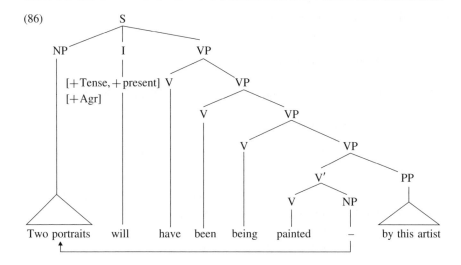

All the movements we have discussed in this chapter have been in a leftward direction. Further types of movement – including rightward movement – will be discussed in Chapter 11.

Key Concepts in this Chapter

verb movement
NP-movement
passive
Subject-to-Subject raising
Subject-auxiliary inversion
Wh-movement
the structure of sentences with multiple auxiliaries

Exercises

1. Draw the trees for (31)–(34) and (36)–(41) in the text. You may use triangles for categories that are not immediately relevant, such as NPs, and you may leave out the Specifier positions of the lower VPs.

2. True or false? In the sentence *Which file can you completely delete?*

   (i)   there are two kinds of movement
   (ii) one of these movements is NP-movement

(iii)   the NP *you* does not move
(iv)   *delete* is an intransitive verb

Draw the tree for this sentence.

3.   Draw the tree for the sentence in (i) below. Show the movements (if any).

(i)   He probably has not written the report.

4.   Take another look at the tree in (86). Are the following statements true or false?

(i)   The VP *painted by this artist* is the Complement of the verb *being*.
(ii)   The PP *by this artist* is an Adjunct in the lowest VP.
(iii)   This tree contains three auxiliary verbs.
(iv)   The verb *been* is the passive auxiliary.

5.   Liliane Haegeman in her book *Introduction to Government and Binding Theory* positions not only modal auxiliaries, but also aspectuals under 'I'. In view of the data in (i)–(iii) below, why is this a problem?

(i)   They must have been dreaming.
(ii)   He will not have broken the mirror. (= (22))
(iii)   She should not be using the phone so late.

*6.   Draw the trees for (74) and (75) in the text. Assume that *live* takes a PP Complement.

*7.   Consider the following sentences.

(i)   Eric has often broken his arm, but Gary never has.
(ii)   ?Eric has often broken his arm, but Gary has never.

For most speakers (ii) would be slightly less acceptable than (i), though it would not be ungrammatical. We can assume that the string *broken his arm* has been deleted from the tail of (i) and (ii). How is (i), as contrasted with (ii), problematic for our account of the syntactic behaviour of non-modal auxiliaries?

*8.   Use the data below to argue either for or against movement of the main verb *be* from its position as Head of the Verb Phrase to 'I'.

(i)   John is not sad.
(ii)   *John not is sad.

Are the data in (iii) and (iv) also of relevance to decide the issue?

(iii)   John is perhaps happy.
(iv)   John perhaps is happy.

*9.   We have seen that if a sentence contains a modal auxiliary verb, as well as an aspectual auxiliary verb, the modal is positioned in 'I', and the aspectual is located in VP. In Section 7.2 we saw that VP-Adjuncts are inside VP (adjoined to V′), and in this chapter we saw that S-Adjuncts are immediately dominated by 'S'. First, how can we use (i) below to show that *intentionally* is a VP-Adjunct which must be positioned in VP?

(i)   He will not have intentionally broken the mirror.

Now draw the tree for (i) above and also for (ii)–(iv) below. Remember that *carefully* and *accidentally* are VP-Adjuncts, while *probably* is an S-Adjunct.

(ii)   Edward will have carefully wrapped the present.
(iii)   He may have broken the vase accidentally.
(iv)   Chuck will probably not have seen it.

*10.   When we discussed Wh-movement in the text, we looked only at Wh-phrases that are arguments. Consider the sentences below, where (ii) can be said to be derived from (i). Draw the trees for both sentences.

(i)   You can eat pancakes WHERE?
(ii)   Where can you eat pancakes – ?

*11.   Describe the movement(s) in the following sentence.

(i)   What has he eaten?

*12.   Draw the tree diagrams for (i) and (ii).

(i)   He will not have written it.
(ii)   He will have not written it.

*13.   In Scottish and Tyneside English and in the southern United States the following sentences are possible:

(i)   I tell you what we might should do.
(ii)   You might could try a thousand K.
(iii)   Could you might possibly use a teller machine?

(Examples from Kortmann 2006)

How are these examples problematic for our model of sentence structure, as exemplified by trees incorporating an I-node?

Further Reading

Movement is a notion found only in *Transformational Grammar* (TG), a theory of language associated with the linguist Noam Chomsky.

In TG there is a special position for moved Wh-elements, called COMP, or simply 'C', which normally hosts complementisers. As I already mentioned at the end of the previous chapter, this position is the Head of a maximal projection called CP. For further discussion of movement processes from a different perspective than the one taken here, see Radford (1988), Haegeman (1994), Ouhalla (1999) and Adger (2003).

Part III
Argumentation

10   Syntactic Argumentation

In Part I of this book we set out to establish the foundations of English syntax, which we elaborated on in Part II by looking at arguments, thematic roles, X'-syntax and movement. In this part of the book we will deal with syntactic argumentation.

Argumentation, as a general notion, is concerned with *reasoning*; more specifically, with the methodological process of arguing in favour of, or against, a point of view, a course of action, an opinion, etc. Syntactic argumentation is about reasoning in the domain of syntax. In this chapter we will address the question how it proceeds, adopting what is called a *hypothesis-falsification approach*. We will address the question what sort of arguments we can use to evaluate an analysis of a particular construction, or to choose between competing analyses, making use of such notions as economy of description, elegance of description and independent justification.

10.1   The Art of Argumentation

How does syntactic argumentation proceed? In this section we'll take a close look at an example of an analytical problem of syntax, and investigate how we might go about tackling it.

Imagine that you are a person who is marooned on a tropical island and to pass the time you decide to write a grammar of English. (The sun has strange effects!) You have a basic knowledge of grammar, but it's very rusty and patchy. Let's assume that you more or less know what nouns, adjectives, verbs and prepositions are, but not much else. You start by focusing your attention on the group of elements that we have labelled 'determinatives' in this book, i.e. words such as *the, a, these, those, all, many, every, several, some*, etc., and you wonder how you might classify them. First you think of some examples involving these words, for example (1) and (2):

(1)   the sunshine
(2)   every palmtree

You then come up with a *hypothesis*, i.e. a supposition, as to what might be the categorial status of the words *the* and *every*. After giving (1) and (2) some thought you notice a parallel between these phrases and phrases like (3) and (4):

(3)   warm sunshine
(4)   tall palmtrees

You observe that words like *the* and *every*, just like *warm* and *tall*, can occur before nouns, and have some sort of modifying function. You now surmise that, by analogy with *warm* and *tall*, words which you know to be adjectives, *the* and *every* are also adjectives. However, you realise that it is not wise to base your conclusions on only a few examples, and at this stage you want to refine your hypothesis, and look for further data that bear on the question of the categorial status of *the*, *every*, etc. In fact, what you want to do is progressively *falsify* your hypotheses by finding counterexamples to them, and in this way continually adjust your initial suppositions. Returning to the problem at hand, let us consider some more data:

(5)   the warm sunshine
(6)   my tall palmtrees
(7)   *my the sunshine
(8)   *the my palmtrees

These examples are problematic for the initial hypothesis that *warm*, *tall*, *the* and *every* are all elements from the same word class. If they were, why is it that *warm* and *tall* can be preceded by *the* or *every*, i.e. an item from our mystery category (cf. (5) and (6)), but that two items from this category cannot co-occur (cf. (7) and (8))? There must be something that distinguishes words like *warm* and *tall* from words like *the* and *every*. Consider next the following phrases:

(9)   beautiful, warm, southern sunshine
(10)   *the every some island

Clearly elements that are indisputably adjectives can be stacked (see Section 7.2), but the same cannot be said for our unknown elements: like (7) and (8), (10) shows that only one of these can be selected. It soon becomes obvious that there are many more examples where there are differences between *warm* and *tall* on the one hand, and *the* and *every* on the other:

(11)   very warm sunshine
(12)   extremely tall palmtrees
(13)   *very the sunshine
(14)   *extremely every palmtree

These examples show that words like *warm* and *tall* can be preceded by an intensifying adverb like *very* or *extremely* (see Chapter 3), while *the* and *every* cannot. In addition, compare (15) and (16):

(15)   Sunshine is warm.
(16)   *Sunshine is the.

It is now clear, on the basis of even a handful of data, that the initial hypothesis that words like *the* and *every* are adjectives must be abandoned.

The next stage is to come up with a new hypothesis. Given the facts above, it would be reasonable to surmise that words like *the*, *a*, *every*, etc. belong to a different word class than the class of adjectives. As we saw above, this new class consists of elements that we have been calling determinatives. We have also seen that at any one time we can select only one determinative. At least, that's what the data we've looked at so far suggest.

Having been on the island for quite a while now, you will have had time to think of plenty more relevant examples, and you come up with (17):

(17)   *All those many good ideas* to get off this island have failed.

What's interesting about this example is that apparently in the italicised string we have *three* determinatives, namely *all*, *those* and *many*. So now we're faced with a situation in which in some cases it's *not* possible to have more than one determinative (cf. (7), (8) and (10)), but in other cases it *is* (cf (17)).

We're now dealing with quite complex structures, and if you think about it, (17) is not only problematic for lone mariners, but for professional grammarians as well. The reason is that the NP we have in (17) cannot easily be accommodated in the X'-theory that we have adopted in this book: after all, in (17) we have three determinatives, but in NPs there is only *one* Specifier position, which is where determinatives are located (cf. Section 7.1). Recall that adjectives that occur in NPs are not problematic in this way. Functionally they are Adjuncts which can recursively be stacked by creating new bar-level nodes (see Section 7.2.). The structure of the Noun Phrase in English is a difficult area of grammar, and the subject of much current research, so we won't attempt to provide a definitive analysis of English NPs.

For our purposes what is most important is that you now have an idea of how argumentation proceeds: it can be seen as an ongoing process of hypothesis refinement by taking into account successively more linguistic data. Where do these data come from? We can either construct them from our knowledge of the language (these are called *introspective data*), or we can collect them from what we hear around us in conversations, on radio or TV, or from what we read in newspapers, books, etc. (these are called *attested data*). There is some debate about the question which kind of data are the most valuable, but the common-sense view is to use any data that are relevant to our concerns.

It's important to stress that our reasoning should be systematic and informed. This is not to say that a certain amount of intelligent guesswork is not part of the argumentative process: especially in the early stages, after first encountering a problem concerning syntactic analysis, we may well find ourselves guessing how we can resolve it. We may even come up with a number of alternative analyses. What is then needed is a procedure for finding support for the conjectured analysis, or for making choices between alternatives.

We now turn to the question of what sort of arguments we can use to evaluate a proposed analysis of a particular construction, and how we can choose between rival analyses.

10.2   Economy of Description: Linguistically Significant Generalisations and Occam's Razor

In this section I will discuss two ways in which *economy of description* should play an important role in analysing a syntactic construction, or in choosing between two or more competing analyses of some phenomenon. It will be intuitively obvious to you that we should rate highest the simplest analysis that successfully accounts for the data, everything else being equal. Simplicity of description can be achieved in two ways: on the one hand by making Linguistically Significant Generalisations, and on the other hand by reducing our terminological repertoire.

10.2.1   Linguistically Significant Generalisations

We start with the notion 'generalisation'. If we're engaged in describing a complex system, *any* complex system, our task is made easier if we can organise the data at our disposal in a systematic way. A systematic description is called a *taxonomy*. Perhaps the most famous taxonomist was the Swedish naturalist Linnaeus (1707–1778), who set up taxonomies of animals and plants. It will be obvious to you that Linnaeus did not achieve fame by providing a random catalogue of animals and plants and a list of their characteristics. He organised the data into patterns in such a way that generalisations could be made. It would take us too far afield to discuss Linnaeus's taxonomy in any sort of detail, but we can get some idea of his system by briefly considering one type of animal, namely cats. We all know that domestic cats, tigers and lions belong to the animal family of felines. If, in setting up a taxonomy, we were to classify each of these animals in a class of their own we would miss the generalisation that they all belong to the family of cats by virtue of certain shared physical characteristics; for example, the shape of their ears, the fact that they have whiskers, etc.

The considerations above regarding animal taxonomies also apply when we attempt to describe the grammar of English. Here too it is important to realise that we don't want a taxonomy in which each element of the language is classified individually. What we want instead is a descriptive system in which we can draw analogies between elements and categories on the basis of their shape and distributional properties. In other words, we want a tightly organised description in which maximum use is made of generalisations. However, we are not interested in *any* generalisation, only in what have been called *Linguistically Significant Generalisations (LSGs)*. These are generalisations that are significant to the extent that they express regular patternings observed in a particular language or across several languages. We now turn to some examples of LSGs.

You may not have realised it, but in previous chapters we have already made extensive use of generalisations. For example, when we looked at word classes in Chapter 3, we grouped words together on principled grounds, namely on the basis of shared syntactic, and in some cases morphological characteristics. So even at that stage we were very much engaged in an argumentative process. Argumentation also played an important role when we discussed the internal structure of phrases in Chapter 7. There we introduced X-bar syntax as a system that achieves cross-categorial generalisations, and we saw that the structure of all phrases in English can be described as in (18):

(18)

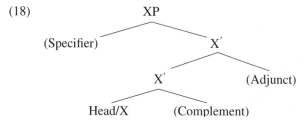

Each phrase XP (where X = N, V, A, P, Adv) contains a Specifier whose sister constituent is a bar-level category. Adjuncts (if present) are sisters of bar-level categories, while Complements (if present) are sisters of lexical categories. As a result of the insights offered by the cross-categorial generalisations of X-bar theory, our description of English syntax is considerably neater and tidier than a system which proposes flat structures for phrases would ever be. The reason is that the need to describe the structure of each phrase individually is obviated.

Cross-categorial generalisations can also range over a smaller set of categories. Consider the sentences below and their variants:

(19)   Kate came to see me. – It was *Kate* that came to see me.
(20)   I met her in Philadelphia. – It was *in Philadelphia* that I met her.
(21)   I made her work. – *It was *work* that I made her.
(22)   I made her happy. – *It was *happy* that I made her.

The second sentences in each case are called *cleft sentences*. They take the following form:

   It + form of *be* + FOCUS (italicised in the sentences above) + *who/that* . . .

I will return to cleft constructions in Chapter 12. For present purposes it is important to observe that there is a restriction on the type of category that can occur in the focus of a cleft sentence. As will be evident from (19)–(22) above, verbs and adjectives cannot occupy that position. These word classes thus seem to pattern in the same way in cleft constructions.

It has been proposed in the linguistic literature that we can capture such generalisations by assigning *syntactic features* to categories. Each of the major word categories is assigned the two features in the following set:

(23)   {± N, ± V}

These features are called *binary features* because they take either the value '+' or '–'. The word classes noun, verb, adjective and preposition can be characterised as follows:

(24)   noun   = $[+ N, - V]$
        verb   = $[- N, + V]$
        adjective   = $[+ N, + V]$
        preposition   = $[- N, - V]$

We can now state the generalisation regarding cleft sentences in more formal terms by saying that only $[- V]$ categories (nouns and prepositions) may be placed in the focus position of a cleft sentence.

Consider next the sentences below:

(25)   Tom likes pizzas.
(26)   Tom is fond of pizzas.
(27)   *Tom is fond pizzas.
(28)   *Tom's fondness pizzas.

These sentences allow us to make the generalisation that NPs can complement verbs or prepositions ((25) and (26)), but adjectives and nouns cannot ((27) and (28)). It is a general fact of English that verbs and prepositions occur in similar patterns as regards their complementation properties, as do nouns and adjectives. The generalisation regarding NP Complements can be stated by observing that only $[- N]$ categories take NP Complements: as you can see from (24), $[- N]$ is the one feature that verbs and prepositions have in common.

Syntactic features can be used to express similarities as well as differences between categories. Some of the combinations of features in (24) are intuitively odd. We might ask, for example, why adjectives are marked $[+ N, + V]$. This is a valid criticism, which I will not attempt to address in this book. I discuss features here because they play a role in the linguistic literature.

10.2.2   Occam's Razor

We turn now to another way in which we can achieve economy of description: cutting back on terminology. It was the English philosopher William of Occam (1280–1349) who put forward the view that in describing a particular phenomenon we should use as few terms as possible: '*entia non sunt multiplicanda praeter necessitatem*' ('entities should not be multiplied beyond necessity'). This idea has become known as *The Principle of Occam's razor*. What Occam intended to say was that in describing something we should cut out (hence the razor, presumably) unnecessary assumptions, categories, terminology and what have you. Put differently, descriptions should be as *constrained* as possible.

We already came across one example of Occam's razor at work in Section 6.4. There we saw that so-called selectional restrictions (imposed on the arguments of predicates) can be handled in terms of thematic roles. The great advantage of this is that the grammar is now simplified, because its stock of terminology has been reduced: the notion 'selectional restriction' has become derivative. In the next two sections we will look at two further examples in which Occam's razor plays a role.

10.2.2.1   *Verb–preposition constructions*

In this section we take a look at constructions in English that involve verbs and prepositions.

Consider the following sentences:

(29)   Valerie sent a memo out.
(30)   Valerie sent out a memo.
(31)   Valerie went out.

In these sentences there is a strong bond between the verbs *send* and *go* and the element *out*, so much so that strings like *send out* and *go out* have been regarded as complex verbs, called *Phrasal Verbs*. Notice that in (29) and (30) there is a Direct Object NP (*a memo*) which can be positioned before or after *out*. (An exception are the pronouns, which must always occur before *out*, cf. **Valerie sent out it*). In (31) there is no DO. We can thus speak of transitive and intransitive Phrasal Verbs. Further examples of Phrasal Verbs are *hand in, heat up, look up, throw away, send back, switch on/off* (transitive), *fall over, fool around* (intransitive), and *break down* (can be both transitive and intransitive).

We can contrast Phrasal Verbs with *Prepositional Verbs*. These are verbs that take a Prepositional Phrase as a Complement:

(32)   He agreed *with his sister.*
(33)   She looked *through the window.*

An important difference with Phrasal Verbs is that the NP cannot occur before the preposition:

(34)   *He agreed his sister with.
(35)   *She looked the window through.

Other examples of Prepositional Verbs are *approve of* (NP), *believe in* (NP), *complain about* (NP), *decide on* (NP), *lean against* (NP), *look after* (NP), *object to* (NP), *rely on* (NP), *wait for* (NP). All of these are intransitive, because there is no Direct Object immediately after the verb. Transitive Prepositional Verbs do have a DO. Examples are *remind* (NP) *of* (NP), *thank* (NP) *for* (NP). There is a further set of verbs in English that involves prepositions, namely so-called Phrasal-Prepositional Verbs (e.g. *put up with* (NP), *let* (NP) *in on* (NP), which we won't discuss here.

I will return to Prepositional Verbs later. In what follows I will concentrate on Phrasal Verbs. Let's start by considering the element *out* in (29)–(31). How is it categorised by grammarians? In quite a few grammars of English it is called a *particle*. A consequence of this is that it necessitates the recognition of a word class of particles *in addition to* the set of word classes we posited in Chapter 3. Now, in view of the principle of Occam's razor, which states that we should not unnecessarily multiply entities, we should be suspicious of proposals for new word classes, the reason being that we must be careful not to make our account of the classification of words more complicated than is strictly necessary. It would seem that in positing a word class of particles we are violating the principle of Occam's razor. Why so? Well, if you look carefully at the 'particle'-elements in the Phrasal Verbs listed above, you will realise that they can also function as Heads of Prepositional Phrases (*in the bank, up the road*, etc.). The simplest assumption we can make which is in harmony with the data is that, because they *look* like prepositions, the 'particle' elements in Phrasal Verbs in fact *are* prepositions. If further investigation supports this view, then we will have avoided 'multiplying entities' in the form of an unnecessary word class of particles.

Treating 'particles' as prepositions initially appears to be unattractive, because 'regular' prepositions are always followed by a Noun Phrase Complement, whereas 'particle' elements in Phrasal Verbs seem to be autonomous elements that do not take dependent phrases, witness the fact that they can occur in different positions in sentences (cf. (29) and (30) above). However, this difference in distributional behaviour is not a real problem if we allow for the possibility that prepositions, like verbs, can be both transitive and intransitive. The prepositions we find in so-called Phrasal Verbs are then simply to be regarded as *intransitive prepositions*, heading an intransitive PP (i.e. a PP in which the preposition is not followed by a Noun Phrase Complement).

We can now analyse sentences involving Phrasal Verbs as below:

(36) Valerie [$_{VP}$ [$_V$ sent] [$_{NP}$ a memo] [$_{PP}$ out]].
(37) Valerie [$_{VP}$ [$_V$ sent] — [$_{PP}$ out] [$_{NP}$ a memo]].
(38) Valerie [$_{VP}$ [$_V$ went] [$_{PP}$ out]].

Here we have simply assumed that a verb like *send* subcategorises for an NP and a PP Complement (cf. (36)), and that *go* subcategorises only for a PP Complement (cf. (38)). The basic position of the Direct Object NP is next to the verb (as in (36)), but it can be moved rightwards, as in (37). The '–' symbol indicates the original position of the Direct Object NP.

Notice that apart from doing away with the word class of particles, we have achieved another economy here: in order to bring out the strong bond between verbs like *send/go* and the element *out* we have said that the former subcategorise for the latter. There is thus no longer a need to posit a separate class of Phrasal Verbs. *Send* and *go* are just like other verbs in their Complement-taking properties. Let's call constructions like (36) and (38) *verb–preposition constructions*.

Now, it is one thing to propose a particular analysis, but another to justify it. When we come up with an analysis of a particular construction, the burden is on us to provide evidence for it. Obviously, everything else being equal, an analysis which is supported by arguments is to be valued more highly than an analysis for which there is little or no support. We can illustrate this point by taking another look at our so-called Phrasal Verbs. Remember that we argued that there is no need to recognise a class of such verbs, and that we are dealing instead simply with verbs that subcategorise either for an NP and an intransitive PP (36), or for an intransitive PP only (38). We should now check whether there is independent evidence that shows that the hypothesised PP behaves like a PP. Consider the following sentence:

(39)   I went in.

In (39) we have another instance of a verb–preposition construction. We can analyse this sentence in the same way as (38), namely as involving a verb (*go*) which subcategorises for an intransitive PP (*in*). Is there a way in which we can show that *in* is not a particle, but a preposition heading a PP?

First, compare (39) with (40):

(40)   I went in the shower.

(This sentence may sound odd to some readers, but it is perfectly acceptable in American English.) Here we see that we can turn the intransitive PP *in* into a transitive one by allowing it to take a Complement NP. The parallel between intransitive/transitive prepositions and intransitive/transitive verbs becomes apparent when we look at verbs like *read* and *eat*. These too can be used intransitively and transitively:

(41)   I was reading.
(42)   I was reading a novel.

(43)   I was eating.
(44)   I was eating a pretzel.

As a further piece of evidence, compare (39) with (45) and (46):

(45)   I went straight in.
(46)   I went straight in the shower.

In (45) *in* is preceded by the modifying word *straight*. That this word can occur in 'regular' PPs as well, as (46) shows, is suggestive of the fact that both *in* and *in the shower* are the same type of phrase, namely a PP. In Chapter 7 we saw that words like *right* and *straight* are Specifiers of P′.

Finally, compare (47) with (39) and (40):

(47)   I went there.

Notice that *there* can replace either *in* on its own or *in the shower*. Independent data tell us that *there* is a substitute for PPs (see also Section 10.3.1 and the next chapter):

(48)   I saw her *in the bank* > I saw her *there*.
(49)   They left her *on the platform* > They left her *there*.

All these considerations constitute independent evidence for the analysis of *in* in (39) as a PP.

Before we move on, here's a brief overview of the differences between the traditional approach to 'Phrasal Verbs' and 'Prepositional Verbs' (Table 10.1), and the account of verb–preposition constructions proposed here (Table 10.2). In the old system we had the following picture:

Table 10.1   The 'old' system of Phrasal and Prepositional Verbs

Phrasal Verbs	**Transitive; with alternation: [verb + NP + particle]** *or* **[verb + particle + NP]** e.g. *hand in, heat up, look up, throw away, send back, switch on/off*, etc. Example: *He handed his essay in./He handed in his essay.*
	Intransitive: [verb + particle] e.g. *break down, cool down, fool around*, etc. Example: *They always fool around at the weekend.*
Prepositional Verbs	**Transitive: [verb + NP + PP]** e.g. *remind NP of NP, thank NP for NP* Example: *I thanked Pete for his help.*
	Intransitive: [verb + PP] e.g. *agree with NP, approve of NP, believe in NP, complain about NP, decide on NP, look after NP, object to NP, rely on NP, wait for NP*, etc. Example: *I agree with Mr Green. (*I agree Mr Green with.)*

Under this view Phrasal Verbs are complex verbs, made up of a verb and a particle, which can be split up by a Direct Object. Prepositional Verbs take a PP as their Complement.

In the new system we recognise only one type of verb–preposition construction:

Table 10.2   Verb–preposition constructions

Transitive	**With alternation; the Head of the PP is intransitive: [verb + NP + PP]** *or* **[verb + PP + NP]** e.g. *hand NP [PP in], heat NP up, look NP up, throw NP away, send NP back, switch NP on/off,* etc. Example: *He handed his essay in./He handed in his essay.*
	Without alternation; the Head of the PP is transitive: [verb + NP + PP] e.g. *remind NP of NP, thank NP for NP.* Example: *She reminds me of my cousin./*She reminds of my cousin me.*
Intransitive	**The Head of the PP is intransitive: [verb + PP]** e.g. *break [PP down], cool down, fool around,* etc. Example: *They always fool around at the weekend.*
	The Head of the PP is transitive: [verb + PP] e.g. *agree [PP with NP], approve of NP, believe in NP, complain about NP, decide on NP, look after NP, object to NP, rely on NP, wait for NP,* etc. Example: *I agree with Mr Green.*

The new system is more constrained and more sophisticated: there is no longer a need for a special word class of particle, nor for the special classes of Phrasal Verbs and Prepositional Verbs. In fact, we don't really need a label at all for verbs involving PPs, as they are no different from other verbs: the special relationship between the verbs in question and their NP and PP Complements is simply handled by the subcategorisation properties of these verbs. This includes the fact that an alternation is possible for some verbs like *hand in* but not for verbs like *remind of.* The label 'verb–preposition construction' is only a convenient term to refer to a group of verbs that syntactically behave comparably.

10.2.2.2   *Achieving economy in the domain of functional terminology*

The discussion in the previous section has shown that we can reduce our inventory of word classes and verb types by abolishing particles, Phrasal Verbs and Prepositional Verbs. We now turn to the domain of functional categories, and we will see that we can achieve similar economies here. Consider the following sentences:

(50)a.   Liam is *very ill.*
   b.   Susie is *Professor of English.*
   c.   Pete is *in France.*

Let's focus on the functional status of the italicised phrases in the sentences above. Traditional descriptive grammars of English often describe the AP and NP following the copular verb *be* in (50)a and (50)b as *Subject Complements*. This term is used because it is argued that such units are instrumental in telling you more about the Subject of the sentence in which they occur: the AP and NP in (50) a/b 'complement' the reference of the Subject. (Notice that the term Complement is used in traditional grammars in a different, more general, sense than in this book. For us a Complement is a phrase or clause whose presence is syntactically required by some Head.)

What about the PP in (50)c? This has been called an *Obligatory Predication Adjunct* in traditional grammar. Although it too tells you more about the Subject, it is thought that the PP in (50)c is an Adjunct because it tells you *where* the Subject is located. Traditional grammars that employ the terminology we just mentioned-need two functional labels to describe the functions of the italicised units in (50)a–c. The drawback of the traditional account is that it foregoes the opportunity to achieve descriptive economy with regard to the sentences in (50), both in the form of a generalisation and in the form of a reduction in terminology. The generalisation vis-à-vis (50)a–c concerns the fact that all three phrases follow a form of the verb *be* and the fact that they are all obligatory. Recall that we already have a functional label for phrases that obligatorily follow a Head (in this case a verbal Head). We call them Complements. So, why not simply say that the AP, NP and PP in (50) are Complements (in the sense used in this book) of the verb *be*? In this way we can make a generalisation by treating all the sentences in (50) in a syntactically identical fashion. We also achieve a terminological economy by doing away with the unnecessary labels *Subject Complement* and *Obligatory Predication Adjunct*.

Consider now (51):

(51)   Craig considers Graham a dunce.

Traditional grammars analyse the two NPs following the main verb (*Graham* and *a dunce*) as a Direct Object and a so-called *Object Complement*, respectively. The latter constituent is said to complement the meaning of the DO, much in the same way as a so-called Subject Complement complements a Subject. This analysis of (51) is quite widespread. It is, however, also unsatisfactory. You may remember that we have come across sentences like (51) before in earlier chapters. We analysed them as involving a clausal object which we called a Small Clause. Sentence (51) was analysed as in (52):

(52)   Craig considers [$_{SC}$ Graham a dunce]

The reasoning behind this analysis was the fact that in (51) Craig is not considering 'Graham' as such, he is considering a proposition, namely the proposition that 'Graham is a dunce'. For that reason the string *Graham a dunce* was analysed as a clause functioning as a Direct Object. The advantage of this analysis over the traditional one is that we can do away with the superfluous functional label

Object Complement. We have thus achieved yet another economy. I will return to structures like (52) in Chapter 15.

What our discussion in this section has led up to is the following: a grammar that can account for the facts of English by making as few ancillary assumptions as possible is to be preferred to a grammar which does need to make such assumptions. The grammar proposed in this book does not need to posit a class of particles, Phrasal Verbs and Prepositional Verbs, and it does away with the functional categories Subject Complement, Object Complement and Obligatory Predication Adjunct. For that reason it is a descriptively more constrained grammar.

10.3 Further Constraints on Description: Elegance and Independent Justifications

In the previous section we discussed the notion of economy in grammar, and why it is desirable to achieve: a description or analysis of some grammatical phenomenon which is constrained in the use of terminology and/or the assumptions it makes is preferable to a description or analysis in which the terminology and assumptions are allowed to proliferate in an uncontrolled way. In this section we turn to two further, closely related, ways of constraining descriptions.

10.3.1 Elegance of Description

We return to prepositions to illustrate a third type of argument that we can use in favour of a particular analysis, namely elegance of description. What do we mean by this? We can say that a proposed analysis of a particular syntactic phenomenon is more elegant than some other analysis, everything else being equal, if it is more tidily organised and more sophisticated in terms of the distinctions it makes.

To illustrate, consider the following sentences:

(53) She repaired the car *expertly*.
(54) He drives his motorbike *slowly*.

(55) They live *there*.
(56) He won't leave *now*.

If I were to ask you what is the formal and functional status of the italicised items in these sentences, your first hunch would probably be that they are adverbs functioning as Heads of Adverb Phrases. After all, they tell us about the 'how', 'where', 'when', etc. of the propositions expressed. These are typically notions expressed by adverbs and their associated phrases. And indeed, this analysis would be the one you would find in the vast majority of grammars and textbooks on the English language. The question we must ask, however, is whether this is the most elegant description from the point of view of the distributional facts of English. It has been proposed instead that *there* and *now* are prepositions, rather than adverbs. At first sight, this may seem a wild idea, but as we will see in a moment, it's not as strange as it may seem.

There are a number of differences between the italicised items in (53)/(54), and those in (55)/(56). Firstly, there is a morphological difference. Both *expertly* and *slowly* end in *-ly*, while *there* and *now* do not. Secondly, there is a semantic difference between the two sets: *expertly* and *slowly* are manner adverbs (see Chapter 3), while *there* and *now* indicate location and time, respectively. Thirdly, and more importantly, the syntactic distribution of *expertly* and *slowly* is different from the distribution of *there* and *now*. This becomes clear from the following sentences:

(57)   She repaired the car *very/extremely expertly*.
(58)   He drives his motorbike *very/extremely slowly*.
(59)   She repaired the car *expertly enough*.
(60)   He drives his motorbike *slowly enough*.
(61)   *She repaired the car *right expertly*.
(62)   *He drives his motorbike *right slowly*.

(63)   *They live *very/extremely there*.
(64)   *He won't leave *very/extremely now*.
(65)   *They live *there enough*.
(66)   *He won't leave *now enough*.
(67)   They live *right there*.
(68)   He won't leave *right now*.

Here we see that *expertly* and *slowly* allow premodification by *very* or postmodification by *enough*, while premodification by *right* is not possible (though (61) and (62) are possible in some dialects). In the case of *there* and *now* the picture is exactly the other way round: premodification by *very* and postmodification by *enough* are not possible, while premodification by *right* is fine. We already know that *very* and *enough* typically modify adjectives or adverbs, while words like *straight* and *right* are typical prepositional modifiers. These facts suggest that *expertly* and *slowly* do not have the same status as *there* and *now*. In fact, *there* and *now* seem to be behaving as prepositions heading PPs. This becomes more apparent if we compare (63)–(68) with (69)–(74).

(69)   *They live *very/extremely on the border*.
(70)   *He won't leave *very/extremely at this moment*.
(71)   *They live *on the border enough*.
(72)   *He won't leave *at this moment enough*.
(73)   They live *right on the border*.
(74)   He won't leave *right at this moment*.

Notice that 'regular' PPs also do not allow premodification by *very* or postmodification by *enough* ((69)–(72)), but they *do* allow the word *right* to precede them ((73)–(74)). These facts confirm the parallel syntactic behaviour of the hypothesised prepositions *there/now* and 'regular' prepositions.

There is more evidence for treating *there* and *now* as prepositions. Consider next the data below:

(75)   Pauline was *reasonably happy.*
(76)   She sang *extremely beautifully.*

(77)   *there happy, *now happy
(78)   *there beautifully, *now beautifully

(79)   *very there, *very now
(80)   *extremely there, *extremely now

(81)   *The people there* are very cheerful.
(82)   *The issue now* is what to do next.

A typical property of adverbs is that they can modify adjectives or other adverbs, as in (75) and (76). However, (77) and (78) show that *there* and *now* cannot perform these functions, which suggests that, in this respect at least, they are not like typical adverbs. Also, while *there* and *now* cannot themselves be modified by adverbs, as (79) and (80) show, they can postmodify nouns, as in (81) and (82). This is also typical of 'regular' PPs:

(83)   *The people at work* are very cheerful.
(84)   *The issue at the moment* is what to do next.

Words like *expertly* and *slowly* cannot postmodify nouns.

A further difference in behaviour between words like *expertly/slowly* and *there/now* is that the latter can replace PPs, as we already saw in Section 10.2.2.1:

(85)   They live *in that house* > They live *there*
(86)   He won't leave *at this moment* > He won't leave *now*

Notice also that *there* and *now* can occur as Complements of copular verbs ((87) and (88)), just like 'regular' PPs ((89) and (90)), but unlike elements such as *expertly* and *slowly* ((91) and (92)):

(87)   The park is there.
(88)   The time to leave is now.

(89)   The park is in the centre.
(90)   The time to leave is at this moment.

(91)   ?The way he drove his car is expertly.
(92)   ?The way he drove his car is slowly.

Finally, observe that words like *there* and *now* can function as Complements of prepositions, whereas true adverbs cannot:

(93)   The car is *out there*.
(94)   *From now* you must pay a fine if you return your books late.
(95)   **From expertly* he devised the plan
(96)   **In slowly* he drove.

Compare (93) and (94) with the phrases below:

(97)   *from under the cupboard*
(98)   *down off the shelf*

Here the 'regular' prepositions *from* and *down* both take PP Complements, namely *under the cupboard* and *off the shelf*. If we treat *there* and *now* in (93) and (94) as Prepositional Phrases, which function as Complements of *out* and *from*, respectively, then we can analyse these structures in the same way as (97) and (98), the only difference between these sets being the fact that the Complements of *out* and *from* in (93) and (94) are intransitive PPs, whereas the Complements of *from* and *down* in (97) and (98) are transitive PPs. Typical adverbs like *expertly* and *slowly* cannot take PP Complements, and cannot therefore be analysed on a par with (97) and (98).

   All these facts suggest that *there* and *now* are not adverbs, but prepositions, more specifically, intransitive prepositions heading PPs.

   What we have achieved in this section is not an economy, as in Section 10.2.2.1, where we did away with so-called particles, Phrasal Verbs and Prepositional Verbs, but a more refined description of the distributional facts of elements such as *expertly*, *slowly*, *there* and *now*. The latter two elements have been reassigned to the class of prepositions. As a result, the adverb and preposition classes have become more tightly defined.

10.3.2   Independent Justifications

Consider again the sentences in (99)–(102), taken from Section 10.2.2.1:

(99)   I was eating.
(100)   I was eating a pretzel.
(101)   I went straight in.
(102)   I went straight in the shower.

We observed a parallel between these two sets, in that in both cases we have an element that can be used both transitively and intransitively. In (99)/(100) this element is a verb, in (101)/(102) it is a preposition. However, it is possible to look at these data differently and say that, although the Complements of the verb and preposition in (99) and (101) are missing, they are nevertheless *understood*. Another way of putting this is to say that there is an *implicit argument* in (99) and (101), which we can represent by the symbol 'Ø':

(103) I was eating Ø.
(104) I went straight in Ø.

In both cases the 'Ø'-symbol stands for a phonetically inaudible, understood Complement Noun Phrase. Now, clearly our positing this element is so far based only on our intuitions: on the grounds that we *sense* that something is missing in (99) and (101) we posited the abstract NP 'Ø'. However, our proposal for positing an abstract element, although attractive intuitively, is open to the perfectly reasonable criticism that its existence is no more than just a supposition. How can we deal with this criticism? If we could find *independent justification* for the element 'Ø', our case would be much stronger. What this means is that we should try to find one or more constructions where there is an independent reason for positing a similar abstract element. If such a construction, or constructions, can be found, then we will have considerably strengthened our case for positing an implicit Complement.

The question is, then, in the case of our element 'Ø': 'can we find a construction in which there is an independent need to posit its existence?' I would like to claim that there is. Consider the sentence below:

(105) Greg painted the wall red.

We will analyse this sentence as involving a Subject NP *Greg*, a Predicator verb *painted*, a Direct Object NP *the wall*, and an Adjunct AP *red*. (Notice that we cannot analyse (105) as involving a Small Clause *the wall red* (cf. (52)), because the NP *the wall* is clearly a DO in the sentence above. After all, Greg did something to the wall, making it a Patient argument of the verb *paint*.)

We can observe two things about (105). First, notice that the AP expresses a *result*: as a consequence of Greg's painting the wall, it has become red. Secondly, despite the fact that it functions as the DO of *paint*, this NP can be regarded as a Subject expression for the AP *red* ('*the wall is red*' after the painting). It is a fact of English that resultative phrases can only take Direct Objects as their Subject expression, not Subjects. Thus, we cannot interpret (105) to mean that Greg painted the wall and as a result he himself became red (e.g. by accidentally painting his fingers). Consider now the advertising slogans in (106) and (107):

(106) Our new washing powder washes whiter!
(107) These revolutionary brooms sweep cleaner!

Notice that the APs *whiter* and *cleaner* express results here. Curiously, however, there is nothing that they can be predicated of. These sentences thus seem to violate our claim that resultative phrases are always predicated of DOs. However, if we posit an implicit Complement NP 'Ø' (a DO) in (106) and (107), which would refer in (106) to 'washable items', and in (107) to 'sweepable surfaces', then our generalisation can be salvaged.

We have now reached a situation in which our positing the element 'Ø' in (103) and (104) has been independently motivated to the extent that we need such an element in a different construction as well, namely (106) and (107). If we had found no independent justification for 'Ø', then our proposal would have been *ad hoc* (from Latin, literally 'to this'; i.e. devised only to solve the problem at hand). An ad hoc proposal is not necessarily wrong, because it may turn out, given advances in our knowledge, that independent evidence is subsequently found. However, if at any point in time there is a need to choose between two analyses of some phenomenon, one ad hoc, the other independently motivated, then the ad hoc analysis is less attractive, everything else being equal. Notice that the notion of independent justification also plays a role in Section 10.2 on economy of description.

10.4   Evaluating Analyses

The three types of arguments presented in this chapter (economy of description, elegance of description and independent justification) can be used as tools for evaluating analyses, or for choosing between two competing analyses. The key word here is *simplicity*: the most highly valued analysis is the one that not only conforms to the general principles of the adopted framework (e.g. X-bar theory), but is also maximally simple, i.e. it is the most economical and elegant, and has the largest amount of independent evidence to support it.

You will have realised that to a great extent the three arguments we discussed are closely interrelated. For example, an analysis that is more economical is also more elegant. Furthermore, as we have seen, we cannot really discuss the notion of economy without appealing to independent justifications. I have nevertheless presented economy, elegance and independent justifications separately. The reasons for this are partly clarity of exposition, and partly the fact that to some extent these notions *can* be discussed independently of each other. For example, as we saw in Section 10.3.1, elegance of description can be achieved independently of economy of description, by reassigning elements such as *now* and *then* to the class of prepositions. Here we achieved a more elegant description, but we did not achieve an economy.

Key Concepts in this Chapter

argumentation
Linguistically Significant Generalisations
economy: Occam's razor
elegance
independent justification

Exercises

1.   Draw trees for the following sentences:

    (i)   She locked her husband out.
    (ii)   We agree with the doctor.
    (iii)   They are looking the information up.
    (iv)   The car blew up.
    (v)   He completely relies on his brother.

2.   Give the subcategorisation frame for the verb *invent*. Then read on.
    It is not unlikely that your subcategorisation frame specified that *invent* requires a Direct Object NP as its Complement. And, indeed, if you look up this verb in a dictionary, you will find that it is invariably labelled a transitive verb. This would seem to be correct on the basis of the fact that if you are engaged in inventing, you must be inventing *something*.
    However, consider now the advertising slogan in (i):

    (i)   Philips invents for you.

    Why is this sentence acceptable?

3.   Consider the sentences below:

    (i)   Marie-Claude is *a social scientist*.
    (ii)   Pete is *very friendly*.

    In this book we have suggested that the functional status of the italicised phrases in (i) and (ii) is simply Complement of the main verb *be*. As we have seen, some grammars of English refer to these units as *Subject Complements*, because they are said to complement the meaning of the Subject. For us there is no need to make use of this additional functional label.
    There is a different way of looking at (i) and (ii). Assuming a raising analysis for these sentences (cf. Section 9.3), as in (iii) and (iv) below, what would you say is the function of *a social scientist* in (i), and *very friendly* in (ii)? You may need to review Section 2.1.

    (iii)   Jill is [– a social scientist]

    (iv)   Pete is [– very friendly]

    Hint: the bracketed strings are Small Clauses.

4.   What do the data below suggest regarding the word class status of *then*?

(i)	the *under-threat* childcare facilities
(ii)	the *then* President of France
(iii)	*the *expertly* engineers

5. In the framework presented in this book, what's wrong conceptually with the label *Obligatory Predication Adjunct*?

*6. In the text we saw that words like *the* and *every* are best analysed as belonging to a different word class than elements like *warm* and *tall*. Apart from the syntactic reasons given in the text, can you think of any *semantic* reasons why these elements are reasonably classed differently? You may find it helpful to think of the kind of meanings these words contribute to the phrases in which they occur.

*7. Consider the data below:

(i)	*Hamid is fond meat.
(ii)	Hamid is fond of meat.
(iii)	*Hamid's fondness meat.
(iv)	Hamid's fondness for meat.

Notice that we can salvage the starred examples by inserting *of* or *for*. In this way we derive (ii) from (i) and (iv) from (iii). Using the syntactic features shown in (24) in the text, repeated in (v) below, formulate an informal rule of preposition insertion.

(v)	noun	=	$[+ N, - V]$
	verb	=	$[- N, + V]$
	adjective	=	$[+ N, + V]$
	preposition	=	$[- N, - V]$

*8. Consider the following data from Joseph Emonds's book *A Transformational Approach to English Syntax* (1976: 173):

(i)	a.	John arrived *before* the last speech.
	b.	John arrived *before*.
	c.	John arrived *before* the last speech ended.

(ii)	a.	I haven't seen him *since* the party.
	b.	I haven't seen him *since*.
	c.	I haven't seen him *since* the party began.

In the present book we have said that the italicised items in the a-and b-sentences above are prepositions, the only difference between them being that the prepositions in the a-sentences are transitive, while those in the b-sentences are intransitive. What about the c-sentences? How have the italicised items been classified in this book? Is there a case for re-classifying them? See also Section 15.4.

*9.   In Quirk et al.'s 1985 grammar a distinction is made between *clause-level functions* and *phrase-level functions*. The former comprise the functions we described in Chapter 2 of this book (i.e. Subject, Direct Object, etc.), while the latter comprise the Head and various types of *Modifiers*. For example, in (i) below *splendid* would be labelled a *Premodifier, canals* is a Head, while *of Amsterdam* is called a *Postmodifier*:

(i)   the splendid canals of Amsterdam.

Compare this treatment to the one presented in this book, and assess the merits of both.

*10.   In the text we saw that *there* and *now* can be reclassified as prepositions, and that the adverb class now consists of at least all adverbial elements ending in -*ly*. However, there are many elements with adverbial meanings that do not end in -*ly*, and we ought to check whether these are adverbs in the narrowed down sense, or perhaps also prepositions. Using the distributional data discussed in Section 10.3.1 as criteria, check whether the following are adverbs or prepositions: *well, when, fast* (as in 'he drives fast') *then, here, home*.

You may find it useful to construct a grid, with *well, fast*, etc. on the vertical axis, and the adverb/preposition criteria on the horizontal axis.

Can you make a generalisation regarding the elements that behave like prepositions?

*11.   In the text I wrote: 'It is a general fact of English that verbs and prepositions occur in similar patterns as regards their complementation properties, as do nouns and adjectives. The generalisation regarding NP Complements can be stated by observing that only [– N] categories take NP Complements.' Why is the phrase *a literature teacher* in Table 7.2 of Chapter 7 a problem for this claim?

Further Reading

Some of the issues we discussed in this chapter pertain to the Philosophy of Science. A good introduction to this field is Chalmers (1999). The idea of falsification is associated with the Austrian philosopher Karl Popper (1902–1994), whose philosophy of science has been very influential in linguistics. One of his most important ideas was that for a theory to be scientific it has to be *falsifiable*. This is true even for the 'best' theory that covers the facts and explains them the most adequately. We find the Popperian method of reasoning everywhere in linguistics: in articles, textbooks and monographs. However, despite its influence, there is some controversy with regard to Popper's methodology, and this has to do with the question what to do with counterexamples. Some have argued that for any proposed theory of a particular phenomenon, counterexamples pose a serious challenge, and that they should in fact invalidate the theory. Others have said that we should not engage in *naive falsificationalism*, i.e. we should not be tempted to discard our theory as soon as we come across a counterexample. Rather, it might be better to 'shelve' counterexamples, when we come across them, in the hope that at a later point, when our knowledge has advanced, we can accommodate them. See especially Chomsky (1981: 149), Lightfoot (1982: 95–9) and Matthews (1993) for discussion.

On determinatives as 'limiting adjectives', see Curme (1935: 46f.).

On the issue of which kinds of data are useful in linguistic studies, see Newmeyer (1983).

An alternative name for Occam's razor which you may prefer is the *KISS-principle*, which can either be rendered as '**K**eep **I**t **S**hort and **S**imple' or, more rudely, as '**K**eep **I**t **S**hort, **S**toopid.'

On Phrasal, Prepositional and Phrasal-Prepositional Verbs, see Quirk et al. (1985: 1152–67) and Aarts (1989, 1992).

On Subject Complements, Object Complements and Obligatory Predication Adjuncts, see Quirk et al. (1985: 1171–4, 1195–208 and 505–10, respectively). Subject Complements are called Subjective Predicative Complements, and Object Complements are called Objective Predicative Complements in Huddleston and Pullum et al. (2002).

On transitive and intransitive prepositions, see Emonds (1976) and Burton-Roberts (1991). The latter also discusses the possibility of reassigning certain adverbs to the class of prepositions.

On subordinating conjunctions and prepositions see Huddleston (1984: 338f.) and Hudson (1995). Huddleston and Pullum et al. (2002) assign all subordinating conjunctions, except the complementisers, to the class of prepositions.

11 Constituency: Movement and Substitution

In this chapter we return to the notion of constituency, and address the important question of how we can use syntactic argumentation to demonstrate that a particular string of words is a constituent. We very often have intuitions about which words make up units in particular sentences, but we really need a more reliable way of establishing how we can carve up sentences. What is required is a set of practical procedures for dividing sentences up into their constituent parts. Applying these procedures we can then tackle sentences whose analysis into constituents isn't immediately obvious.

You will remember that constituents are strings of one or more words that syntactically and semantically behave as a unit. We defined constituents formally in terms of the notion of dominance. To refresh your memory, consider the tree diagram in (2) for the sentence in (1):

(1) My father admires my mother.

(2)

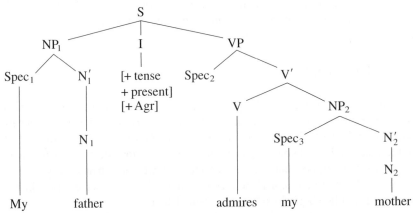

'Constituent' and 'immediate constituent' were defined as follows:

Y is a constituent of X if and only if X dominates Y.
Y is an immediate constituent of X if and only if X immediately dominates Y.

In the tree in (2) S dominates every single individual node, as well as the lexical items *my, father, admires, my* and *mother*. Thus, in (2) all the elements under S are constituents of S. Also, S *immediately* dominates NP_1, 'I' and VP, and so NP_1, 'I' and VP are immediate constituents of S. Furthermore, $Spec_1$ and N'_1 are immediate constituents of NP_1; $Spec_2$ and V' are immediate constituents of VP; V and NP_2 are immediate constituents of V' and so on.

At this point we may well ask how we can *show* that (2) is the correct representation for (1)? Why not analyse (1) as in (3)?

(3)

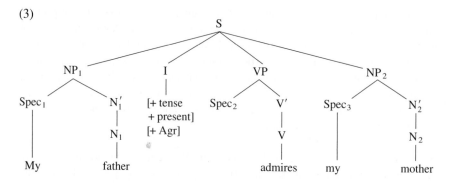

In this tree S has four immediate constituents instead of three (namely NP_1, 'I', VP and NP_2). What we want to be able to do with regard to (2) and (3) is give *reasons* for taking either of these representations to be the correct way of analysing (1). In this chapter we will see that we can use a number of *constituency tests* to determine whether or not a particular sequence of words is a constituent. We will turn to these tests in the following sections, starting with Movement.

11.1   Movement

In Chapter 9 we came across the phenomenon of the displacement of elements when we discussed Verb Movement, NP-Movement and Wh-Movement. In this chapter we will be looking at additional types of movement. The main issue I want to focus on here is how we can relate the idea of movement to constituency.

Linguists have argued that one way of finding out whether a particular sequence of words behaves like a unit is by trying to move it to another position in the sentence. The following principle can be established:

Movement

If we can move a particular string of words in a sentence from one position to another, then it behaves as a constituent.

Another way of putting this is to say that if some sequence of words in a particular sentence can occur in a different position in that same sentence, this is an argument for analysing the sequence in question as a constituent.

In English, apart from Verb Movement, NP-Movement and Wh-Movement, there exist a number of further types of movement. Here we will be looking at Topicalisation, VP-Preposing and *Though*-Movement (movements to the left), as well as Heavy-NP-Shift and Extraposition from NP (movements to the right). These movements are generally regarded as *stylistic*. In contrast to Verb Movement, NP-Movement and Wh-Movement, which are obligatory, they are carried out optionally in English to achieve different effects as regards the way in which information contained in sentences is presented.

11.1.1   Movements to the Left

11.1.1.1   Topicalisation

Here's a fragment of an imaginary interchange between two people:

(4)   Flora   Do you like Belgian beer and Belgian wine?
      Ben   [Belgian beer] I like — , but [Belgian wine] I hate —

Ben's response is somewhat out of the ordinary. He could simply have said (5):

(5)   I like Belgian beer, but I hate Belgian wine.

Instead, he chose a different syntactic structure, one which involves movement of the Direct Objects in (4) from the positions marked by '–' to a clause-initial position. This movement process is called *Topicalisation*. Ben answers the way he does because he wants the phrases *Belgian beer* and *Belgian wine* to be more prominent (more topic-like) than they would be if they occurred in their normal position following the verb, as in (5). In other words, his answer in (4) literally *brings to the fore* the topics Belgian beer and Belgian wine, as well as the contrast between what he thinks of these drinks.

Our principal concern here is that the strings *Belgian beer* and *Belgian wine* must be constituents because we can move them, as the contrast between (4) and (5) shows. Because the most prominent words in *Belgian beer* and *Belgian wine* are nouns, namely *beer* and *wine* respectively, we must be dealing with displaced Noun Phrases.

Topicalisation can involve complex phrases as the following set of sentences shows:

(6)   Nobody liked [$_{NP}$ the books about New York that she bought].

(7)   [$_{NP}$ The books about New York that she bought] nobody liked —

Notice that we cannot leave behind any of the component parts of the moved NP:

(8)   *[NP The books about New York] nobody liked — that she bought.

Not only NPs can be topicalised, other phrases can too:

(9)   Wendy: Is Elly always so nervous?
       Al: [Neurotic] I would say she is – , not nervous.
(10) Kate: Does Greg really keep his pets in his attic?
       Len: [In his attic] he keeps his plants – , not his pets.
(11) Nicky promised to write an essay, and [write an essay] he will –

In (9) we've fronted an AP, in (10) a PP, and in (11) a VP.
   With regard to Topicalisation we can establish the following principle:

Topicalisation
If we can topicalise a string of *elements* whose principal element is an X (where X stands for N, A, P or V), then that string is an XP (i.e. a phrase headed by X).

We turn now to a more detailed discussion of VP-Topicalisation, better known as VP-Preposing.

11.1.1.2   VP-Preposing

Consider the sentence in (12):

(12) Ralph says that he will clean his room,

                              and [clean his room] he will —

A movement process has taken place here, such that the string *clean his room*, a verb with its Direct Object, has moved from a position at the end of the second clause to the beginning of that clause. Because the principal element of this string (i.e. its Head) is the verb *clean*, we conclude that we must be dealing with a Verb Phrase. We refer to the movement process in (12) as VP-Preposing. VP-Preposing involves movement of a Verb Phrase from its normal position in the clause to the beginning of that clause, and as such is a special type of Topicalisation. Here are some more examples:

(13) Sally says that she will return my book,

                              and [return my book] she will —

(14)   Drew says that he will wash the dishes,

and [wash the dishes] he will —

Interestingly, (12)–(14) show that the Direct Objects are part of the Verb Phrases of the sentences in which they occur, and this is because they are fronted along with the main verb that precedes them. We cannot leave the DOs behind:

(15)   *Ralph says that he will clean his room, and [clean] he will – his room.
(16)   *Sally says that she will return my book, and [return] she will – my book.
(17)   *Drew says that he will wash the dishes, and [wash] he will – the dishes.

These data are a confirmation of the structure of Verb Phrases that we posited in Chapter 7, and at the beginning of this chapter (see (2)). You will remember that we said that Direct Objects are sisters of the main verb inside VP, as in the tree diagram below, which represents the VP of (12):

(18)

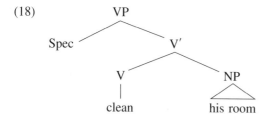

When VP-Preposing applies, the VP is moved to a clause-initial position. We will assume that the entire VP is moved, including the empty Spec-position.

Notice that VP-Preposing can only apply if the sentence in question contains an auxiliary verb, such as *will* in the examples we have looked at, or *did* in (19):

(19)   Sally said that she returned my book, and [return my book] she did —

The following is impossible:

(20)   *Sally said that she returned my book, and [returned my book] she —

Another notable fact about (12)–(14) is that in each case *will* is left behind. This means that modal auxiliary verbs are *not* part of the VP of the sentence in which they occur. If they were, they would have been fronted along with the main verb and Direct Object. (21) shows that the auxiliary in (12) cannot also be preposed:

(21)   *Ralph says that he will clean his room,

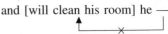

and [will clean his room] he ——

Here again we have confirmation of our analysis in Chapter 8. We said there that modal auxiliaries are dominated by 'I', not by VP.

What's important about VP-Preposing is that we can use it as a test to see whether a particular element or string of elements is part of VP. In (12)–(14) VP-Preposing established that the VPs of these sentences are *clean his room*, *return my book* and *wash the dishes*. Consider now the sentence below in which an Adverb Phrase functioning as an Adjunct has been added:

(22)   Ralph says that he will clean his room meticulously.

Recall that in Chapter 7 we claimed that Adjuncts like *meticulously* are sisters of V′ inside VP, as in the tree in (23):

(23)

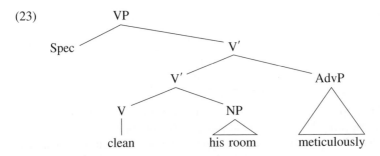

We now want to know whether we can *show* that the AdvP in (22) is indeed part of the VP or not. Let's apply VP-Preposing and see:

(24)   Ralph says that he will clean his room meticulously, and [clean his room meticulously] he will –
(25)   *Ralph says that he will clean his room meticulously, and [clean his room] he will – meticulously.

The result of preposing the VP is that the AdvP must be moved along with the main verb and its Direct Object, and is therefore inside VP. Leaving the AdvP behind, as in (25), leads to an ungrammatical result. (The sentence is OK if there is a long pause after *will*. In this case *meticulously* can be regarded as an after-thought.)

At this point we are only concerned to show that the AdvP is indeed inside VP. We still need to demonstrate, however, that the internal structure of the VP is as shown in (23). This we leave to Section 11.2.2.

So far we have established that DOs are inside VP, as are Adjuncts following the DO (cf. (22)–(25)), and that modal auxiliaries are outside VP. What about Adjuncts that *precede* the main verb, as does *carefully* in (26)?

(26)   Ralph says that he will carefully clean his room.

Exercise

Apply VP-Preposing to check whether the AdvP *carefully* is part of the VP of (26).

The results should look like this:

(27)   Ralph says that he will carefully clean his room, and [carefully clean his room] he will –
(28)   *Ralph says that he will carefully clean his room, and [clean his room] he will carefully –

We see from these sentences that, just like Adjuncts that follow the DO, Adjuncts that precede the main verb are also inside VP, because they cannot be left behind when we move a string of elements that includes the main verb. The structure of the VP in (26) is as in (29):

(29)

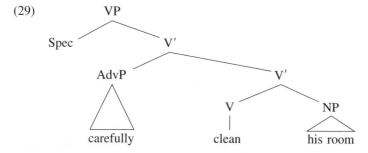

All the sentences involving VP-Preposing that we have looked at so far conform to the same pattern: there is always an auxiliary verb at the end of the second clause. This is because VP-Preposing can only operate in sentences that contain an auxiliary verb. As we have seen, VP-Preposing is an important constituency test, but does the restriction on VP-Preposing that we just noted mean that we cannot use it as a constituency test when there is no auxiliary in the sentence? No, it doesn't, because we can always create a context in which an auxiliary is *added*. How does this work? Let us assume that we come across a sentence without an auxiliary before the main verb, and we want to determine what its VP is, for example *Simone dances the samba competently*. To create a context in which we can move a string of elements minimally containing the main verb (i.e. a VP) we apply a few simple steps:

1.　Make the sentence a *that*-clause Complement of a verb of saying, e.g. *say, claim*, etc.: *Simone says that she dances the samba competently*. Notice that the Subject of the original sentence is now the main clause Subject, while the Subject of the Complement clause is a pronoun.
2.　Add the coordinator *and*, then repeat the original sentence, changing its Subject into a pronoun, and placing an auxiliary verb in front of the main verb in both clauses: *Simone says that she will dance the samba competently, and she will dance the samba competently*.
3.　Now prepose a string of elements which minimally contains the main verb. If the result is good, the string is a VP. If the result is bad, the string is not a VP.

　　*Simone says that she will dance the samba competently, and [dance] she will—the samba competently.
　　*Simone says that she will dance the samba competently, and [will dance] she—the samba competently.
　　*Simone says that she will dance the samba competently, and [will dance the samba] she—competently.
　　*Simone says that she will dance the samba competently, and [dance the samba] she will—competently.
　　Simone says that she will dance the samba competently, and [dance the samba competently] she will –

Here we have moved different strings: main verb only; auxiliary verb + main verb; auxiliary verb + main verb + Direct Object, and so on. Only the fifth sentence is good, and we conclude that the VP of the sentence *Simone dances the samba competently* is *dances the samba competently*.

Exercise

Determine what is the VP in each of the following sentences. In applying the steps above use the main verb *say* and the modal auxiliary *will*.

(30)　Frank flies to New York tomorrow.
(31)　The Head of Department holds a meeting at 4 p.m.

The correct results of applying the steps above are as follows:

(32)   Frank says that he will fly to New York tomorrow, and [fly to New York tomorrow] he will –
(33)   The Head of Department says that he will hold a meeting at 4 p.m., and [hold a meeting at 4 p.m.] he will –

The results of movement show that the bracketed constituents are VPs.

11.1.1.3 Though-*Movement*

The next type of movement is *Though*-Movement, a term used to describe the displacements in sentences like (34)–(38):

(34)a.   Though students are fare dodgers, they're not thieves.
   b.   [Fare dodgers] though students are – , they're not thieves.
(35)a.   Though Ken usually is quite happy, today he is sad.
   b.   [Quite happy] though Ken usually is – , today he is sad.
(36)a.   Though she works very hard all day, at night she's lazy.
   b.   [Very hard] though she works – all day, at night she's lazy.
(37)a.   Though she is in debt, she's very generous.
   b.   [In debt] though she is – , she's very generous.
(38)a.   Though he ate the mushrooms, he hasn't been sick.
   b.   [Eat the mushrooms] though he did – , he hasn't been sick.

The term *Though*-Movement is misleading because it isn't the word *though* that moves, as the sentences above show. I have retained the terminology, however, because it is in general use in the linguistic literature. As you can see from (34)–(38), in each case a string of words has moved to a clause-initial position: an NP in (34), an AP in (35), an AdvP in (36), a PP in (37), and a VP in (38).

The movement exemplified in (38) confirms the results of the VP-Preposing test: Verb Phrases consist of a main verb + a Direct Object (if there is one).

Though-Movement, like VP-Preposing, is useful when we want to establish the exact delimitation of the VP of a particular sentence. Consider (39) and (40):

(39)   Though Ralph will clean his room meticulously, he'd rather watch TV.
(40)   Though Ralph will carefully clean his room, he's normally untidy.

We now want to check whether the Adverb Phrases *meticulously* and *carefully* are inside the VP of these sentences. We can apply *Though*-Movement to find out.

This is the result:

(41)   [Clean his room meticulously] though Ralph will – , he'd rather watch TV.

(42)   *[Clean his room] though Ralph will – meticulously, he'd rather watch TV.

(43)   [Carefully clean his room] though Ralph will – , he's normally untidy.

(44)   *[Clean his room] though Ralph will carefully – , he's normally untidy.

(All these to be read with a short pause where the dash is positioned.)

These results confirm those of the preceding section: in (39) and (40) if we move a string of words that involves the main verb *clean*, then *meticulously* and *carefully* must be moved along with it. This means that both Adjuncts that precede the main verb, as well as those that follow the Direct Object, are positioned inside VP. (The trees for the VPs in (41) and (43) are shown in (23) and (29) above).

11.1.2   Movements to the Right

11.1.2.1   Heavy-NP-Shift

A feature of all the movements that have been discussed so far in this book is that they were *leftward movements*; that is, an element or string of elements was moved to a position to the left of its original position. In this section and in the next one we'll be looking at some examples of *rightward movements*. Consider the following sentences:

(45)   We brought – into the country *six boxes of excellent French wine.*

(46)   She sold – at the market *the prints that she had made.*

Because Direct Objects as a rule occur immediately to the right of the verb that subcategorises for them, it is reasonable to assume that in (45) and (46) the italicised NPs have moved to the right from the position indicated by the dash. These movements are triggered by the relative 'heaviness' of the NPs in question caused by the PP *of excellent French wine* in (45) and by the relative clause *that she had made* in (46). For this reason this type of movement is called *Heavy-NP-Shift (HNPS)*.

   A restriction on HNPS is that we cannot move Indirect Objects or Objects of prepositions to the right:

(47)   *I sent – a postcard *my cousin from London.*

(48)   *I sent a postcard to – yesterday *my cousin from London.*

For present purposes it is important to see that HNPS can be used as a constituency test. In this connection, consider (49) below:

(49)   I travelled the world from Moscow to Rio in three weeks.

With regard to this sentence we might wonder whether the string *from Moscow to Rio* is a postmodifying phrase, and as such part of the NP headed by *world*, or whether it is perhaps a separate phrase. If the string *the world from Moscow to Rio* is indeed an NP, it should be possible to move it, because of its 'weight'. If it is not an NP, then displacement should not be possible. If we apply HNPS to (49) the result is (50):

(50)   *I travelled – in three weeks *the world from Moscow to Rio.*

The result is bad, and we conclude that *the world from Moscow to Rio* is not an NP constituent.

11.1.2.2   *Extraposition of Subject Clauses*

Consider (51) and (52) below:

(51)   *That the film ended so soon* was a shame.
(52)   It was a shame *that the film ended so soon.*

In (51) the Subject of the sentence is the clause *that the film ended so soon*. We can move ('extrapose') it from a clause-initial to a clause-final position, as (52) shows. The pronoun *it* is inserted in the position vacated by the Subject clause. This movement establishes the constituent status of the Subject clause.

11.1.2.3   *Extraposition from NP*

Consider the following sentences:

(53)   Six women – appeared *with yellow hats.*
(54)   We employed two people – last week *from European Union countries.*
(55)   The dogs – escaped *that were chained to the house.*

In (53) the PP *with yellow hats* has been extraposed out of the Subject NP *six women*, while in (54) the PP *from European Union countries* is moved out of a Direct Object NP. In (55) a relative clause has been displaced. We call this kind of movement *Extraposition from NP (ENP)*. ENP seems to be more acceptable if the Verb Phrase is relatively light; for example, if it consists of an intransitive verb or a Raising verb (*seem, appear, become,* etc.). The following sentence, which contains a transitive verb, seems to be much less good:

(56)   ?*Three men – noisily left the theatre *who were drunk.*

Just like HNPS, this type of movement can be used as a constituency test, as the example that follows will make clear. We might ask whether the string *with yellow hats on their heads* in (57) below is one constituent, or whether it should really be regarded as two separate PPs, namely *with yellow hats* and *on their heads*:

(57)   Six women *with yellow hats on their heads* appeared.

If the former possibility is correct, we should be able to move the whole string under ENP; if the latter possibility is correct we should be able to move only the PP *with yellow hats*. The result of applying ENP to (57) is (58):

(58)   Six women – appeared *with yellow hats on their heads*.

This sentence is fine, which means that *with yellow hats on their heads* is one constituent. By contrast, (59) is barred:

(59)   *Six women – on their heads appeared *with yellow hats*.

This suggests that in (59) *with yellow hats* is not a constituent: we cannot move it without also moving *on their heads*. As you will have realised, the PP *on their heads* is an Adjunct of the Head *hats*. The tree for the italicised string in (58) looks like this:

(60)

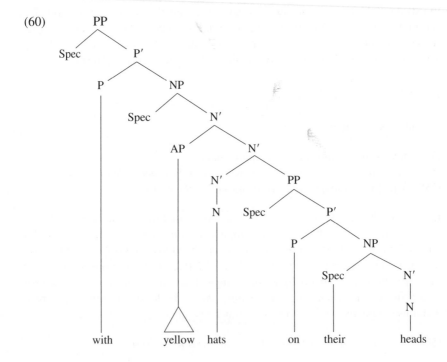

Notice that *with yellow hats* is not a constituent here. (Review Section 4.4 if this is not clear to you.)

Summarising, in Section 11.1 we looked at Movement, and we saw that it can be used as a diagnostic test to determine constituency. A very important result to come out of the discussion is that Direct Objects are inside VP, and that modal verbs are *not* inside VP. The latter are best analysed as being located in 'I'. We concluded that (1) should be analysed as in (2), not as in (3), i.e. S-nodes immediately dominate three constituents, not four.

11.2 Substitution

In the previous section we saw that Movement always affects constituents. In this section we'll be looking at the notion of *Substitution* (i.e. replacement) as applied to language. The idea here is that a particular string of words must be a constituent if it can be replaced by something else: by a single word, by another string of words, or even by nothing at all. Like Movement, Substitution can affect full phrases, but we will see that it can affect clauses and bar-level constituents too.

11.2.1 Substitution of nominal projections: NP and N'

Consider again sentence (1), repeated as (61):

(61)   My father admires my mother.

Let's concentrate on the strings *my father* and *my mother*, which you will intuitively have recognised to be Noun Phrase constituents, because the main words in both cases are nouns. We now want to be able to actually *demonstrate* that *my father* and *my mother* are constituents, other than by moving them. We can do so by means of *Substitution*. We will say that a particular sequence of words is a constituent if it can be replaced by a so-called *proform*, a word or word-sequence that 'stands in' for some other word or word-sequence. We establish the following principle:

Proform Substitution
A particular string of words is a constituent if it can be substituted by a suitable proform.

Obviously, there should be no change in meaning as a result of this Substitution. Let's see how this works with regard to (61). To verify our intuition that *my father* and *my mother* are indeed constituents, the question we must ask is the following: 'can we replace either *my father* or *my mother* with something else?' If so, then these two groups of words must be constituents. Notice that both *my father* and *my mother* refer to people, one a man, the other a woman. As you know, we can refer to males and females not only by using full NPs, as in (61), but also by using personal pronouns, words such as *she, her, he, him, they, them*, etc. Notice now that *my father* can be replaced by *he*, and *my mother* by *her*:

(62)   *He* admires *her*.

The pronouns *he* and *her* function as proforms here, because they stand in for the NPs *my father* and *my mother*. We have already seen that the term 'pronoun' is really a misnomer, because a sentence like (62) clearly shows that the pronoun replaces not a noun, as its name suggests, but an NP. 'Pro-NP' would therefore be a better term. Notice that the meaning of (62) has not changed, because *he* refers to the same individual as *my father*, and *her* refers to the same individual as *my mother*, assuming that the sentence is uttered in the same context as (61). What (61) and (62) show is that a Noun Phrase can be replaced by another Noun Phrase.

Exercise

Replace the Noun Phrase constituents in the following sentences with pronouns.

(63)   The boys saw six blue Rolls Royces.
(64)   Harriet sold her computer to my friends from Edinburgh.

In (63) we can replace *the boys* by *they* and *six blue Rolls Royces* by *them*. In (64) we can substitute *Harriet* by *she*, *her computer* by *it*, and *my friends from Edinburgh* by *them*. This means that *the boys, six blue Rolls Royces, Harriet, her computer* and *my friends from Edinburgh* must be constituents. As their most prominent words in each case are nouns, they must be Noun Phrases.

Pronouns can replace quite complex NPs:

(65)   I like *those funny people who eat with their hands and sing at the dinner table*.
       >
       I like *them*.

Other phrase types, and even clauses, can be replaced by proforms too, as the following sentences demonstrate:

(66)   They say that Wayne is *very unhappy* and *so* he is.

(67)   Our neighbours will go on holiday *on Sunday*, and we will leave *then* too.

(68)   Tim sat *on the couch* and stayed *there*.

(69)   Janet drove her car *too fast*, and Sam rode his bike *likewise*.

(70)   He believes *that politics is a dirty game*. We all believe *that*.

(71)   He said *that the operation will be successful*. I certainly hope *so*.

In (66) the AP *very unhappy* has been replaced by *so*, while in (67) and (68) *then* and *there* replace the PPs *on Sunday* and *on the couch*, respectively. In (69) *likewise* replaces the AdvP *too fast*, and in (70) and (71) *that* and *so* replace clauses. VPs too can be replaced, as we will see in the next section.

We again see that the constituency of a particular sequence of words can be established by replacing it with a proform. Substitution by proforms is thus a useful test for constituency. It can also be useful for determining the categorial status of a particular constituent (i.e. what type of phrase it is). To see how this works, consider the italicised portion of the following sentence:

(72)   *The French* are hospitable people.

Exercise

Before reading on, and mindful of the preceding discussion, give some thought to the question to which phrasal category *the French* belongs.

At first sight it may appear that we are dealing with an Adjective Phrase here, because the Head of this string is clearly an adjective (cf. *a French village, the French President*, etc.). There are, however, quite a few reasons for saying that *the French* is not an AP, but a Noun Phrase. One reason is that it occurs in Subject position, a very common position for Noun Phrases. Another is that the phrase is introduced by the definite article *the*, which is typically found in NPs. Thirdly, and here Substitution plays a role, we can replace *the French* by a pronoun: 'They are hospitable people'. We conclude that phrases such as *the French, the Dutch, the Portuguese*, etc. are NPs.

So far we have seen that proforms in the form of personal pronouns (*he, she, it*, etc.) can replace full NPs. English also possesses a word that can replace *less* than a full NP, and this is the proform *one*. Consider (73):

(73)   Mark is a dedicated teacher of language, but Paul is an indifferent one.

In this sentence, *one* replaces *teacher of language*. This proform cannot be a full NP, because it is preceded by the determinative *a* and the AP *indifferent*. We can show this more clearly in a tree diagram. You'll remember from Chapter 7 that inside NPs Adjective Phrases are adjoined to N′, and that Complements are sisters of the Head, as in (74):

(74)

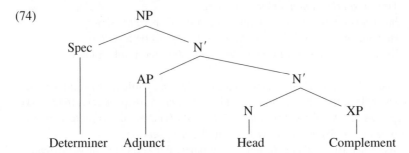

The NPs *a dedicated teacher of language* and *an indifferent one* in (73) have the following structures:

(75)

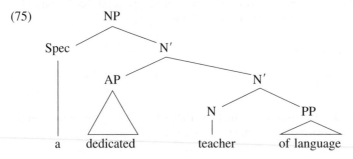

(76)

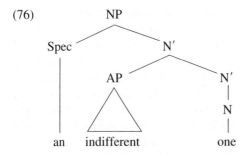

In these trees the APs *dedicated* and *indifferent* are analysed as pre-head Adjuncts, and the PP *of language* is regarded as a nominal Complement (cf. *he teaches language*). As *one* in (76) replaces *teacher of language* in (75) it must be replacing an N'. We thus reach the following conclusion:

One-Substitution
The proform *one* replaces N'-constituents

This is interesting confirmation of the X-bar theoretical conception of the internal structure of phrases. If we allowed phrases to have only two levels, for example the phrase level and the Head level, as in many grammars, we would not be able to explain the fact that *one* can refer to a unit that is not an NP or a noun, but something in-between.

One-Substitution, apart from clearly establishing the existence of bar-level categories, also has a practical use in establishing constituency. Consider the NP *a student of English*. We might wonder whether the PP *of English* is a Complement of the noun *student*, or an Adjunct. We know that if it is a Complement, then *student* + *of English* (N + PP) together form an N′, and *one* should be able to refer back to this N′. If, by contrast, the PP *of English* is an Adjunct, then this phrase must be a sister of an N′. In that case both *student* and *student of English* are N-bars which *one* can refer back to. The alternative structures of the NP *a student of English* can be represented as in (77) and (78):

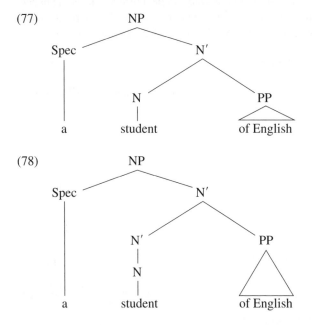

(77)

(78)

Let's now see whether we can use *one*-Substitution to decide in favour of either of these representations.

Exercise

In the following sentence, can *one* replace *student of English*?

(79) Ben likes the Italian student of English, but not the Spanish *one*.

The answer to this question is 'yes'. Notice that this answer is consistent with both (77) and (78), because *student of English* in both cases is an N′.

We therefore still need a way of choosing between (77) and (78). Consider (80). Can *one* replace *student* here?

(80)   Ben likes the Italian student of English, but not the Spanish *one* of literature.

The answer is 'no', and you should place an asterisk in front of (80): *one* can refer only to *student of English*, not to *student* alone. We therefore conclude that *student of English* is an N', but that *student* on its own is not. The tree in (78) is therefore incorrect, because here *student* is an N' (as well as an N). *Student* must be a Head noun which takes the PP *of English* as its Complement, as in (77).

In some of the Noun Phrases we have come across so far in this section there was more than one N'-node. Our claim that *one* can be a pro-N' raises the expectation that if there is more than one N'-constituent in any one NP, the proform *one* should be able to replace each of these N-bars. Consider the following NP:

(81)   a clever Italian student of English

The tree for (81) is simply an expanded version of (77): we add two AP modifiers (*clever* and *Italian*), and hence two N'-nodes:

(82)

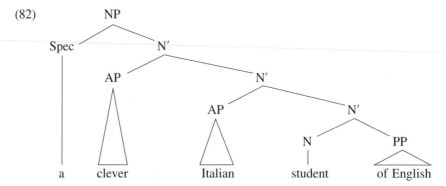

Now try the following exercise.

Exercise

Determine which constituents *one* can replace in the following ambiguous sentence:

(83)   Marco is certainly a clever Italian student of English, but Paolo is an absolutely brilliant one.

One can replace the italicised strings in (84) and (85):

       Marco is certainly a clever Italian student of English,...

(84) ...but Paolo is an absolutely brilliant *Italian student of English*.
(85) ...but Paolo is an absolutely brilliant *student of English*.

These sentences show that (83) can receive more than one interpretation, depending on which N' *one* replaces. It can replace either *Italian student of English*, in which case both Marco and Paolo are students of English of Italian extraction, or it can replace only *student of English*, in which case all we know about Paolo is that he studies English.

Exercise

Consider again sentence (83). Can we interpret it to mean (86)?

(86) Marco is certainly a clever Italian student of English, but Paolo is an absolutely brilliant student.

In other words, can Paolo be something other than a student of English, say a student of geography?

The answer is 'no': *one* must minimally replace the string *student of English*. This again shows that *student* on its own is not an N', and that the structure of the NP *an Italian student of English* is as in (82), with the noun *student* taking the PP *of English* as its sister.

11.2.2 Substitution of Verbal Projections: VP and V'

In the preceding sections we looked at proforms that can replace phrases, or parts of phrases, and clauses. When we looked at Noun Phrases we saw that maximal projections as well as bar-projections can be replaced by proforms: pronouns replace full NPs and *one* replaces N-bars. In this section we will take a closer look at the Substitution of verbal projections. I will begin with a discussion of VP-Substitution, and then move on to V-bar Substitution.

Consider the following exchanges:

(87) 'Will you please leave the room?'
'OK, I will – !'

(88) 'Can you play the piano?'
'Yes, I can – '

(89) 'You take chances, Marlowe.'
'I get paid to – '   (from *The Big Sleep*)

In (87) and (88) the strings *leave the room* and *play the piano* following the modal verbs *will* and *can* have been deleted, while in (89) *take chances* following the infinitival marker *to* has been left out. We can regard this deletion process as a special case of Substitution, and say that *leave the room, play the piano* and *take chances* have been substituted by a *null proform* (i.e. by nothing), instead of by an *overt* proform (like, for example, *one* in the previous section). Now, we have seen that proforms can only replace constituents. It follows that, by virtue of being a special form of Substitution, Deletion too applies only to constituents. Returning now to (87)–(89), recall that we argued in chapter 8 that modal verbs like *can* and the infinitival marker *to* are positioned in 'I'. If you now turn back to the tree in (2) at the beginning of the chapter it will be clear that what must have been deleted in (87)–(89) are Verb Phrases. We will therefore refer to the deletion process in (87)–(89) as *VP-Deletion*.

Sentences (87)–(89) again confirm the syntactic structure that we posited for sentences (cf. (2), as opposed to (3)), because it turns out that V + DO sequences indeed behave like constituents, not only with regard to movement (cf. the discussion on VP-Preposing), but also with regard to Substitution by a null proform.

The question now arises whether proforms can stand in for something *less* than a full VP. Before proceeding, recall that we argued that the structure of Verb Phrases in English is as in (90):

(90)

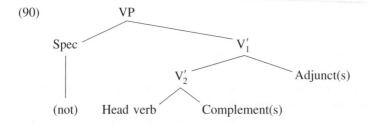

In this tree, as before, Complements are analysed as sisters of the Head verb, and Adjuncts are analysed as sisters of V'. The negative element *not* (if present) is positioned in the Specifier slot.

Notice that the tree in (90) makes a specific claim, namely that V'_1 is a constituent that is made up of V'_2 and the Adjunct position, and that V'_2 is a constituent made up of the Head verb and a Complement position. In Chapter 7 we posited this structure with only very little justification. The question we must now ask ourselves is whether there is evidence that V'_1 and V'_2 are constituents. To answer this question, consider first the sentence below:

(91)   Dawn cleaned the windows diligently.

In this sentence the NP *the windows* is a Direct Object, and the AdvP *diligently* is an Adjunct. The posited structure of its VP is as shown in (92):

(92)

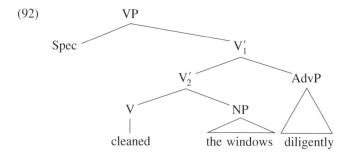

Consider now (93) and (94):

(93)   Dawn cleaned the windows diligently, and Sean *did so* too.
(94)   Dawn cleaned the windows diligently, but Sean *did so* lazily.

Here we have a new proform, namely *do so*, which replaces different lexical material in the two sentences above: in (93) it replaces *cleaned the windows diligently*, while in (94) it replaces *cleaned the windows*. We have seen that proforms can only replace constituents, so we conclude that these strings are constituents, thus confirming that V′₁ and V′₂ in (92) are units. This leads us to the following generalisation:

Do so-Substitution
do so replaces V′-constituents.

Here are some more examples:

(95)   Barry hired a big Jaguar, and Milly *did so* too.
(96)   Lenny sent Will a postcard, and Gemma *did so* too.

Exercise

What lexical material is replaced by *do so* here?

In these cases what has been replaced are the strings *hired a big Jaguar* (V + DO) and *sent Will a postcard* (V + IO + DO). We have claimed that verbs and their Complements together form V′-constituents, so here again *do so* replaces V-bars. The structure of the VPs of the initial clauses in (95) and (96) is as in (97)a and

(97)b. *Do so* replaces the V-bars:

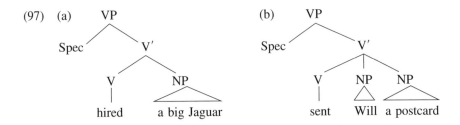

(97) (a) VP — Spec, V' (V | hired, NP | a big Jaguar)
(b) VP — Spec, V' (V | sent, NP | Will, NP | a postcard)

Do so can never replace *less* than a V'. The following sentences are out:

(98)   *Barry hired a big Jaguar, and Milly *did so* a Volkswagen.
(99)   *Lenny sent Will a postcard, and Gemma *did so* a present.

In (98) the proform replaces only the main verb, but, as you can see in (97)a, although this is a constituent, it is not a V'-constituent. In (99) *do so* replaces the verb and only one of its Complements, namely the Indirect Object. Again, this is not allowed, because these two nodes do not together form a V'-constituent.

     Do so-Substitution is a very practical test because we can use it to see whether a particular element, or string of elements, is inside VP. The line of reasoning is as follows: if we can show, using *do so*-Substitution, that some element is part of the V' of a sentence, then that element is also part of the VP of that sentence, because all V-bars are dominated by a VP. Let's see how this works. Consider the following sentence:

(100)   Ray rudely interrupted the speaker.

On the basis of various tests, VP-Preposing and VP-Substitution among them, we already know that the Direct Object, the NP *the speaker*, is inside VP, but we may be unsure about the Adverb Phrase *rudely*. As it is positioned immediately before the main verb, there is the possibility that it is inside VP, like the DO. We can apply the *do so*-Substitution test to find out. This is done by adding a clause in the form *and X does/did so too* to the original sentence:

(101)   Ray rudely interrupted the speaker, and Vincent *did so* too.

Here, clearly *do so* has replaced *rudely interrupted the speaker*, which must therefore be a V'. Because V-bars are dominated by VPs, we conclude that the AdvP is indeed inside VP.

Exercise

The AdvP *rudely* clearly functions as an Adjunct inside VP. Draw the tree for the
VP of the first clause in (101) (*Ray rudely interrupted the speaker*), and circle the
V′ that *do so* replaces in the second clause of this sentence.

This tree looks like this:

(102)

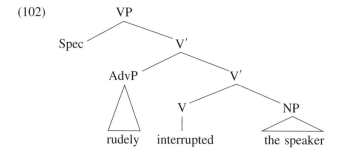

It is the higher of the two V-bars that *do so* replaces in (101). What about the lower
V′? Can we replace that too with *do so*? Yes, we can, as (103) shows:

(103)   Ray rudely interrupted the speaker, while Vincent politely *did so*.

Exercise

Identify the V-bar constituents in the following sentences. Use the frame *X...,
and Y does/did so too*, in the same way we did, for example, for (95) and (96)
above. There may be more than one possibility!

(104)   William bought the bread in the supermarket. (and Iris...)
(105)   Janet ran. (and Frank...)

The results are as follows:

(106)   William bought the bread in the supermarket, and Iris did so in the corner
        shop.
(107)   William bought the bread in the supermarket, and Iris did so too.
(108)   Janet ran, and Frank did so too.

In (106) *do so* replaces *bought bread*, while in (107) it replaces *bought bread in
the supermarket*. In (108) the proform replaces *ran*.

What we have seen in this section is that *do so* replaces V-bars, and that *do so-*Substitution is a useful test for determining whether a particular element, or group of elements, is inside the Verb Phrase of a sentence.

There exists another process that affects V-bars, called *V'-Deletion*. Consider again (91), repeated here as (109):

(109)   Dawn cleaned the windows diligently.

We saw above that *diligently* is inside VP, and we analysed the VP of (109) as in (110):

(110)

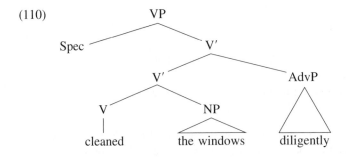

Consider now (111):

(111)   Dawn will clean the windows diligently, but Sean will – lazily.

In (111) we deleted the string *clean the windows*. As we have seen, Deletion is a special case of Substitution, and we will say that *clean the windows* has been substituted by a null proform. Because proforms can only replace constituents, it follows that a sequence like *clean the windows* must be a constituent. In (110) we analysed this string as a V'-constituent, so that in (111) we are dealing with *V-bar Deletion* (alternatively spelt V'-Deletion). Sentences like (111) furnish further evidence for our claim that V + DO sequences are constituents. Direct Objects (if they are present) are therefore dominated by V' and VP, as in (110).

As a further example of V'-Deletion consider the following sentence:

(112)   Ray will rudely interrupt the speaker, but Bruce will politely –

We showed above, using *do so*-Substitution as a test, that an Adjunct like *rudely* in the first clause in (112) is inside VP, in a position where it is adjoined to V', as in (113) below. (Recall that the modal verb is positioned in 'I'.)

(113)

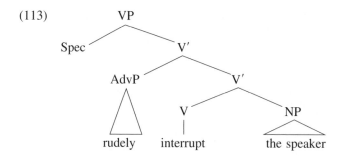

In the second clause of (112) we have deleted the string *interrupt the speaker*. Now, because this string contains the main verb *interrupt*, and we have a stranded Adjunct here (*politely*), we must be dealing with a deleted V'-constituent. Notice that this time the Adjunct is positioned *before* the deletion site. Because Adjuncts like *rudely* and *politely* are adjoined to V', we know that the string *rudely/politely interrupt the speaker* is also a V'.

In this chapter we looked at Movement and Substitution as tests for constituency. In the next chapter we'll be looking at a few additional tests.

Key Concepts in this Chapter

constituency
constituency tests
Movement test
Substitution test

Exercises

1. Draw the trees for the following sentences. Give reasons for your analysis.

    (i)   The big blue balloon exploded.
    (ii)   I will buy some chocolates this afternoon.
    (iii) She could act extremely well.
    (iv)   She believes that her best friend is a genius.
    (v)   We quickly decided that we should leave.

2. In the text we assigned the following structure to the PP (six women) *with yellow hats on their heads* (cf. (60)):

(i)

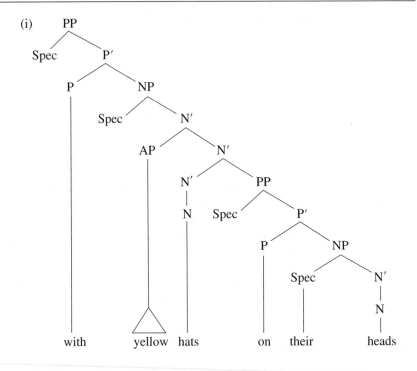

A further possible analysis is shown in (ii):

(ii)

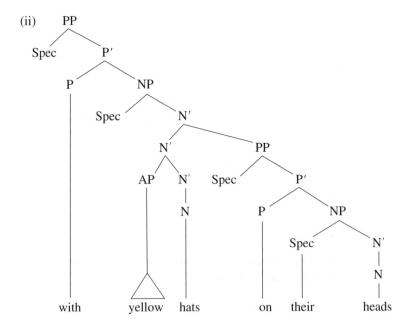

The difference between (i) and (ii) is that in (i) *yellow hats* is not a constituent, whereas in (ii) it is. Conversely, *hats on their heads* is a constituent in (i), but not in (ii). Both (i) and (ii) conform to X′-theory, but they might be said to represent very slightly different meanings for the string *hats on their heads*, namely 'hats which are yellow and on their heads' and 'yellow hats on their heads'. Which structure corresponds with which meaning? Explain your answer.

3.   When we discussed VP-Preposing in Section 11.1.1.2 we saw that this process always leaves behind an auxiliary verb. Consider now the following sets of sentences in which there is more than one auxiliary verb:

(i)   They say he may have been killing flies, ...

   (a)   ... and [killing flies] he may have been –
   (b)   ... and [so] he may have been –
   (c)   ... [which] he may have been –

(ii)   They say he may have been killing flies, ...

   (a)   ... and [been killing flies] he may have –
   (b)   ... and [so] he may have –
   (c)   ... [which] he may have – .

(iii)   They say he may have been killing flies, ...

   (a)   ... and [have been killing flies] he may –
   (b)   ... and [so] he may –
   (c)   ... [which] he may –

Assuming that these sentences are all grammatical (not everyone will agree), and also assuming that Verb Phrases have been preposed in the a-sentences, or substituted by the proforms *so* or *which* in the b and c-sentences (and then preposed), draw the tree structure for the sentence *He may have been killing flies*. Does the structure you have produced accord with the structure of sentences with multiple auxiliaries proposed in Chapter 8?

4.   In many textbooks on English syntax it is assumed that Verb Phrases only contain verbs. Below you will find two common analyses of the Verb Phrase in English. The example sentence used is *Nicholas will burn the toast*:

(i)

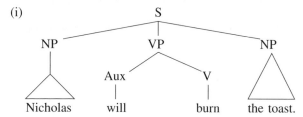

(ii)

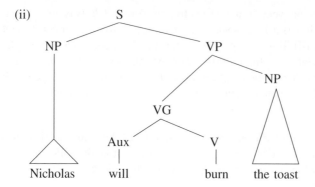

VG = Verb Group

Give distributional arguments in favour or against these analyses (i.e. use the tests introduced in this chapter). Are there also *semantic* reasons for adopting or rejecting these analyses?

5. Now do the same for the analysis below (advocated in Warner 1993):

(i)

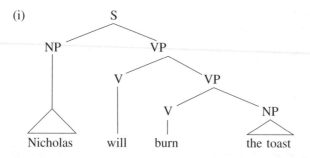

*6. Consider (i) below:

(i) For him to kill that poor fly was wrong.

In this sentence we might wonder whether the string *for him to kill that poor fly* is a unit, or whether we should subdivide it into two independent constituents, namely *for him*, which would then be a PP, and *to kill that poor fly*, which would be a clause without an overt Subject (but whose Subject would be interpreted to be the same as the Complement of the preposition, i.e. *him*). Using the tests discussed in this chapter, show which of these options is correct. Make sure that the meaning of the sentence does not change if you apply Movement.

*7. Although we haven't discussed NP-Movement as a test for constituency in this chapter, we *can* use it as such. Consider the sentences below:

(i)   Charlie saw the book on the table.
(ii) Charlie put the book on the table.

Using NP-Movement as a test, show how the constituency of these sentences is different, despite their superficial similarity as NP–V–NP–PP structures. Draw the trees for (i) and (ii).

*8.   Show how the Substitution test discussed in this chapter confirms your analyses of (i) and (ii) in Exercise 8.

*9.   Our discussion of movement in Chapter 8 and in this chapter has not dealt with all possible displacements in English. In this exercise we will look at further possibilities, specifically some types of *inversion* in English. Here are two examples:

*Inversion around **be***
(i)   a.   New York is the ultimate city in the world.
      b.   The ultimate city in the world is New York.

This inversion process can be used as a test to demonstrate the constituent status of the strings *New York* and *the ultimate city in the world*. You might initially have been tempted to suppose that *in the world* does not form a unit with *the ultimate city*. How does (ii) below put you on the right track?

(ii) *The ultimate city is New York in the world.

Consider next the sentences below:

Subject-Auxiliary-Inversion (SAI)

(iii) a.   Katie will pass her driving test.
      b.   Will Katie pass her driving test?

Here we see that a Subject and an auxiliary verb (a modal) have swapped places. Inversion is one of the NICE properties of auxiliaries that we introduced in Chapter 3. How can we use the pair of sentences in (iii) to bolster our claim (made in Chapter 8 and in this chapter) that modal auxiliaries are not inside VP, but are dominated by a separate node which we labelled 'I'?

*10. In Section 11.1.2.2 we discussed the extraposition of Subject clauses, as in *That Henry made that comment* obviously irritated her > *It* obviously irritated her *that Henry made that comment*. Consider now the sentences below:

(i)   I consider *it* a problem *that you didn't write that report.*
(ii) *I consider *that you didn't write that report* a problem.

What's going on here? As a starting point, think about the functional status of the extraposed *that*-clause in (i).

*11.   Use the examples in (i) and (ii) to demonstrate that the proforms *so did* and *did the same* can be used as VP proforms. How do *so did* and *did the same* differ from *do so*?

(i)   Ben drafted a new proposal effortlessly.
(ii)   Elly vainly admired herself.

Further Reading

On constituency tests see also Radford (1988) and Haegeman (2006). On constituency and sentential reorderings, see also Huddleston (1984), Section 1.2 and Chapter 14, as well as Rochemont and Culicover (1990) and Birner and Ward (2006).

12 Constituency: Some Additional Tests

In the previous chapter we looked at movement and substitution as tests for constituency. In this chapter we'll be looking at a few additional tests: the Coordination Test, the Cleft and Pseudocleft Test, the Insertion Test, the Constituent Response Test, the Somewhere Else Test and the Meaning Test. I have grouped them together in a separate chapter, because they are not always as reliable as Movement and Substitution. The order in which they are discussed roughly reflects their degree of reliability, the first being the most reliable.

12.1 Coordination

Coordination was briefly discussed in Chapter 3. We saw there that it involves the linking of two or more strings by a coordinating conjunction, typically *and, or* or *but*; for example, *[very clever] and [extremely eager], [in the box] or [on the floor], [handsome] but [stupid]*, etc. The claim now is the following:

Coordination
Only constituents can be coordinated

Let's see if coordination facts can confirm the constituent structure of Verb Phrases that we posited in Chapter 7. Consider the following sentences:

(1)   Frank washed his shirts yesterday.
(2)   Michael loudly announced the election victory.

For (1) we posited a structure like (3), while we assigned a structure like (4) to (2):

(3)

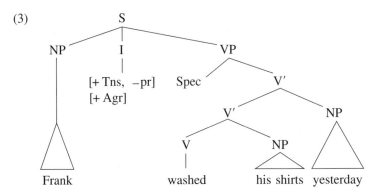

(4)

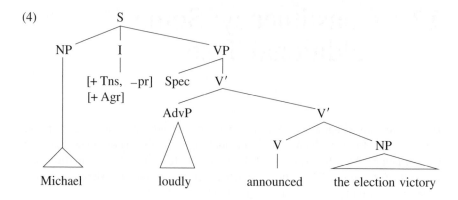

The constituents inside the VPs of both (3) and (4) are the (empty) Specifier position, the higher V′, the lower V′, the main verb and the Direct Object NP, as well as the Adjunct NP in (3), and the Adjunct AdvP in (4). The constituent status of all of these is confirmed by the fact that they can be coordinated with other similar units:

(5)   Frank *washed and ironed* his shirts yesterday. (coordinated main verbs)
(6)   Frank *washed his shirts* and *polished his shoes* yesterday. (coordinated lower V-bars)
(7)   Frank washed his shirts *yesterday* and *last week*. (coordinated Adjunct NPs)
(8)   Frank *washed his shirts yesterday* and *polished his shoes last week*. (coordinated higher V-bars)

(9)   Michael loudly *announced* and *decried* the election victory. (coordinated main verbs)
(10) Anna loudly *announced the election victory* and *gave an interview to the press*. (coordinated lower V-bars)
(11) Anna *loudly* and *cheerfully* announced the election victory. (coordinated Adjunct AdvPs)
(12) Anna *loudly announced the election victory* and *cheerfully gave an interview to the press*. (coordinated higher V-bars)

We will call the type of coordination exemplified above *Ordinary Coordination*. Consider now (13)–(15):

(13) Frank washed the shirts, and Dick ironed the shirts.
(14) Frank will wash the shirts, but Dick won't wash the shirts.
(15) Frank will iron the shirts tomorrow, but Dick won't iron the shirts tomorrow.

We can apply a second type of coordination to these sentences which we will call *Right Node Raising* (RNR). Here are some examples:

(16)   Frank washed – , and Dick ironed – , *the shirts.*
(17)   Frank will – , but Dick won't – , *wash the shirts.*
(18)   Frank will – , but Dick won't – , *iron the shirts tomorrow.*

In (16) the main verbs *wash* and *iron* both take *the shirts* as Direct Object. Because Direct Objects are always on a right-hand branch inside V′ they are 'right nodes'. In (16) *the shirts* has been raised from the positions indicated by the dashes, and one copy of this NP is placed at the end of the sentence, hence the term Right Node Raising. In (17) we have raised a V′-constituent consisting of a main verb and its Direct Object, while in (18) another V′, this time consisting of a main verb + DO + Adjunct, has been raised. We can now make the following observation:

Right Node Raising
Only constituents can undergo RNR.

The data in (16)–(18) show once again that Direct Objects, V + DO strings and V + DO + Adjunct strings form constituents, as in (3) and (4).

There are problems for our claim that only constituents can be coordinated. Here is a classic counterexample:

(19)   Alison gave my brother a T-shirt and my sister a CD.

We know that the ditransitive verb *give* takes two Complements: an IO and a DO, and that both these Complements are sisters of the main verb inside V′:

(20)

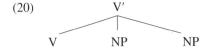

The units that appear to be coordinated in (19) are *my brother a T-shirt* and *my sister a CD*, i.e. IO + DO strings. The problem now is that in both cases the two NPs together (IO + DO) do not form a constituent, because the node that dominates them also dominates V, as is clear from the tree diagram above. However, (19) can be regarded as only an apparent counterexample, if we assume that the verb *gave* has been omitted before *my sister* in (19):

(21)   Alison [gave my brother a T-shirt] and [gave my sister a CD].

In this sentence we can then say that we have coordinated two V-bars.

12.2   Cleft and Pseudocleft Sentences

Our next constituency test involves so-called Cleft and Pseudocleft sentences, examples of which are given below:

(22)	Frank washed his shirts yesterday.	'Regular' sentence (= (1))

(23)	It was *Frank* who washed his shirts yesterday.	Cleft
(24)	It was *his shirts* that Frank washed yesterday.	Cleft
(25)	It was *yesterday* that Frank washed his shirts.	Cleft

(26)	What Frank washed yesterday was *his shirts*.	Pseudocleft
(27)	What Frank did yesterday was *wash his shirts*.	Pseudocleft
(28)	What Frank did was *wash his shirts yesterday*.	Pseudocleft

Clefts and Pseudoclefts are special constructions in English which enable language users to highlight a particular string of words in a sentence. We already briefly came across cleft sentences in chapter 10.

Clefts and Pseudoclefts are easily recognisable, because they have a typical structure. They always start with the same word: *it* in the case of the Cleft construction and *what* (and a few other Wh-items) in the case of the Pseudocleft. The skeletal structures of Clefts and Pseudoclefts are as follows:

Cleft

It	+	form of *be*	+	FOCUS	+	*who/that...*
It		was		*Frank*		who washed his shirts yesterday

Pseudocleft

Wh-item	+	...	+	Form of *be*	+	FOCUS
What		Frank did		was		*wash his shirts yesterday*

Both Clefts and Pseudoclefts always contain a form of the copular verb *be* (*is/was/were*). The position following this copular verb is called the *focus position* (italicised in the examples above). The elements that occur here receive special prominence. Different elements are able to occupy the focus position in Clefts and Pseudoclefts, and for this reason a sentence can have more than one Cleft or Pseudocleft version.

For current purposes the following principle is important:

Cleft and Pseudocleft
Only constituents can occur in the focus position of a Cleft or Pseudocleft.

From the discussion in the previous section you will remember that we argued that the Verb Phrase in (22) has the structure in (3). The data in (23)–(28) confirm that *Frank, his shirts, yesterday, washed his shirts* and *washed his shirts yesterday* in

(22) are indeed constituents, as in (3). The verb alone cannot occur in the focus position of Clefts and Pseudoclefts.

In view of the fact that only constituents can occur in the focus position of Clefts and Pseudoclefts, we can use these constructions as tests for constituency. Consider the sentence in (29) (= (2)):

(29)   Michael loudly announced the election victory.

The structure we posited for this sentence is (4).

Exercise

Give the Cleft and Pseudocleft versions of (29), and underline the elements in the focus position.

The Cleft versions are as in (30)–(32):

(30)   It was *Michael* who loudly announced the election victory.
(31)   It was *the election victory* that Michael loudly announced.
(32)   It was *loudly* that Michael announced the election victory.

The Pseudocleft versions are as follows:

(33)   What Michael loudly announced was *the election victory.*
(34)   What Michael did loudly was *announce the election victory.*
(35)   What Michael did was *loudly announce the election victory.*

We conclude that the italicised strings above are constituents, and this confirms the structure in (4).

12.3   The Insertion Test

Another way of testing the constituent structure of a particular construction is to see whether it can be interrupted by so-called *parenthetical elements*. These are individual words or phrases that are not syntactically integrated in the sentence, but often relate to the sentence as a whole from the point of view of meaning. Typical examples are sentence adverbs such as *however*, *probably* and *frankly* (see Sections 3.6 and 9.1). Here's an example:

(36)   I myself won't be going on holiday this summer. Pam, *however*, will take two weeks off in August.

However can be positioned in various locations in (36), as (37)–(39) below show:

(37)   Pam will, *however*, take two weeks off in August.

(38)   *However*, Pam will take two weeks off in August.
(39)   Pam will take two weeks off in August, *however*.

Further examples of parenthetical elements are: *as you know, would you believe,* vocatives, and so on. The generalisation that we can make with regard to parenthetical elements is as follows:

The Insertion Test
Parenthetical elements can only occur between S-constituents.

By 'S-constituent' I mean a constituent that is immediately dominated by S. Thus, in (36) *however* occurs between NP and 'I'; in (37) it occurs between 'I' and VP, while in (38) and (39) it occurs at the beginning and end of the sentence, respectively. The Insertion Test, as formulated above, raises the expectation that if a parenthetical element occurs in a position other than between S-constituents, the result will be bad. This expectation is borne out:

(40)   *Pam will take, *however*, two weeks off in August.

(40) is clearly ungrammatical. The reason for this is that a parenthetical element intervenes between the main verb and its Direct Object. These are not S-constituents, but constituents of VP.

   Recall that in Chapter 8 we argued that modal auxiliary verbs are positioned inside 'I'. We now have further confirmation that this is indeed the case by pointing to sentences such as (36) and (37), which show that the node in which the modal auxiliary is positioned must be an S-constituent.

12.4   The Constituent Response Test

When we are asked a question in the form of an open interrogative (see Section 4.3.2) we often give a short response, rather than a lengthy one, as in the interchange below:

(41)   Dick: Where did you buy this bread?
       Frances: In the supermarket.

Frances could have responded with the full sentence *I bought this bread in the supermarket*, but it would have taken more time to utter. With regard to shortened answers like the one in (41) the assumption now is the following:

The Constituent Response Test
Only constituents can serve as responses to open interrogatives.

If you look back at some of the sentences we discussed earlier, you'll see that this seems to be a correct generalisation. Take (42), repeated from Chapter 11:

(42)   Ray rudely interrupted the speaker.

With regard to this sentence we can ask the following

Who rudely interrupted the speaker?
How did Ray interrupt the speaker?
Who did Ray (rudely) interrupt?
What did Ray do rudely?
What did Ray do?

The responses are *Ray, rudely, the speaker, interrupt the speaker* and *rudely interrupt the speaker.* The fact that these strings can be responses (though some are more acceptable than others) shows that they must be constituents. This is confirmed by the other tests that we applied to this sentence in Chapter 11.

12.5   The Somewhere Else Test

This test relies on the following premise:

The Somewhere Else Test
If a string of words whose constituent status is unclear occurs as a constituent in some other construction, then this constitutes weak support for the possibility of analysing it as a constituent in the first construction as well.

How does the Somewhere Else Test work? Consider the sentence below:

(43)   *That 'The Sound of Music' is a bad film* is obvious.

The Subject of this sentence is the italicised *that*-clause. This clause must be a constituent because it can be extraposed to the end of the sentence. The dummy element *it* is then inserted in its original position:

(44)   It is obvious *[that 'The Sound of Music' is a bad film]*.

Another reason for regarding the *that*-clause in (43) as a constituent is that it can be replaced by a proform:

(45)   *It* is obvious.

Now, notice that a *that*-clause such as the one in (43) can occur as a constituent in a different syntactic environment, for example after a main verb:

(46)   Everyone believed *that 'The Sound of Music' is a bad film.*

Compare (46) with (47)–(49):

(47)   *That 'The Sound of Music' is a bad film* was believed by everyone
(48)   It was believed by everyone *that 'The Sound of Music' is a bad film.*
(49)   Everyone believed this: *that 'The Sound of Music' is a bad film.*

These data can be regarded as weak confirmation of the contention that the *that*-clause in (43) is a constituent. They don't actually *prove* it, in the way that Movement and Substitution in (44) and (45) do, but they could be said to constitute support for that claim, to the extent that such clauses do seem to behave naturally as constituents in a variety of constructions. We will say that (46)–(49) constitute *suggestive evidence* for the constituency of the *that*-clause in (43).

Consider next (50):

(50)   Ivan wants the train to depart.

In Chapter 5 we said that the Direct Object of this sentence is a nonfinite clause, namely *the train to depart*. That such a string can act as a constituent is confirmed by the Somewhere Else Test:

(51)   It might be better for *the train to depart.*

Here *the train to depart* occurs after *for*. Again, the fact that this string occurs as a unit in (51) doesn't conclusively prove that it is also a constituent in (50). All we can say is that (51) shows that such strings can be constituents, and hence the analysis of (50) as involving a constituent *the train to depart* becomes more plausible than it might have seemed at first sight.

Care should be taken when applying the Somewhere Else Test. Consider the NP *the garden of the hotel* in the sentence below:

(52)   *The garden of the hotel* was beautifully maintained.

We might wish to investigate whether the string *the garden* is a constituent inside the italicised phrase. At first blush, and from the point of view of the Somewhere Else Test, it might seem obvious that it is. After all, it can occur in a variety of typical NP positions (e.g. **The garden** is beautiful, We dined in **the garden**, etc.). However, notice that we cannot apply the Movement or Substitution tests to this string:

(53)   *Of the hotel was beautifully maintained the garden.
(54)   *It of the hotel was beautifully maintained.

In the first sentence of this pair we have moved *the garden* to the right, and this results in ungrammaticality. You will find that other movements are also ruled out. In the second sentence *the garden* has been replaced by *it*, again with an ungrammatical result.

Exercise

Draw the tree diagram for the NP *the garden of the hotel*, treating *of the hotel* as a PP Adjunct of the Head *garden* (i.e. it should be adjoined to an N′-constituent). Include all Specifier positions. Explain why *the garden* on its own is not a constituent

---

Your tree should look like this:

(55)

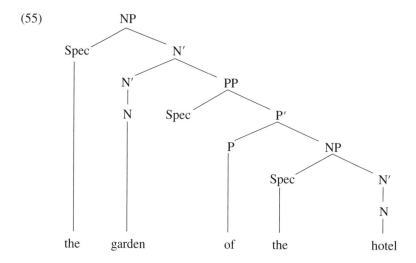

Clearly, in this tree the sequence *the garden* does not form a constituent. (Review Section 4.4 if this is not clear to you.)

12.6 The Meaning Test

On the assumption that where possible we should aim to match the syntactic analysis of a sentence with its meaning, constituency can often be established on semantic grounds. Consider again sentence (50) above. If you think about what this sentence actually means, you'll find that the object of Ivan's wanting is not 'the train', but a proposition, namely 'that the train departs'. On these grounds it is possible to argue that the propositional string *the train to depart* is a constituent, and that this sequence, not the NP *the train* on its own, functions as the Direct Object of *want*.

12.7 A Case Study: the *Naked Pizza Eating*-Construction

In this section we will bring together all the tests that were introduced in Chapter 11 and this chapter, and apply them to what I will call, for lack of a better term, the *Naked Pizza Eating-Construction* (henceforth: the NPEC). This construction is exemplified in (56) below:

(56)   Josh ate the pizza naked.

From left-to-right this sentence contains a Subject (*Josh*), a Predicator (*ate*), a Direct Object (*the pizza*) and a phrase (the AP *naked*) that tells us something more about the Subject of the sentence. We interpret the AP as telling us that 'Josh ate the pizza *while* he was naked'. The AP thus has an 'Adjunct feel' to it. Pizza eating in the nude is a somewhat unusual activity, to be sure, but you may be surprised to hear that sentences like (56) have been widely discussed in the linguistic literature, and very seriously too!

A problem with (56) is the question whether the AP *naked* is inside VP or not. As an initial hypothesis we might surmise that it is not, and that a natural division of (56) is as follows:

(57)   [s [NP Josh] [I] [VP ate the pizza] [AP naked]]

The associated tree diagram is as in (58):

(58)

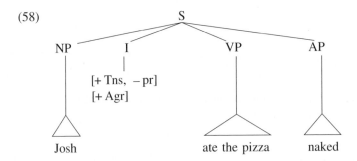

In this tree the AP *naked* is an immediate constituent of S. However, because it occurs right next to the VP, we should investigate whether perhaps it is part of that VP. If *naked* is indeed inside VP, then the string *ate the pizza naked* should behave as a constituent, if we apply our various tests. So let's give it a try.

We start with Movement. Recall that two Movement tests were relevant to VPs, namely VP-Preposing and *Though*-Movement. Can these be used? Let's try VP-Preposing first:

VP-Preposing

(59) Josh says that he will eat the pizza naked, and [eat the pizza naked] he will –.

(60) *Josh says that he will eat the pizza naked, and [eat the pizza] he will – naked.

These results show that if a string of words is fronted that involves the main verb *eat*, i.e. a Verb Phrase, then the AP *naked* must also move, suggesting that it is part of the VP. Now let's apply *Though*-Movement:

Though-Movement

(61) *Eat the pizza naked* though he will – , Josh wants to be paid for it.

(62) **Eat the pizza* though he will – naked, Josh wants to be paid for it.

The outcome confirms our earlier conclusion that *naked* is inside VP.

 The rightward movement tests, i.e. Heavy-NP-Shift and Extraposition from NP, are of no use in establishing whether the AP *naked* is inside VP or not.

 Our next battery of tests involves Substitution. We start with VP-Deletion. Here we reason as follows: if we can delete (i.e. substitute by nothing) a string of elements that involves the main verb and the AP *naked*, then the AP must be inside VP. Consider (63):

VP-Deletion

(63) Josh will eat the pizza naked, but Ennio won't – .

Under VP-Deletion, apart from the main verb and Direct Object, *naked* is also removed from the second clause in (63). We can therefore again conclude that Subject-related APs like *naked* are inside VP.

 Can we also apply *do so*-Substitution to the NPEC? If *do so* can replace a V'-sequence that includes *naked*, then this Adjective Phrase is inside V', and hence also inside the VP which dominates it. Let's apply the test and see what the result is:

(64) Josh ate the pizza naked, and Ennio *did so* too.

In (64) *do so* has replaced the sequence *ate the pizza naked*, which is therefore a V'. (64) thus shows that the AP *naked* is inside V', and hence also inside the VP which dominates it.

 We have now demonstrated that the AP *naked* is not an immediate constituent of S, but is in fact *inside* the VP, contrary to our initial expectations. We revise (57) as (65):

(65) [$_S$ [$_{NP}$ Josh] [$_I$] [$_{VP}$ ate the pizza naked]]

We turn now to the additional tests we discussed in Sections 12.1–12.6. If, as our tests have so far suggested, *ate the pizza naked* is a constituent, as in (65), we would expect it to be possible to coordinate this string with a structurally identical string. Sure enough, this is possible:

Ordinary Coordination

(66)   Josh *ate the pizza naked*, but *ate the doughnut fully clothed*.

Right-Node-Raising too can apply:

Right-Node-Raising

(67)   Josh said he would –, but Deirdre said she couldn't possibly –, *eat the pizza naked*.

The string *eat the pizza naked* cannot be the focus of a Cleft, but it *can* be the focus of a Pseudocleft:

Cleft and Pseudocleft

(68)   *It was *eat the pizza naked* that Josh did.
(69)   What Josh did was *eat the pizza naked*.

I will return to (68) in Section 12.8.

As for the Insertion Test, notice that the following example is of dubious acceptability:

The Insertion Test

(70)   ?Josh ate the pizza, would you believe it, naked.

This suggests that the boundary between *pizza* and *naked* is not an S-constituent boundary, but a VP-internal boundary. It must be conceded, however, that the example is not completely unacceptable.

Turning now to the Constituent Response Test, we find that *eat the pizza naked* can occur as a constituent in an exchange like the following:

The Constituent Response Test

(71)   Edgar: What did you do in the restaurant?
       Fran: *Eat a pizza naked.*

And the Somewhere Else Test shows that *eat the pizza naked* can be a constituent in a sentence like (72):

The Somewhere Else Test

(72)   This he refuses to do: *eat the pizza naked.*

Finally, the **Meaning Test** leads us to say that meaningwise *eat the pizza naked* is a unit, because this string predicates something of the Subject. In fact, it tells us two things about the Subject, namely that Josh performed an act of pizza eating, and that he was in a state of undress when he did so.

12.8   Some Caveats Regarding the Tests

The constituency tests of Chapter 11 and this chapter should be applied with some care. I have already pointed out that not all the tests we discussed are equally reliable. For example, you will have realised from the discussion in Sections 12.5 and 12.6 that the Somewhere Else Test and the Meaning Test have a different status from the other tests that we dealt with, in that they seem useful only in *indicating* or *suggesting* constituent structure. They are the least reliable of all the tests. The procedure to follow if you're investigating the constituent structure of a particular construction is first to apply the tests of Chapter 11, then those of Sections 12.1–12.4, and to use the Somewhere Else Test and the Meaning Test only in conjunction with the other tests as a supplementary check.

A general constraint that applies to the tests is that they work in only one direction. Thus, for example, with regard to Movement we can say that if we can move a certain string of words, it must be a constituent, but if we *cannot* move a string of words, that string is not necessarily *not* a constituent. An example will make this clear:

(73)   *[About New York], nobody liked the books — .

This sentence is ungrammatical, because the PP cannot be moved in the way indicated. However, the fact that leftward PP-Movement is illicit in this example should not immediately lead us to conclude that the PP is not a constituent. Before drawing such a conclusion we should try to apply other tests. For example, (74) below shows that the PP *about New York* can be coordinated with another PP:

(74)   Nobody liked the books *about New York* and *about Los Angeles.*

We can also use the Somewhere Else Test to find a different context in which a PP which is structurally identical to the one in (73) *can* be moved, and in which it therefore *does* function as a unit. Sentence (75) is an example:

(75)   He never mentioned London, whereas [about New York] he could talk – for hours.

Here *about New York* has moved from the position following the main verb of the subordinate clause to the position following the complementiser *whereas*.

We won't go into the question why (73) is bad, but we will simply say that its ungrammaticality must be due to some constraint in the grammar that prohibits leftward Movement of PPs out of NPs.

We can use other examples to illustrate the one-directionality of the constituency tests. Consider again (68), repeated here as (76):

(76)   *It was *eat the pizza naked* that Josh did.

(76) considered in isolation might lead us to suppose that *eat the pizza naked* cannot be a constituent, because it cannot occur in the focus position of a Cleft sentence. However, to take *only* this sentence into account would be wrong, in view of the overwhelming evidence presented in Section 12.7 that showed that *eat the pizza naked* does behave as a constituent. The fact that (76) is bad is simply due to a general constraint which disallows strings involving verbs to be placed in the focus position of Clefts (cf. also **It was eat that he did/*It was eat the pizza that he did.*).

To conclude, when using constituency tests, it is imperative to bear in mind that some are more reliable than others, and that they only work in one direction. More generally, it is a good idea to apply not just one, but several tests to a sentence whose constituency you are investigating, as we have done in the case of the NPEC.

Key Concepts in this Chapter

constituency tests
coordination test
cleft and pseudocleft tests
insertion test
constituent response test
somewhere else test
meaning test

Exercises

1.   The following sentence is ambiguous. Draw the tree structures that correspond to the different meanings. Give arguments based on distributional evidence to support your analyses.

  (i)   I saw the policeman with the binoculars.

2.   Use the constituency tests discussed in Chapter 10 and this chapter to investigate whether the Adjective Phrase *dry* is positioned inside VP in (i) below.

(i)   Jeff rubbed the plates dry.

Notice that under the most likely reading of (i) the AP is related to the Direct Object *the plates*. Notice also that the AP expresses a result, i.e. as a result of Jeff's rubbing the plates, they became dry. (The AP can also – just about – be related to the Subject, as in the NPEC, in such a way that Jeff was dry when he rubbed the plates, but we will disregard this meaning.)

3.   Check to see which of the constituency tests discussed in Chapter 11 and this chapter, apart from the Elsewhere and Meaning Tests, confirm the constituent status of *the train to depart* in (50), repeated here as (i):

(i)   Ivan wants *the train to depart.*

4.   In Section 5.4 we analysed a sentence like (i) as in (ii).

(i)   I saw you paying this bill.
(ii)   I saw [you paying this bill].

How does the sentence in (iii) support the analysis in (ii)?

(iii)   There may have been a delay between you paying this bill and the issue of this notice. (From a telephone bill.)

*5.   In the text we used the following sentences to illustrate Right-Node-Raising:

(i)   a.   Frank washed the shirts, and Dick ironed the shirts.
             –RNR→
       b.   Frank washed – , and Dick ironed – , *the shirts.*
(ii)   a.   Frank will wash the shirts, but Dick won't wash the shirts.
             –RNR→
       b.   Frank will – , but Dick won't – , *wash the shirts.*
(iii) a.   Frank will iron the shirts tomorrow, but Dick won't iron the shirts tomorrow.
             –RNR→
       b.   Frank will – , but Dick won't – , *iron the shirts tomorrow.*

In these sentences it may appear to be the case that as a result of RNR new structures come about in which the strings *Frank washed* and *Dick ironed* in (i)b, and *Frank will* and *but Dick won't* in (ii)b and (iii)b are being co-ordinated. This would suggest that these strings are constituents. However, this cannot be correct, i.e. these strings cannot be constituents, if the general structure we've posited for sentences is correct. Why not? (Refer to the tree structures in (3) and (4) in answering this question.) Is there a way around this problem?

*6.   In the section on the NPEC we saw that Subject-related Adjective Phrases are inside VP (see (65)). We can go further and ask whether the AP is a Complement of the main verb inside VP, or an Adjunct. The two possible structures of the VP *eat the pizza naked* are shown in (i) and (ii) below:

(i)

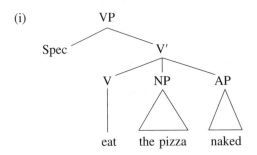

(ii)

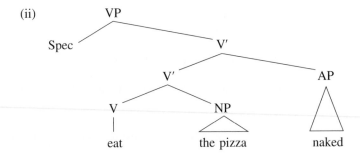

In (i) the AP is a Complement of the verb *eat*, in (ii) it is an Adjunct. How do we decide between these representations? Here's a hint: notice that in (i) there is one V′, whereas in (ii) there are two V-bars. We now predict that if (i) is correct, we should be able to replace the V′ by *do so*, whereas if (ii) is correct we should be able to replace both the higher and lower V-bars by *do so*. Use the sentences in (iii) and (iv) to decide in favour of either (i) or (ii) as the correct representation of the VP in *Josh ate the pizza naked*.

(iii)   Josh ate the pizza naked, and Ennio *did so* too.
(iv)   Josh ate the pizza naked, and Ennio *did so* fully clothed.

*7.   Huddleston (1984: 215–17) discusses the following sentence:

(i)   Ed intended Liz to repair it.

He presents two analyses of this sentence in the form of tree diagrams (which I have modified slightly):

(ii)

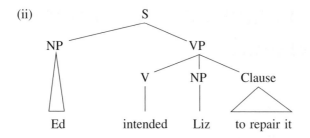

(iii)

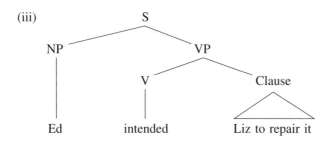

Huddleston observes that (iii) 'matches the meaning more closely' than (ii), but '[f]rom a syntactic point of view...there are grounds for preferring the analysis shown in [ii]'. One argument in favour of (ii) that Huddleston gives is that 'a sequence like *Liz to repair it* does not occur elsewhere as a constituent: we cannot say, for example, **Liz to repair it was intended, *Liz to repair it would be useful, *The intention was Liz to repair it, *What he intended was Liz to repair it.*' Which constituency test is Huddleston invoking here? Can you think of a sentence which would disprove his claim that *Liz to repair it* cannot occur elsewhere as a constituent?

*8.   What do the parenthetical insertions (cf. Section 12.3) in the sentences below (from Chomsky 1955/1975: 475–6) tell us about the strings *in every possible place* and *up the case*? How would you grammatically analyse these sentences?

(i)   He looked, as you can see, in every possible place.
(ii) *He looked, as you can see, up the case in the records.

Further Reading

On the NPEC and related structures, see Aarts (1995).

13 Predicates and Arguments Revisited

In this chapter we return to the notions of predicate and argument that were first introduced in Chapter 6. We will look at cases where it is not so straightforward what the arguments of a particular predicate are, and we will discuss ways in which we can establish argumenthood, i.e. whether or not a particular element is an argument of some predicate. The notion of argumenthood is intimately related to constituency, as will become clear as we go along.

To refresh your memory, recall that predicates are linguistic expressions that require arguments to satisfy them. Here are some examples:

(1) <u>Penny</u> **admires** <u>Judith</u>
(2) <u>Imelda</u> **sent** <u>Darren</u> <u>presents</u>
(3) <u>Pam</u> **thinks** <u>that she is clever</u>
(4) <u>Being here</u> **annoys** <u>me</u>

The elements in bold represent predicates, while the underlined elements represent arguments. In English, predicates take minimally one, and usually no more than three arguments. In most cases it is not difficult to decide how many arguments a particular predicate requires, especially if we are dealing with simple sentences like those in (1)–(4). There is also usually no problem in deciding what is the categorial status of the arguments that are needed. In the sentences above they are either Noun Phrases or clauses. However, there do exist some controversial cases. We turn to them in the next section.

13.1   Establishing Argumenthood

In deciding whether a particular element is an argument of some predicate we have recourse to a number of tests for argumenthood: meaning, dummy elements, idiom chunks and passivisation. We will look at each of these in turn.

13.1.1   Meaning

In the previous section we looked at a number of simple predicate-argument combinations. We saw that in each of these cases it was quite straightforward to decide which arguments the predicates required. The number and type of arguments that a particular predicate needs is clearly determined to a large extent by the *meaning* of the predicate in question. The meanings of predicates are stored in our mental lexicon, along with information about the number of arguments they require, as well as their categorial status (NP, clause, PP, etc.). Furthermore, recall that for an element to be an argument of some predicate there must be a thematic relationship between the argument and predicate in question. Information about the thematic roles borne by arguments is also stored in the mental lexicon. When we interpret a sentence, the information that is stored in our mental lexicon about the predicate(s) that the sentence contains is retrieved. As an example, take the sentence below:

(5)   Ed believes the story.

In (5) the meaning of *believe*, a two-place predicate, is such that it requires some-body who does the believing (a Subject) as well as a specification of what is being believed (a Direct Object). These functions are performed by the NPs *Ed* and *the story*, respectively. *Ed* carries the thematic role of Experiencer, while *the story* carries the role of Patient.

Consider now (6):

(6)   Ed believes that the story is false.

Here again we have the predicate *believe*, which differs from the verb in (5) only with respect to the categorial status of the arguments it takes: in (5) it takes two NP arguments, whereas in (6) it takes an NP Subject and a clausal Direct Object. Notice that both the NP *the story* in (5) and the clause *that the story is false* in (6) are DOs which carry the thematic roles of Patient and Proposition, respectively.

It is worth stressing again the fact that for some element to act as an argument of some predicate it must bear a thematic relation to that predicate. Keeping this in mind, consider next (7):

(7)   Ed believes the story to be false.

This sentence is a little less straightforward. Apart from the matrix clause Subject, which again is clearly the NP *Ed*, we might wonder how many further arguments *believe* has in this sentence. There are a number of possible analyses we can assign to (7). One common analysis involves taking the NP *the story* to be a Direct Object, and *to be false* to be a further infinitival Complement. Under this view *believe* is a three-place predicate. What might be the arguments for such an analysis? One reason for taking *the story* to be a DO is that when we passivise (7) it is this NP that is fronted:

(8)   The story is believed — to be false by Ed.

Furthermore, if we have a pronominal NP following *believe*, this pronoun must take objective case:

(9)   Ed believes *him* to be a traitor.

It is said to be typical of Direct Objects that they are fronted under passivisation, and that they take objective case if they are pronouns. Let us take a closer look at these arguments. As for passivisation, while it is true that in traditional grammar the possibility of fronting a phrase under Passivisation has always been a hallmark of Objects (both DOs and IOs), there is nothing God-given about the generalisation that only Objects can be fronted under Passivisation. When we discussed NP-Movement in Chapter 9, we saw that both Subjects and Objects can be fronted, the former under raising, the latter under Passivisation. Recall that the terms 'Raising' and 'Passivisation' are convenient labels for the same process of NP-Movement. We'll see in a moment that the NP following the main verb in (7) is more plausibly regarded as the Subject of a subordinate clause, and hence we will be saying that in (8) a Subject, not an Object, has been fronted.

Turning now to the objective case on postverbal pronominal NPs, the fact that we have *him* in (9), rather than *he* is necessary, but not sufficient evidence for the objecthood of this NP. As is well-known, case is governed by verbs (as well as prepositions), and in (9) we have *him* rather than *he* simply by virtue of the fact that the verb *believe* and the pronoun are adjacent to each other. If something intervenes between the verb and the pronoun, for example a complementiser, as in (10), then the pronoun receives subjective case.

(10)   Ed believes that *he* is a traitor.

Not only are the arguments in favour of an analysis of *the story* as a Direct Object in (7) not wholly convincing, they lead to a serious problem: if *believe* indeed takes this NP as its DO, we would expect there to be a thematic relationship between *believe* and *the story*, such that *believe* assigns the thematic role of Patient to *the story*, exactly as in (5). Meaningwise, this entails that 'Ed believes the story'. Clearly, this is not what (7) means. Quite the contrary: (7) expresses Ed's incredulity with regard to the story in question. This suggests that *the story* is not a Direct Object argument of *believe*, but the Subject of the string *the story to be false*. We conclude that the string *the story to be false* is a clausal Object of *believe*. Notice that (6) and (7) have a parallel structure: in both cases the verb *believe* subcategorises for a clausal Object. In (6) this Object takes the form of a *that*-clause, while in (7) it is an infinitival clause. In the next section we turn to further arguments for analysing (6) and (7) in a parallel fashion.

13.1.2   Dummy Elements and Idiom Chunks

In this section we will discuss so-called *dummy elements* and *idiom chunks* and their importance for establishing argumenthood. What are they?

Dummy elements are lexical elements without semantic content, i.e. they are meaningless. English has two such elements, namely *it* and *there*. Here are some example sentences containing these words:

(11)   *It* is raining.
(12)   *It* is cold.

(13)   *There* are a number of solutions to this problem.
(14)   *There* has been an increase in crime in America.

Dummy *it* and *there* are semantically contentless, because they do not refer to anything, and they are said simply to fill the Subject slots in sentences like those above. Because they are meaningless, there can be no thematic relationship between them and the following predicate. Put differently, no thematic role is assigned to them, and for that reason they cannot act as arguments. Dummy *it* and *there* (also called *expletive* or *pleonastic* elements) *always* occur in Subject position and should be distinguished from referential *it* and locative *there*:

(15)   I don't like his pipe. *It* stinks.
(16)   Los Angeles? I have no desire to go *there*.

Obviously, *it* and *there* do carry meaning here, and refer to an object and a location, respectively.

We turn now to idioms and idiom chunks. Idioms are language-particular expressions with a characteristic meaning that is not, or only vaguely, predictable from the component parts. Perhaps the most cited instance in English is *kick the bucket*, the composite meaning of which is 'die'. As the name suggests, idiom chunks are subparts of idioms. The phrase *the bucket* is an Object idiom chunk. Idioms in which the verb and an Object are the central elements are by far the most frequent in English. Idioms containing Subject idiom chunks are far less frequent. For our concerns, however, these are the most interesting. Consider the following:

(17)   The coast is clear.
(18)   The fat is in the fire.

In these examples *the coast* and *the fat* are Subject idiom chunks. These NPs cannot be replaced by different NPs without the particular meanings associated with the full expressions being lost. As for the semantics of (17) and (18), notice that their meanings are not predictable. (17) means 'there is nobody or nothing to hinder us', while (18) roughly means 'something has been done from which adverse consequences can be expected'.

Before we proceed it's a good idea to remind ourselves of the following: wherever there is a predicate-argument relationship, there is a thematic relationship between the predicate in question and its argument(s). How is this observation relevant in the context of a discussion of dummy elements and idiom chunks?

Dummy elements and Subject idiom chunks can be used to show that the NP in *believe* + NP + *to*-infinitive structures like (7) cannot be analysed as a Direct Object. In this connection consider the data below:

(19) Ed believes *it* always to be raining in London.
(20) Ed believes *there* to be a traitor in the company.

These sentences pose problems for frameworks in which the NP in *believe* + NP + *to*-infinitive structures is analysed as a Direct Object. The reason is that dummy elements *must* occur in Subject position, as we have seen, and they cannot be analysed as Direct Objects, because an element must have a thematic relationship with a preceding main verb for it to occur in the Direct Object slot. Because dummy *it* and *there* are meaningless, they cannot enter into a thematic relationship with a preceding verb, and there is therefore no thematic role associated with them. The conclusion is that they cannot function as Direct Object arguments. We therefore analyse them as Subjects of subordinate clauses. Thus, both in (19) and (20) *believe* takes a clausal DO (*it always to be raining in London* and *there to be a traitor in the company*, respectively).

We can pursue a similar line of reasoning for Subject idiom chunks. Because they are invariably associated with the Subject slot of the idiomatic expressions of which they form a part, we cannot analyse them as Direct Objects in the following sentences:

(21) Ed believes *the coast* to be clear.
(22) Ed believes *the fat* to be in the fire.

We conclude that the idiom chunks *the coast* and *the fat* are the Subjects of the subordinate clauses *the coast to be clear* and *the fat to be in the fire*.

13.1.3   *Passivisation*

Apart from arguments based on meaning, dummy elements and idiom chunks, there is an additional argument we can use to show that the NP in *believe* + NP + *to*-infinitive constructions is not a Direct Object. Consider the following data:

(23) Ed believes the jury to have given the wrong verdict.
(24) Ed believes the wrong verdict to have been given by the jury.

The first thing we can say about this pair of sentences is that *they mean the same*: Ed holds a belief in the content of a proposition, namely the proposition that the jury has given the wrong verdict. As in the other *believe* + NP + *to*-infinitive constructions that we looked at, it is *not* the case that 'Ed believes the jury' in (23), or that 'Ed believes the wrong verdict' in (24). In other words, there exists no thematic relationship between *believe* and the NPs *the jury* in (23) and *the wrong verdict* in (24). These phrases cannot therefore function as the Direct Objects of *believe*. Yet again we are led to an analysis in which the postverbal NP in the *believe* + NP + *to*-infinitive construction should be taken to be the Subject of a subordinate clause, rather than the Direct Object of the matrix clause. The verb *believe* has a thematic relationship with a proposition, not with an NP in these instances. The syntactic difference between (23) and (24) is the Passivisation process that has taken place in the clausal Complement of *believe*.

With regard to (23) and (24) the generalisation we can now make is that if we can passivise the postverbal portion in any verb + NP + *to*-infinitive construction without a resulting change in meaning, then the postverbal NP is not a Direct Object, but the Subject of a subordinate clause. (23) and (24) are bracketed as follows:

(25)   Ed believes [the jury to have given the wrong verdict]
(26)   Ed believes [the wrong verdict to have been given by the jury]

Incidentally, do not confuse the passive in (24) with an alternative passive version of (23), namely (27):

(27)   The jury is believed to have given the wrong verdict by Ed.

Here the *matrix clause*, rather than the subordinate clause, has been passivised.

13.2   Two Further Types of Verb + NP + *to*-Infinitive Construction: *persuade* and *want*

In the previous section we looked at ways of testing argumenthood in a very specific construction of English: *believe* + NP + *to*-infinitive. In this section we will look at two further types of verb + NP + *to*-infinitive construction, this time involving the verbs *persuade* and *want*. We will see that these verbs are very different.

13.2.1   Persuade

Take a look at the following sentence:

(28)   Ed persuaded Brian to interview Melanie.

The issue with regard to (28) is which elements are the arguments of *persuade*. Clearly, *Ed* is the Subject, but is *Brian* a Direct Object, or does it function as the Subject of a subordinate clause, like the NP in the *believe* + NP + *to*-infinitive construction?

To answer this question, let us first see what (28) actually means. Unlike in the *believe* + NP + *to*-infinitive construction, notice that there is a thematic relationship between the verb *persuade* and the NP that follows it: in (28) the individual Brian undergoes Ed's act of persuasion, and the NP *Brian* can therefore be said to function as a Direct Object.

Now, if the postverbal NP in the *persuade* + NP + *to*-infinitive construction is indeed a Direct Object, we would not expect it to be possible for this position to be occupied by dummy elements, as these can only occur in Subject position. This expectation is borne out:

(29)   *Ed persuaded it to be hot in the room.
(30)   *Ed persuaded there to be a party.

The position following *persuade* can only be filled by elements that can be assigned a thematic role. As dummy elements are meaningless, they cannot stand in a thematic relationship with *persuade*. Idiom chunks also cannot occupy the position following *persuade*:

(31)   *Ed persuaded the coast to be clear.
(32)   *Ed persuaded the fat to be in the fire.

This is what we would expect if the NP slot after *persuade* is a Direct Object position: given the fact that *the coast* and *the fat* are Subject idiom chunks, they cannot appear in Direct Object position.

What about the Passivisation test? Consider the following pair of sentences:

(33)   Ed persuaded Brian to interview Melanie.   (= (28))
(34)   Ed persuaded Melanie to be interviewed by Brian.

Unlike in the case of the *believe* + NP + *to*-infinitive construction, we can establish a thematic relationship between the verb and the postverbal NPs here, i.e. between *persuade* and *Brian* in (33), and between *persuade* and *Melanie* in (34). Put differently, Ed persuaded an individual in both cases, not a proposition.

Recall that we said that if we can passivise the postverbal portion in a verb + NP + *to*-infinitive construction without a change in meaning, then the postverbal NP is *not* a Direct Object, but the Subject of a subordinate clause. Clearly, (33) and its passivised version (34) do not mean the same, and we therefore conclude that the NP in the *persuade* + NP + *to*-infinitive construction is a Direct Object. We can regard the string of words containing the *to*-infinitive as a Complement clause, so that *persuade* is a three-place predicate. The implied Subject of this

Complement clause has the same referent as the DO of the matrix clause. In a labelled bracketing we can indicate this implied Subject using the symbol 'Ø', which we introduced in Chapter 10 to denote implied arguments. In addition, we indicate the fact that the matrix clause DO and the Subject of the Complement clause are coreferential (i.e. share the same referent) by using a subscript letter 'i'. The representation for (28) is then as in (35):

(35)   Ed persuaded Brian$_i$ [Ø $_i$ to interview Melanie]

13.2.2   Want

Like *believe* and *persuade*, the verb *want* can also occur in the verb + NP + *to*-infinitive construction. Here is an example:

(36)   Kate wants Ralph to get out of her life.

Is *want* like *believe* or like *persuade*, or different again? As before, the issue is the question which are the arguments of the verb *want*. Clearly, *Kate* is the Subject argument of the verb *want*, but what about the NP *Ralph*? Is it a Direct Object (as with *persuade*), or is it perhaps the Subject of a subordinate clause (as with *believe*)? To answer this question, let us see what (36) means. If the first possibility is correct, namely that *Ralph* is a Direct Object, then we expect there to be a thematic relationship between the verb *want* and the NP *Ralph*, i.e. we expect it to be the case that 'Kate wants Ralph'. This is obviously not the case, because what the sentence expresses is exactly the opposite: Kate wants to lead her life without Ralph, and hence we can confidently say that she does not want him. What is it, then, that Kate wants? Clearly, what she wants is a situation, and situations are described by propositions, in this case 'that Ralph gets out of her life'. In other words, the thematic relationship in (36) holds between *want* and its Subject *Kate*, and between *want* and the string *Ralph to get out of her life*. The latter is a nonfinite clause which takes *Ralph* as its Subject. It functions as a Direct Object.

It appears, then, that *want* is like *believe*. Before drawing this conclusion, however, let's apply our other tests. Consider (37) and (38):

(37)   Kate wanted it to rain on Ralph's birthday.
(38)   Ralph wanted there to be a ceasefire between him and Kate.

In these sentences the dummy elements *it* and *there* appear in postverbal position. We know that they cannot be Direct Objects, because there can be no thematic relationship between a verb and an element that is devoid of meaning. We must therefore analyse *it* and *there* as the Subjects of subordinate clauses. The same conclusion can be drawn from sentences that contain idiom chunks:

(39)   Kate wants the coast to be clear, in order for her to escape from Ralph.

(40)   Kate doesn't want the fat to be in the fire, because of some stupid action of
        Ralph's.

Turning now to the Passivisation test, we find that, if we passivise the postverbal
string of a *want* + NP + *to*-infinitive construction, the meaning of the overall
sentence remains constant:

(41)   Kate wanted Janet to poison Ralph.
(42)   Kate wanted Ralph to be poisoned by Janet.

Again, we conclude that there is no thematic relationship between *want* and the
NPs that follow it, namely *Janet* in (41) and *Ralph* in (42).

It seems, then, that our earlier supposition that *want* is like *believe* is warranted.
However, this is only partially the case. The similarity between *believe* and *want* is
that both verbs take a clausal postverbal argument in the verb + NP + *to*-infinitive
pattern. The difference is that in the case of *believe*, but not in the case of *want*,
the matrix clause can also be passivised:

(43)   Ed believes the jury to have given the wrong verdict. (= (23))
(44)   The jury is believed to have given the wrong verdict by Ed. (= (27))

(45)   Kate wanted Janet to poison Ralph. (= (41))
(46)   *Janet was wanted to poison Ralph by Kate.

This is a general difference between *believe* and *want*, which also shows up when
these verbs take simple Direct Objects in the form of a Noun Phrase:

(47)   Ed believed the wild allegations.
(48)   The wild allegations were believed by Ed.

(49)   Ed wanted a new CD player.
(50)   ?*A new CD player was wanted by Ed.

Summarising our results so far: we have looked at verb + NP + *to*-infinitive constructions involving the verbs *believe*, *persuade* and *want*, and found them to be
different in each case. The differences resulted from the distinct argument-taking
and passivisation properties of these verbs. In Chapter 15 we will discuss a further
construction instantiating the verb + NP + *to*-infinitive pattern, namely *allow* +
NP + *to*-infinitive.

13.2.3   Overview

To conclude our discussion of verb + NP + *to*-infinitive constructions compare
sentences (7), (28) and (36), repeated here as (51), (52) and (53):

(51) Ed believes the story to be false.
(52) Ed persuaded Brian to interview Melanie.
(53) Kate wants Ralph to get out of her life.

All three sentences conform to the pattern verb + NP + *to*-infinitive, and yet they are syntactically different: in the *believe* + NP + *to*-infinitive construction the postverbal NP functions as the Subject of a subordinate clause, while the NP in the *persuade* + NP + *to*-infinitive construction functions as a Direct Object. In the *want* + NP + *to*-infinitive construction the postverbal NP is also the Subject of a subordinate clause, but, unlike the postverbal NP in the *believe* + NP + *to*-infinitive construction, it cannot be fronted when the matrix clause is passivised.

With regard to verb + NP + *to*-infinitive constructions we can now set up three classes of verbs:

Believe class
Verb + Direct Object clause in the form of an NP + *to*-infinitive. The NP can be fronted under passivisation.

Examples: [$_S$ Ed [$_{VP}$ believes [$_{Clause}$ the story to be false]]]
The story is believed — to be false by Ed.

Other verbs: *consider, expect, intend, know, suppose, understand*
(Note: this list is not exhaustive, and some of these verbs can also appear in other patterns.)

Persuade class
Verb + Direct Object NP + second Complement in the form of a *to*-infinitive clause with an implied Subject that is coreferential with the matrix clause DO. The NP can be fronted under passivisation.

Examples: [$_S$ Ed [$_{VP}$ persuaded [$_{NP}$ Brian]$_i$ [$_{Clause}$ Ø$_i$ to interview Melanie]]]
Brian was persuaded — to interview Melanie by Ed.

Other verbs: *advise, convince, notify*
(Note: this list is not exhaustive, and some of these verbs can also appear in other patterns.)

Want class
Verb + Direct Object clause in the form of an NP + *to*-infinitive. The NP cannot be fronted under Passivisation.

Example: [s Kate [vp wanted [Clause Brian to interview Melanie]]]
            *Brian was wanted — to interview Melanie by Kate.

Other verbs: *demand, hate, hope, love, prefer, wish*
               (Note: this list is not exhaustive, and some of these verbs can
               also appear in other patterns.)

13.3 Concluding Remarks

In order to establish the argument-taking properties of a particular predicate we can use tests based on meaning, on the distribution of dummy elements and idiom chunks, as well as on Passivisation. In this chapter we have applied these tests to verb + NP + *to*-infinitive patterns.

It is important to be aware of the fact that the way we resolve issues pertaining to predicates and arguments in particular sentences has consequences for the way that those sentences are analysed into constituents. Thus, for example, we have seen that the NP in the pattern *believe* + NP + *to*-infinitive is arguably not a Direct Object of the verb. The consequence is that the functional bracketing of this pattern should be as in (54) below, not as in (55):

(54)   *believe* [DO NP *to*-infinitive]
(55)   *believe* [DO NP] [Complement *to*-infinitive]

The tests that we have looked at have a use beyond the verb + NP + *to*-infinitive constructions discussed here. In the next chapter we will see how we can use the argumenthood tests, together with the constituency tests, to set up verb complementation patterns in English.

Key Concepts in this Chapter

argumenthood
tests for argumenthood
    the meaning test
    the dummy elements test
    the idiom chunks test
    the passivisation test

Exercises

1. Construct verb + NP + *to*-infinitive constructions with the 'other verbs' given in the three verb classes at the end of Section 13.2.3, and think of possible further verbs that might fit these patterns.

2. In the text we claimed that the NP in *persuade* + NP + *to*-infinitive constructions is a Direct Object. How is the following example a problem for this claim?

(i) We persuaded Charlie to cook and Nick to do the washing up.

3. As we have seen, traditional and modern descriptive grammars of English often use two criteria for establishing whether a particular NP is a Direct Object or not: objective case and passivisation. So, for example, in sentence (i) below *him* is regarded as the DO of *believe*, because this pronoun carries objective case, and because the clause can be passivised, resulting in *him* being fronted, cf. (ii).

(i) She believes him to be an Adonis.
(ii) He is believed to be an Adonis by her.

How does a sentence like (iii) below pose problems for such an account?

(iii) She wants him to be more considerate.

4. Discuss the function of the NP following *prevent* in (i) below. Base your discussion on the sentences in (ii)–(iv).

(i) Des prevented the council from granting planning permission.
(ii) Des prevented planning permission from being granted by the council.
(iii) Des prevented there from being an outcry over the council's planning policy.
(iv) Des prevented the fat from being in the fire.
(v) In Soviet times artificial means were often used to prevent it from raining.

5. In this chapter we have seen that expletive elements like *it* and *there* cannot occur in Direct Object position (cf. Section 13.1.2). The reason is that they do not carry meaning, and cannot therefore be assigned a thematic role. Because DO positions are always assigned a thematic role, expletives are barred from appearing in this position. Postal and Pullum (1988) have challenged the claim that expletives cannot occur in DO position. They cite expressions like those below.

(i) Beat it.
(ii) Cool it.
(iii) Move it.
(iv) Hop it.

How are these examples problematic for the claim that expletives cannot occur in subcategorised positions? Is there a way of dealing with these data without abandoning our claim?

*6. Consider the following sentences, taken from T. Givón's *English Grammar* (1993: 125).

   (i) They elected him president.
   (ii) They appointed her judge.
   (iii) We consider them members.
   (iv) They judge him a good man.
   (v) She deemed their marriage a fiasco.

  Givón treats all these sentences as being syntactically the same. More specifically, he claims that their main verbs all take *two Direct Objects*. Assess this claim paying particular attention to the thematic roles each of the individual verbs assigns to its arguments in (i)–(v). You will of course first need to establish which are the arguments of each of these verbs.

*7. In Morenberg's *Doing Grammar* (first edition, 1991) the following observation about Direct Objects is made.

  [o]ften the subject of a transitive verb 'does something to' the object noun phrase.

                    (1991: 6)

  In the following sentences Morenberg regards the postverbal NPs as Direct Objects:

   (i) American analysts *consider* Kaddafi a terrorist.
   (ii) Soviet music critics *consider* the Rolling Stones decadent.

  Do you agree that the Subject 'does something to' the postverbal NPs here? Morenberg goes on to observe that:

  In the first example, *consider* is followed by a noun, *Kaddafi*, that functions as a direct object, and that is in turn followed by a noun phrase, *a terrorist*, that functions as a COMPLEMENT. Similarly, the [verb] in the second example is followed by a noun, *the Rolling Stones*, and then by an adjective, *decadent*. Whether it is an adjective or noun, by the way, this type of complement that follows a direct object in a sentence with a [verb like *consider*] is called an OBJECT COMPLEMENT...A complement in grammar is rather like one in mathematics: it completes something, not a 90° angle, but an idea. In the example sentences above, 'American analysts' don't simply 'consider Kaddafi', but they 'consider him *a terrorist*'; nor do Soviet music critics 'consider the Rolling Stones', but they consider the Rolling Stones *decadent*.

                   (1991: 8–9)

Write a short critique of these passages. (Be aware of the fact that Morenberg uses different terminology from that used in this book. In fairness, in subsequent editions of his book, Morenberg changed the passage above.)

*8.   In Section 13.2.2 we analysed the sentence *Kate wanted Janet to poison Ralph* (= (41)) as in (i) below:

(i)   Kate wanted [$_{DO}$ Janet to poison Ralph]

We saw that we cannot passivise the main clause:

(ii)   *Janet was wanted to poison Ralph by Kate. (= (46))

And then we saw that in general *want* does not allow Passivisation:

(iii)   Ed wanted a new CD player.
(iv)   *A new CD player was wanted by Ed.

How can we use the data above to support the claim that *want* is in fact like *believe*, and not in a class of its own?

Further Reading

The criteria for argumenthood presented in this chapter are often not mentioned or explained in grammars or textbooks dealing with English syntax, or, if they are mentioned, they are not dealt with systematically in one place. It is therefore difficult to recommend further reading. However, you may wish to consult Huddleston (1984), Palmer (1987), Radford (1988) or Haegeman (2006) which deal with some of the material discussed here, but you will need to make deft use of the tables of contents and indexes of these works.

Part IV
Application

14   Grammatical Indeterminacy

Argumentation plays an important role in linguistics, because at every stage of linguistic inquiry we have to make motivated choices in favour or against particular analyses. These choices often have repercussions. For example, analysing *him* in a sentence like *I believe him to be friendly* as the Subject of a subordinate clause means that we have to drop the traditional assumption that only Direct Objects can be fronted under Passivisation; after all, in *He is believed to be friendly* a Subject has been fronted (namely the Subject of the subordinate clause *him to be friendly*), not a Direct Object. The importance of argumentation is especially clear when we deal with issues pertaining to constituency and argumenthood, as we have seen in previous chapters. However, it is not just in these areas that argumentation is important, but at just about every stage of analysis. For this reason it is essential that you have a good understanding of the way argumentation proceeds. The aim of this part of the book is two-fold: in this chapter we will look more closely at categorisation and the important role it has played, and continues to play, in linguistics. Specifically, we will be looking at what we might call 'grammatical indeterminacies', that is, cases where it is not immediately obvious which category to assign a particular element to. The aim of Chapter 15 is to engage you in syntactic argumentation yourself. To this end we will discuss a number of case studies which illustrate the kind of reasoning involving argumentation that has come to play such a crucial role in linguistics.

14.1   Category Boundaries and Gradience

So far in this book we have classified words, phrases and clauses into a number of different categories, like noun, verb, Noun Phrase, Adjective Phrase, main clause, subordinate clause, etc. Many of these categories have been in use for centuries. Ideas on classification have been strongly influenced by Aristotle (384–322 BC) who held that elements are assigned to categories if a number of defining criteria jointly apply. If one of the defining criteria of a class α does not apply to a particular element, then it cannot be a member of α. Aristotle also claimed that elements cannot belong to more than one category at the same time, and that all members of a category have equal status. However, work in psychology has shown that the Aristotelian view of categorisation is too strong. For example, when people are shown a series of pictures of different types of birds, they do not consider all birds as being equally 'birdy'. Instead, they will pick out the sparrow as a typical representative of the category of birds, while birds like penguins and emus are regarded as less typical because they cannot fly. Typical exemplars are called 'prototypes'. In grammar too we can observe that there are typical members of grammatical categories and less typical members as regards their distributional properties. I refer to this phenomenon as *Subsective Gradience* (SG). We can also observe in grammar that some elements share properties of more than one word class. This is called *Intersective Gradience* (IG). I will look at some examples of SG and IG in the next two sections.

14.2　Subsective Gradience

14.2.1　Nouns

Consider the words *dog* and *there*. The first is clearly a noun if we apply the criteria for nounhood from Chapter 3, namely (c1)–(c4):

c1　The phrase of which the item is the Head can function as Subject and/or Direct Object, which are typical NP positions: *the dog chased the cat/the vulture ate the dog.*

c2　The item can be preceded by a determinative like *a* or *the*: *a/the dog.*

c3　The item can take a genitival suffix: *dog's.*

c4　The item can take a plural suffix: *dogs.*

If we apply these criteria to the word *information* we find that Criteria (c1)–(c3) apply, but not (c4). What about the word *there*? In this case we find that this word is an even less typical noun because it cannot be preceded by a determinative, nor can it take a genitival or plural suffix. However, as we have already seen, it *is* possible for *there* to occur in Subject position (though not in Direct Object position): *there are four dogs in the kitchen.* We can say, then, that *there* is a 'defective' noun, less typical than *dog* and *information*. We can show the difference in behaviour between *dog, information* and *there* in a matrix:

Nouns	c1	c2	c3	c4
dog	√	√	√	√
information	√	√	√	x
there	√	x	x	x

Arguably also less typical nouns are so-called *pluralia tantum*. These are words like *scissors, trousers*, etc. which only appear in the plural.

14.2.2 Adjectives

Within the class of adjectives a word like *nice* is a typical member because all the adjective criteria that we discussed in Chapter 3 apply to it, namely:

c1.   ability to appear in attributive position: *a nice house*
c2.   ability to appear in predicative position: *that house is nice*
c3.   ability to be preceded by an intensifier like *very*: *very nice*, and
c4.   ability to take comparative and superlative forms: *nice/nicer/nicest.*

A word like *utter* is less typically adjectival, the reason being that it cannot be preceded by *very*, has no comparative or superlative forms, and cannot appear in predicative position.

Exercise

Which of the criteria above apply to *ill* in your speech?

For some speakers this word is a central member of the class of adjectives because it conforms to all the adjective criteria, while for others *ill* is a peripheral adjective because for them an NP like *the ill student* is not acceptable. What about the adjective *alive*? The number of speakers who would reject *alive* occurring in attributive position (as in *an alive rat*) is probably quite large, and for them this word is a peripheral member of the class of adjectives. However, there are signs that *alive* is becoming a more central member of its class, witness the following example I came across in a newspaper:

> Snow, who lives in Kentish Town, has *an alive presence*, an abiding awareness, a serious desire to seek the truth and make some sense of life amid the vortex of confusion in the modern world that daily manifests itself on screen, along with his charismatic ties.

In this example *alive* occurs before the Head noun, maybe by analogy with the structure of the following NPs (*abiding awareness, serious desire*), thus creating neatly parallel patterns. We thus see a cline of typicality of membership within the class of adjectives, which can again be shown in a matrix:

Adjectives	c1	c2	c3	c4
nice	√	√	√	√
ill	?	√	√	√
alive	?	√	?	?
utter	√	x	x	x

14.2.3   Verbs

In this book we have taken auxiliary verbs to be main verbs, an analysis that is controversial, but nevertheless fairly widely adopted (for example in Huddleston and Pullum's *Cambridge Grammar of the English Language*, published in 2002). This is not to say, of course, that there are no differences between the 'auxiliaries' and 'regular main verbs'. As we saw in Chapter 3, auxiliaries display the NICE properties, while main verbs do not. In addition, notice that auxiliaries do not take verbal endings like the third person singular -*s* or -*ing*, as the following examples make clear:

(1)   *He musts go to Paris.
(2)   *She wills eat fish and chips.
(3)   *We are canning to open the door.

Notice also that while most auxiliary verbs have morphological past tenses (*will/would, shall/should, can/could*, etc.), the verb *must* has no past tense form (**musted*). Again, then, we see that within the class of verbs, different elements distributionally behave differently. This can lead us to do two things: either we say that there are two different classes, namely auxiliary verbs and main verbs, or we say that all these elements belong to a single class of verbs whose members are more or less typical exemplars of their class. The first strategy is often called 'splitting', the second 'lumping'. In this book we have opted to lump together the auxiliaries and main verbs in one class, because there are enough properties that all these elements share.

14.2.4   Prepositions

As we have seen, prepositions are usually short monosyllabic words followed by a Noun Phrase Complement (*in the house, on the mat*). Many prepositions allow 'stranding', which occurs when an NP Complement is moved to the front of a sentence, as in the following examples:

(4)   What are you looking at –? (cf. I am looking *at the window.*)
(5)   Which book did you get a discount for –? (cf. I got a discount *for all the books.*)

However, not all prepositions allow stranding felicitously, especially complex ones:

(6)   ?What did he put the document inside –? (cf. He put the document *inside the box*)
(7)   ?Who did she leave without –? (cf. She left *without her sister.*)

This leads us to set up a gradient of 'prepositionhood' which looks like this:

more typically prepositional > less typically prepositional

strandable prepositions > non-strandable prepositions

But we're not quite there yet, because we also have a number of items which have sometimes been called 'marginal prepositions'. They include for example *not-withstanding* which is an odd word because it can be a *pre*position, as in *notwith-standing his excellent results*, as well as a *post*position, as in *his excellent results notwithstanding*. The words *apart* and *aside* behave similarly syntactically. We can now refine the gradient above as follows:

more typically prepositional > less typically prepositional

strandable prepositions > non-strandable prepositions > marginal prepositions

We have seen, then, that it is possible to recognise a number of items within the class of prepositions as being more typical exemplars of the class than others.

14.3   Intersective Gradience

In the sections that follow we will look at a number of cases where elements appear to belong to more than one class at the same time. We will see, however, that in all of these cases a particular set of word class properties outweighs another set of properties.

14.3.1   Word Classes: Adjective or Adverb?

Consider the Noun Phrase below:

(8)   the *then* President of America

The question we need to address here is which word class we should assign *then* to. Although it looks like an adverb, it would not be unreasonable to hypothesise that this word is in fact an adjective, because it is positioned immediately in front of the Head noun *President*, a typical adjectival position. We should then investigate whether *then* behaves like an adjective in other respects too. For example, we might ask whether it can be preceded by a modifier like *very*. The answer is clearly 'no', as the following phrase shows:

(9)   *the *very then* President of America

Next, we might see whether *then* takes comparative or superlative forms. It turns out that it is impossible to form comparative or superlative forms for *then*:

(10)   *the *more/most then* President of America

You will recall from Chapter 3 that another typical property of adjectives is that they can occur predicatively (review Section 3.3 if you've forgotten what this term means).

Exercise

Try to construct a sentence in which *then* occurs in predicative position after a linking verb.

You will have found that *then* cannot occur predicatively:

(11)   *The President of America was *then*.

We have to conclude that *then* shares only one of the properties of adjectives, namely the ability to occur in attributive position in Noun Phrases. However, this is not a sufficient reason for assigning this word to the adjective class. What we will say is that *then* is an adverb which can exceptionally be placed in front of a noun, in the same way that some nouns can be placed in front of other nouns (as in, e.g., *the fan heater*).

14.3.2   *Word Classes: Verb or Noun?*

Consider the following examples, taken from Quirk et al.:

(12)   some paintings of Brown's
(13)   Brown's paintings of his daughters
(14)   The painting of Brown is *as skilful as that of Gainsborough.*
(15)   Brown's deft painting of his daughter *is a delight to watch.*
(16)   Brown's deftly painting his daughter *is a delight to watch.*
(17)   *I dislike* Brown's painting his daughter.
(18)   *I dislike* Brown painting his daughter. (when she ought to be at school)
(19)   *I watched* Brown painting his daughter. (*'I watched Brown as he painted'/'I watched the process of Brown('s) painting his daughter'*)
(20)   Brown deftly painting his daughter *is a delight to watch.*
(21)   Painting his daughter, *Brown noticed that his hand was shaking.*
(22)   Brown painting his daughter that day, *I decided to go for a walk.*
(23)   The man painting the girl *is Brown.*
(24)   The silently painting man *is Brown.*
(25)   *Brown* is painting *his daughter.*

(1985: 1290–1)

At the top end of this sequence the word *painting* is clearly a noun: it has a deter-minative in front of it and is followed by a PP. At the bottom end *painting* is clearly verbal by virtue of being part of a progressive construction. Somewhere in the middle of the sequence we run into some less clear-cut cases. How should we categorise *painting* in (16)? There appears to be a mixing of different types of properties: nominal and verbal. Let's look at these properties in more detail, starting with the nominal ones. It turns out that *painting* has only two nominal properties:

- It is the head of a phrase positioned in the Subject slot, which is a typical position for NPs to occur in, and
- It occurs with a genitival determinative: *Brown's*

The number of verbal properties is as follows:

- *painting* has a verbal inflection;
- it occurs with an NP Complement;
- it is preceded by a manner adverb;
- it can be preceded by *not*;
- Passivisation of the italicised string is possible: *His daughter's being deftly painted by Brown* is a delight to watch;
- a perfective auxiliary can be inserted: *Brown's having deftly painted his daughter* was a true feat.

What can we conclude from these facts? Well, what at first sight appears to be a hybrid structure that displays both nominal and verbal properties is in fact probably best regarded as verbal, because the latter properties outweigh the former. All this leads us to analyse the string *Brown's deftly painting his daughter* in (16) as a clause which functions as the Subject of the overall sentence.

14.3.3   *Phrases: Adjective Phrase or Prepositional Phrase?*

So far we have looked at Intersective Gradience between word classes. What about phrases? Can we have gradience between phrasal categories? Consider the following examples:

(26)   *off-campus* facilities
(27)   *with-profits* shares

These are set phrases used in the worlds of education and finance, respectively. Sometimes these items are listed as adjectives in dictionaries. We can also come across more creatively used examples, such as the following attested example:

(28)   the *under-construction* stadium

In each of these cases we have what look to be PPs in typical pre-noun adjective positions. Now, recall from Section 10.2.2.1 that we have two types of prepositions: transitive and intransitive, the latter occurring in verb-preposition constructions such as *let the dog out, look up the facts*, etc. If we regard *in, through, up* and *above* in the examples that follow as intransitive prepositions then again we have PPs in attributive position:

(29)   the *in* crowd
(30)   a *through* road
(31)   the *down* escalator
(32)   the *above* examples

So are we dealing here with PPs modifying the Head or are we dealing with Adjective Phrases? The latter analysis would be misguided because occurring in attributive position is the only adjectival property that the italicised items in (26)–(32) possess. Other adjectival properties (see Section 14.2.2) do not apply: the items in question can't be placed in predicative position; it is impossible to put intensifiers in front of them and they do not have comparative or superlative forms. But we should also note that the PP modifiers *right* and *straight* (see Section 10.2.2.1) cannot be put in front of the italicised items. If we look at these examples in terms of which properties predominate, we would have to say that calling the italicised items PPs makes most sense, but this is by no means a secure conclusion. If they are PPs, they are certainly not typical ones.

14.3.4   Constructional Gradience

In Quirk et al.'s *Comprehensive Grammar of the English Language* (1985: 1218f.) we find a cline (or gradient) between V + NP + *to*-infinitive patterns of the type we discussed in Chapter 13:

(33)   We like *all parents* to visit the school.
(34)   They expected *James* to win the race.
(35)   We asked *the students* to attend a lecture.

They say that in (33) the italicised NP is clearly not an argument of the verb while in (35) it certainly is. By contrast, in (34) the postverbal NP has both Subject properties and Direct Object properties: it is Subject-like with respect to the verb *win*, but Object-like with respect to *expect*.

Exercise

Referring to chapter 13, what would you say are the Subject-like properties of *James* in (34), and what are its Direct Object-like properties?

James is Subject-like because this NP has the role of Agent with respect to the predicate *win*. Also, *expect* can be followed by non-referential *it*, by existential *there* and by Subject idiom chunks. What's more, if we passivise the subordinate clause the meaning does not change (*they expected James to win the race = they expected the race to be won by James*). By contrast, what makes *James* Direct Object-like is the fact that if we replace this name by a pronoun, it must be a pronoun in the objective case (*they expected* him *to win*). Also, we can say *James was expected to win the race*, where the main clause has been passivised. We thus seem to have gradience between the following structures: V NP [*to*-infinitive] and V [NP + *to*-infinitive]. As we saw in Chapter 13, the solution to this grammatical indeterminacy has been to say that on balance there is rather more evidence for saying that *James* is a Subject in (34). However, it is important to stress that not everyone would agree. Some linguists would argue that although *James* is not a *semantic* argument of *expect*, *grammatically* it is still a Direct Object.

14.4   Concluding Remarks

Gradience, conceived of as grammatical indeterminacy, pervades grammar. In this chapter I have distinguished between two types: Subsective Gradience and Intersective Gradience. We have seen that the former involves the recognition that members of grammatical categories can be more or less typical exemplars of their class, while the latter involves the phenomenon of particular elements displaying distributional features of two classes. Despite this, with IG we should not conclude that the elements in question belong to two classes at the same time. Instead, there is usually a preponderance of distributional features associated with one of the two classes, which then 'wins out'.

Key Concepts in this Chapter

grammatical indeterminacy
gradience
Subsective Gradience
Intersective Gradience
  constructional gradience

Exercises

1. In the following Noun Phrases is the italicised element a verb or an adjective? Give reasons for your answer.

(i)   a *disappointing* result
(ii)   a *waiting* taxi
(iii)   a *moving* film
(iv)   a *moving* target

2. To which word class would you assign the italicised elements in the bracketed Noun Phrases below? Give reasons for your answer.

(i)   [The *freeing* of the hostages] was a dangerous enterprise.
(ii)   [This *computer* virus] was developed by a hacker in America.

3. In (i) below, is *broken* an adjective or a verb? How do you decide?

(i)   The window was broken.

4. Consider the word *fun*. Which word class would you assign this word to? Next, consider the sentences below. Do they confirm or refute your answer?

(i)   I want to have some fun today.
(ii)   For children running up and down the stairs is fun.
(ii)   He's fun to be with and friendly.
(iii)   It was so fun!
(iv)   Now let's think of someone fun. (*Oxford English Dictionary*)
(v)   This is the funnest thing I've ever done.

Further Reading

There is a vast literature in psychology and linguistics on prototypes, but less work on gradience in grammar. However, see, for example, Taylor (2003) on linguistic categorisation. For a collection of texts on vagueness, prototypes and the like, see Aarts, Denison, Keizer and Popova (2004). The problems we encounter in assigning words to word classes are discussed in Huddleston (1984), Chapters 3 and 9, and in Aarts (2007a). The latter is a monograph on gradience in grammar, and contains a wealth of further references.

15 Case Studies

This final chapter will give you the opportunity to practise syntactic argumentation by working your way through a number of case studies which centre on specific problem areas in the syntax of English. In each case we'll be tackling the problems in the same way: we start out with a hypothesis as to how to solve the problem at hand, and we then proceed to find arguments that either support or disconfirm the initial analysis. Sometimes we will arrive at a conclusion, sometimes we won't. This last point is important, as you will come to realise that there are many unsolved issues in English syntax.

15.1 Negated Modal Auxiliaries

In Chapter 11 we discussed the processes of VP-Deletion and V'-Deletion. To refresh your memory, here are some of the sentences we looked at:

(1) 'Can you play the piano?'
    'Yes, I can – .'

(2) 'You take chances, Marlow.'
    'I get paid to –.'   (from: *The Big Sleep*)

(3) Dawn will clean the windows diligently, but Shawn will – lazily.
(4) Ray will rudely interrupt the speaker, but Bruce will politely – .

We argued that in (1) and (2) VPs have been deleted, while in (3) and (4) V-bars have been left out.
   Let's now look at some further examples:

(5) Nick should read more books, but he can't – .
(6) Millie can lend her sister some money, but she won't – .

Exercise

What lexical material has been deleted here?

In (5) we have deleted a V + DO sequence (*read more books*), while in (6) a V + IO + DO string (*lend her sister some money*) has been left out. The question now arises how to account for these sentences. The problem centres around the negated modal verbs *can't* and *won't*. Recall that we argued that modals are positioned in

'I'. We also claimed that negative elements like *not* are positioned in the Specifier-of-VP position. But we haven't yet dealt with elements like *can't, won't, mustn't,* etc. in which the negative element is tagged onto the modal. The problem with negated modals is that they appear to be units. But this is irreconcilable with the fact that the modal itself belongs to the I-node, while the negative bit *-n't* belongs to VP. There are now two possible analyses for sentences like (5) and (6).

One way of looking at (5) and (6) is to say that in the *but*-clauses the negative element *not* first moves up to 'I' and then merges with the modal, after which the VP-shell is deleted. This process is shown in (7) for (5), and in (8) for (6):

(7)   Nick should read more books, but...

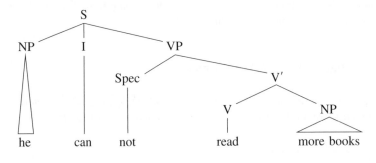

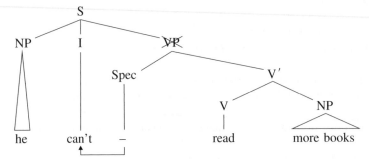

(8)   Millie can lend her sister some money, but...

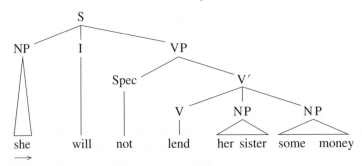

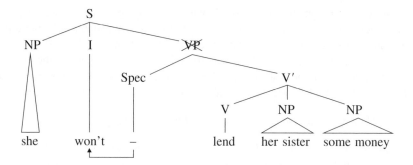

An alternative way of looking at (5) and (6) is to assume that in the *but*-clauses the negated modals are positioned in 'I' and that what gets deleted is the following VP as a whole. Under this view we take negated modals to be lexical elements in their own right and there is no movement.

(9)   Nick should read more books, but...

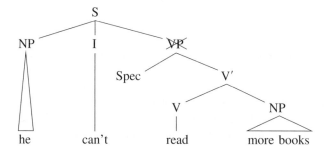

(10)   Millie can lend her sister some money, but...

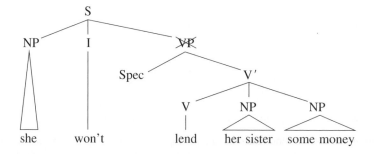

Which of these views is correct? You will have realised that the two accounts are only very subtly different, but it should nevertheless be possible to give arguments which favour one or the other analysis. Recall that in (7) and (8) we have a movement process, while in (9) and (10) we are regarding the negated modal as a lexical element in its own right.

Notice that under the first view, shown in (7)/(8), we need a new rule of *not-movement*. Of course, there is nothing to stop us positing such a rule, but unless we can find independent justification for it (see Section 10.3.2), this strategy is unappealing. However, even if we were to find some independent justification, the rule would be complicated to state. The reason is that it would not be exception-less, because not all modal verbs can contract with the negative element *not*:

(11)　He may not arrive early./ *He mayn't arrive early.

Furthermore, notice that unlike contractions like *he will > he'll*, where *will* is simply tagged onto the pronoun and two letters are omitted, negative elements do not combine with the modals in such a straightforward way. Thus, we have *will + not > won't* and *shall + not > shan't*, etc., which show that contraction would involve idiosyncratic modifications such as vowel changes.

What about the second proposal, in which the negated modals are regarded as lexical items in their own right? The first point to observe is that it is much more simple: we assume that the grammar selects negated modals directly from the lexicon and inserts them in 'I'. Is there any more to say? Consider (12):

(12)　You can't not invite your boss.

You can imagine somebody saying this to a colleague who has just announced that he is not going to invite his boss to a party. What's interesting about (12) is that, in addition to -*n't* being tagged onto the modal, there is a second negative element, namely *not*, which is placed immediately before the verb *invite*. (Notice, incidentally, that it is stressed.) We can account for the structure of this sentence straightforwardly if we assume that the negated modal is positioned in 'I', while *not* is positioned in the Specifier-of-VP position:

(13)

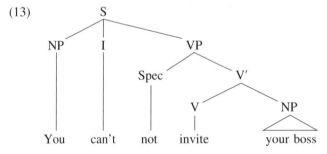

If we assumed movement of *not* to 'I', we would be able to account for the first, but not for the second, negative element in this sentence. Consider next (14):

(14)　You can't kiss her and not touch her.

Here again we have a negated modal and a second negative element further to the right in the sentence. Assuming once more that the negated modal is positioned

in 'I', we can easily account for the syntax of this sentence, by coordinating two
VPs, as below:

(15)

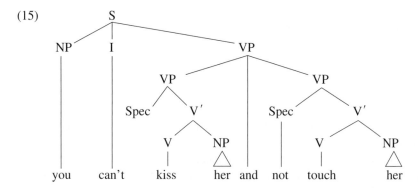

If we assumed *not*-movement, we would have to explain why the first *not* moves,
but not the second. Furthermore, (15) accounts naturally for what are called the
scope properties of the first negative element: what (14) means is that what you
cannot do is 'kiss her and not touch her'. What it doesn't mean is that you can 'not
kiss her and not touch her', which would be the expected meaning if the first *not*
originated inside the leftmost of the coordinated VPs.

The conclusion of this discussion must be that negated modals are positioned in
'I', and that there is no process of *not*-movement.

15.2 Noun Phrase Structure

In this section we will be looking at some problems in the structural analysis of
Noun Phrases.

15.2.1 A Lot of Books

When we discussed X-bar syntax in Chapter 7 we saw that all phrases must be
properly headed. Thus, a Verb Phrase must be headed by a verb, a Prepositional
Phrase must be headed by a preposition, and so on. There are cases, however,
where it is not clear which particular element is the Head. In this section we will
be looking at Noun Phrases of the type in (16) below:

(16)   a lot of books

In this NP we have *two* nouns, namely *lot* and *books*, and we might wonder
which is the Head of the overall NP. Your first inclination might be to say that

the first noun must the Head, with the structure in (17) for the NP as a whole:

(17)

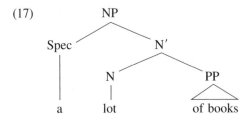

Here we have analysed the PP *of books* as a sister (i.e. Complement) of the Head noun *lot*.

Another possibility is to take the second noun (*books*) in (16) to be the Head. It then becomes more difficult to decide what would be the tree structure representation of the NP. Structures like those in (18) and (19), among others, have been put forward in the linguistic literature:

(18)

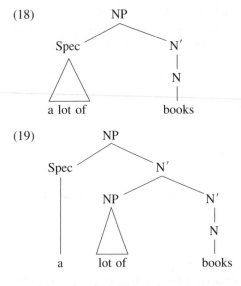

(19)

In (18) the sequence *a lot of* is regarded as a complex Specifier, while in (19) *a* is the Specifier and *lot of* is a complex modifying string.

How do we decide between these three representations? You will have realised that the nature of the problem we are dealing with here concerns the constituency of the NP in (16). Can we use any of the constituency tests of Chapters 11 and 12 to help us out? Let us take a closer look at each of the trees in (17)–(19).

With regard to the structure in (17) notice that it parallels noun + Complement sequences of the type we have in (20) which we analysed in Chapter 7 in the same way as in (17), namely as a noun taking a PP as its sister:

(20)   This newspaper publishes *a review of books* every month.

However, recall that whereas we can draw a parallel between *review of books* in (20) and the verbal construction *[they] review books*, the string *of books* in (16) seems to be a different kind of Complement from the PP in (20) to the extent that the noun *lot* cannot be related to a verb in the way that *review* can. So from the point of view of meaning there doesn't seem to be much support for (17). We should now ask whether analysing the PP *of books* in (17) as a constituent can be motivated *syntactically*. By proposing an analysis along the lines of (17) we are making an important claim regarding the constituency of (16). Notice that the words *of* and *books* together form a Prepositional Phrase. It should be possible for us to test whether this string actually behaves like a constituent. Not all of our tests are applicable to this structure, but quite a few are. We consider movement first. Compare the following pairs of sentences:

Movement

(21)   *[Of books] we buy a lot – .
(22)   We don't publish a review of CDs, but [of books] we do (publish a review –).

Here in both cases the PP *of books* has been moved to the left under Topicalisation. Clearly, the result is much worse in (21) than it is in (22). This suggests that there is a difference between the *of*-string in (21) and the undisputed Complement *of books* in (22).

So far we have only looked at leftward movement. Let's now see if the *of*-string in question can be moved to the right. In the following passive sentences we cannot move the *of*-string from a NP containing the noun *lot*, but moving the same string from a NP headed by *review* causes no problems:

(23)   *A lot – were rubbished [of books by new young novelists].
(24)   A review – was published [of books by David Lodge].

Again we see that the string introduced by *of* in (23) behaves differently from that in (24).

The data in (22) and (24) *prove* that the *of*-strings are constituents. In (21) and (23), however, we must be careful: here we cannot draw any firm conclusions about the constituency of the PPs. Remember that the movement test works only in one direction: if we can move a string of words it is a constituent, but if we cannot move a string of words, it is not necessarily not a constituent. We need to look at some further data before we can draw any conclusions.

The substitution test isn't of any use to us in this case, because only locative PPs can be replaced by a proform (namely *there*, see Section 10.2.2.1).

Of the tests of Chapter 12, only coordination and the cleft construction are useful. Compare first the sentences below:

Coordination

(25)   *We buy a lot [of books] and [of records].
(26)   We published a review [of books] and [of CDs]

In (25) it is impossible to coordinate the *of*-strings, whereas this poses no problems in (26). This again suggests that the PPs are constituents in (26), but not in (25).

We turn now to the cleft construction:

Cleft construction

(27)   *It is [of books] that he buys a lot.
(28)   It is [of books] that we publish a review.

Once again we end up with a contrast in grammaticality: (27) is clearly bad, while (28) is perhaps somewhat clumsy, but certainly markedly better than (27). The constituency of the PP in (28) is again established, whereas the *of*-string in (27) is likely not to be a constituent.

We have so far looked at data which strongly suggest that the *of*-string in the *review of books*-NP is a true constituent, whereas the *of*-string in the *lot of books*-NP is not. We turn next to a piece of evidence that will clinch the matter. Consider (29):

(29)   A lot of books were destroyed by the fire.

This example is very instructive. Notice that the verb *were* agrees in number with what is evidently a *plural* Noun Phrase. As the number of an NP is determined by its Head, we conclude that *books* is the Head of the NP *a lot of books* in (29).

Summarising the evidence we have amassed so far, we can say that there are three different processes (movement, coordination and clefting) which suggest that the sequence *of books* in the NP *a lot of books* is not a constituent. Furthermore, the observed number concord between *a lot of books* and a following plural verb leads us to conclude that *books* is the Head of the overall NP.

Notice that both (18) and (19) reflect the fact that *of books* is not a constituent and that *books* is the Head. We now need to decide between these two analyses. One thing that will immediately strike you is that in (18) *a lot of* and in (19) *lot of* are analysed as constituents. This looks a bit funny, as intuitively we don't feel these strings to be units. I will return to this matter in a moment.

Deciding between (18) and (19) is quite straightforward. Recall that we established that *books* is the Head of the NP *a lot of books*. If this is so, then the representation in (19) is automatically ruled out because Specifiers must agree with their Heads (cf. *those book*, *this windows*), as you'll remember from earlier chapters. In (19) the Specifier is singular, while the Head is plural.

The correct representation of the NP *a lot of books*, pending further possible evidence, would seem to be (18), where *a lot of* is regarded as a complex Specifier.

Additional support for this analysis comes from the fact that we can substitute *many* for *a lot of*.

An objection to (18), hinted at above, could be the fact that intuitively *a lot of* doesn't look like a constituent. However, if we allow ourselves to view grammar in a slightly different way than we have been doing so far, namely as a system that is constantly in a state of flux in which shifts in patternings can occur, then maybe (18) becomes less strange. We could hypothesise that initially *lot* was the Head of the NP *a lot of books*, but that over time users of the language have begun to feel that *a lot of* somehow functions as a complex Specifier. A process like this is an instance of *grammaticalisation*, which happens when elements which formerly behaved like individual lexical items regroup and attain a particular grammatical function (e.g. Specifier, Adjunct, etc.). All of this is speculative, and you may want to look at the Further Reading section at the end of this chapter for references to discussions of this topic in the linguistic literature.

15.2.2 A Giant of a Man

We now turn to a construction that bears some similarities to the one discussed in the previous section.

(30)   a   A *giant* of a *man*
       b   That *idiot* of a *policeman*
       c   These *nitwits* of *politicians*
       d   Those *geniuses* of *doctors*

Because they contain two prominent nouns we will call NPs like those in (30) *Binominal Noun Phrases (BNPs)*. I will refer to the leftmost noun as N^1, and to the rightmost noun as N^2. Just like the construction we discussed in the previous section, it is not immediately obvious which of the two italicised nouns in the examples above is the Head of the BNP. In discovering what the best analysis is for binominal NPs we will follow the same line of argumentation as we did in the previous sections.

Let's start by looking at some of the characteristics of BNPs. First of all, they are often used as negative qualifications, though not always, as (30)d shows. Notice that the NPs that can occur in this construction can be either singular ((30)a–b), or plural ((30)c–d). In the singular *both* nouns are singular and N^2 is always preceded by the determinative *a*. In the plural *both* nouns are plural, and nothing precedes N^2. Any plural determinative can precede N^1.

Exercise

Draw two trees for the NP *a giant of a man*. In one of these assume that *a* is a determinative, *giant* is the Head and *of a man* its Complement. In the other tree, again take *a* to be a determinative, *giant of a* to be a complex Adjunct in the shape of an NP, and *man* to be the Head. Use triangles for the complex Adjunct and for the PPs.

The trees are as follows:

(31)

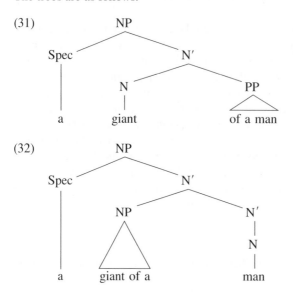

(32)

In (31) N^1 is the Head and the PP *of a man* is its Complement. By contrast, in (32) N^2 is the Head and *giant of a* is regarded as a constituent that modifies *man*. (I have assigned the label 'NP' to *giant of a* which may seem somewhat odd, but this problem is peripheral to our present concerns.) We now need to see which of the representations above fits in best with the evidence we can gather.

At first sight (31) looks more plausible than (32). This is because intuitively we don't feel that *giant of a* in (32) forms a unit. However, we shouldn't be relying on our intuitions, at least not exclusively, but should argue systematically for or against either of these analyses.

Before discussing the trees above further, let us briefly return to the phrases in (30). Recall that the issue that we are investigating is which of the two nominals is the Head of the BNP. A criterion for headedness that has been put forward by linguists stipulates that the Head of a construction is the element of which the phrase as a whole is a kind. With regard to the BNPs in (30) it is easy to see that N^2 qualifies as the Head in each case. After all, *a giant of a man* is a kind of man, not a kind of giant and *an idiot of a policeman* is a kind of policeman, not a kind of idiot, etc. So there is some initial evidence for an analysis of BNPs along the lines of (32) where N^2 is the Head.

Now, let us take a closer look at (31). The syntactic claim that this tree structure makes is not only that N^1 is the Head, but also that *of a man* is a constituent. We should now test whether this is indeed the case. Contrast the following sentences:

(33)   *[Of a man], he was a giant – .
(34)   The company didn't announce the release of the record, but [of the CD] they did (announce the release –).

Moving the *of*-string to the left results in ungrammaticality in (33), but not in (34). Again, as in (21) and (22), we notice a difference between the *of*-string in (33) and the undisputed Complement *of the CD* in (34) (cf. *They released the CD.*). The different behaviour of the two *of*-strings is likely to be due to the fact that in (33) *of a man* is not a constituent.

What about rightward movement?

Exercise

In the following sentences, try moving *of a man* and *of a CD by the Pope* to the right (cf. (23) and (24) above):
(i)   A giant of a man was arrested.
(ii)   The release of a CD by the Pope was announced.

The results are as follows:

(35)   *A giant – was arrested [of a man].
(36)   The release – was announced [of a CD by the Pope].

Again, the string introduced by *of* in (35) behaves differently from that in (36). As we have seen, in (36) the *of*-string is without doubt a Complement, but not in (35).

Let's now try to apply the coordination test. We get the following results:

(37)   *We spotted a giant [of a man] and [of a woman].
(38)   We announced the release [of a CD] and [of a record]

In (37) it is impossible to coordinate the *of*-strings, whereas this poses no problems in (38). This again suggests that the PPs are constituents in (38), but not in (37).

Exercise

Now, using (27) and (28) as a model, apply the cleft test to the *of*-strings in (i) and (ii) of the previous exercise.

The results are as in (39) and (40):

(39)   *It was [of a giant] that a man was arrested.
(40)   It was [of a CD by the Pope] that the release was announced.

All the data we have been looking at show that in the second sentence of each of the pairs the *of*-string is a constituent. The ungrammaticality of the first sentence in each pair suggests that the *of*-strings are not constituents.

At this point in our discussion it is beginning to look as though (31) is not an appropriate representation for the BNP *a giant of a man*. In other words, there are strong reasons for taking N^2 to be the Head of BNP constructions. What other evidence can we find that could decide the matter? What about Subject-verb agreement when we pluralise BNPs? Recall that when we discussed the NP *a lot of books* we saw that a following verb must be plural, cf. (29), repeated here:

(41)   [A lot of books] *were* destroyed by the fire.

On the basis of this sentence we decided that *books* is the Head in the bracketed NP above. In the case of BNPs we cannot use this test, because both N^1 and N^2 are either both singular or both plural:

(42)   A giant of a man *was* arrested after the incident.
(43)   Giants of men *were* arrested after the incident.

Consider next the following BNPs (all attested examples, so no apologies for their political incorrectness):

(44)   this oceanic barge of a woman
(45)   another bitchy iceberg of a woman

I want to concentrate here on the Adjective Phrases that precede N^1 in these examples. Notice that in (44) *oceanic* is an appropriate Adjunct for *barge*, but not for *woman*. However, in (45) the situation is the other way round: *bitchy* is an appropriate Adjunct for *woman* but not for *iceberg*. Our analysis of BNPs must allow for an AP that precedes N^1 to modify either N^1 or N^2. Now, if we adopt a structure like (31) for (44) and (45) the trees would look like this:

(46)

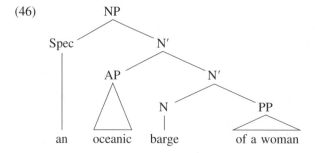

(47)

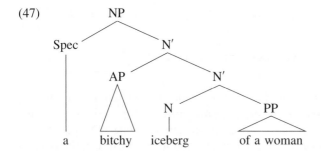

What these structures encode is that in (46) *oceanic* modifies *barge of a woman* and in (47) *bitchy* modifies *iceberg of a woman*. While (46) is not ruled out, the structure in (47) is clearly inappropriate because *bitchy* should modify a constituent which has the noun *woman* as its Head.

If we now adopt structures like (32) for our NPs in (44) and (45) we get the following results:

(48)

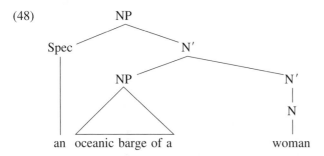

(49)

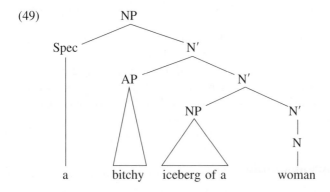

Here we get the right results in both cases: in (48) *oceanic* modifies *barge*, while in (49) the strings *bitchy* and *iceberg of a* modify *woman*. Notice that both Adjuncts are sisters of N'.

The answer is that there would then be a semantic clash between these two elements, as the combination *oceanic woman* is meaningless. It appears, then, that tree
structures like (48) and (49) make the right predictions regarding (44) and (45).

As a final piece of evidence in favour of an analysis in which N^2 is the Head in
BNPs consider the phrase below:

(50)   a hell of a problem

Hell of a-BNPs are common in English. If our proposed analysis of BNPs is
correct then *problem* is the Head, as in (51):

(51)

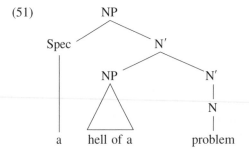

This analysis is corroborated by the fact that in spoken English we can contract
the sequence *hell of a* to *helluva*. Even in written English this contraction has
been attested.

All in all, we have overwhelming evidence in favour of an analysis of BNPs
in which N^2 is the Head. Again, as in the case of the string *a lot of* in NPs like *a
lot of books*, a sequence like *hell of a* in (51) seems to be an unlikely constituent.
However, almost certainly this construction is in an intermediate stage of devel-
opment, and our grammar should allow for patterns like (51), as there is support-
ing evidence for them.

15.3   Verb Complementation

In this section we will be looking at *verb complementation*, an area of English
grammar about which much has been written, and about which there is a great
deal of disagreement among linguists. The term verb complementation refers to
the description of the Complement-taking properties of verbs: i.e. which Complements they take, and how these Complements are realised.

In Chapter 5 we looked at ways in which the grammatical functions (GFs) of English (Subject, Direct Object, etc.) can be realised. Some of these function-form pairs were quite straightforward, and needed little justification. Thus, the claim that Direct Objects can be realised as NPs (as in *I kicked [NP the ball]*), or as finite clauses (as in *Everyone thinks [Clause that she is lovely]*) is an uncontroversial one. Other function–form relationships are less straightforward (e.g. that DOs can be realised as nonfinite clauses, as in the type of constructions we discussed in Chapter 13). In these cases it is often hard to establish which string of words in a sentence realises a particular GF. In Chapter 5 we made a number of tacit assumptions about these less obvious cases. Having acquainted ourselves in the preceding chapters of this book with the skills to set up reasoned analyses of sentences, we are now in a position to assess those early claims.

Before proceeding let us briefly recapitulate the subdivision of the class of main verbs in English. As we have seen, main verbs can be either *transitive* (i.e. they take internal arguments) or *intransitive* (no internal arguments). Because they do not pose any analytical problems we'll leave intransitive verbs aside, and deal only with transitive verbs.

The main area of disagreement among linguists with regard to English verb complementation concerns sentences that conform to one of the following patterns:

Pattern 1   V + to-infinitive

(52)   Jim wanted [to leave London].

Pattern 2   V + NP + to-infinitive

(53)   My sister believes [Jim to be a loner].
(54)   We persuaded [Jim][to stay].
(55)   My friends want [Jim to stay].
(56)   The prime-minister allowed [the finance-minister to increase taxes].

Pattern 3   V + NP + {NP, AP, PP}

(57)   I considered [Jim a dunce].
(58)   I considered [Jim foolish].
(59)   I want [the kids in the car].

Pattern 4   V + NP + bare infinitive

(60)   I heard/made [Jim leave the flat].

Pattern 5   V + NP + -ing participle clause

(61)   I saw [Jim leaving the flat].

Pattern 6   V + NP + -ed participle clause

(62)   I had [the TV repaired].

In each of these example sentences the brackets indicate the analyses we've been assuming in this book. It's time now to justify these analyses, and look for the arguments that underpin them. In this chapter we will be concentrating on patterns 1–3.

15.3.1   Pattern 1: V + to-*infinitive*

The first example sentence for pattern 1 above involves the verb *want*. The analysis implied in (52) is that *to leave London* is the Direct Object of this verb. This DO takes the form of a clause whose Subject remains implicit, but is interpreted as having the same referent as the matrix clause Subject. You will remember that we indicate implied arguments with the symbol 'Ø'. Sentence (52) can then be represented as in (63):

(63) Jim_i wanted [$Ø_i$ to leave London]

The subscript letter 'i' indicates coreferentiality. What is the evidence for analysing *to leave London* as the DO of *want*? We need to show that both from a semantic and a syntactic point of view the bracketed string in (52) functions as a constituent.

Let's start with semantic reasons for our analysis. By semantic reasons I mean evidence pertaining to argumenthood. The question is the following:

Exercise

Can we reasonably say that *to leave London* is a Direct Object argument of *want* in (52)? In other words, is 'leaving London' what Jim wanted?

The answer to this question is surely 'yes'. If this is indeed the case, i.e. if *to leave London* is indeed the DO of *want*, then this string ought to behave as a constituent. So let's apply the tests we set up in Chapters 11 and 12 one-by-one to see if there is syntactic support for the analysis in (52).

First we look at Movement. The question we must ask ourselves is whether it is possible to move the string *to leave London* in (52). We could hypothesise that *to leave London* is a Complement of the verb *want* in the form of a VP. One way to test this hypothesis is to apply VP-Preposing. If we do this it turns out that only (64) is possible (though stylistically somewhat clumsy), whereas (65) is completely out:

(64) ?Jim says that he will want to leave London, and [leave London] he will want to – .

(65) *Jim says that he will want to leave London, and [to leave London] he will want – .

The element *to* cannot be moved along with the main verb and DO.

If we apply *Though*-Movement the result is (66):

(66) [Leave London] though he wanted to –, he still loves the place.

(67) *[To leave London] though he wanted – , he still loves the place.

Again, only the verb and its DO can be moved. Infinitival *to* is left behind, and cannot also be moved. (Notice that these data confirm our conclusion in Chapter 8 that the infinitival marker *to* is not part of VP, but positioned inside 'I'.)

The data we have looked at so far show that *to leave London* in (52) is not a VP-constituent. However, even if it is not a VP, it could be some other type of constituent. In (63) we analysed this string as a clausal Direct Object of *want* with an implicit Subject. Can we apply Passivisation, also a Movement process, to this DO? The answer is 'no', as (68) shows:

(68) *[To leave London] was wanted by Jim.

It now seems that *to leave London* is not a constituent, VP or otherwise. I use the word *seems* advisedly here, because it is important to remember that the constituency tests work in only one direction: if a string of words can be moved, it must be a constituent; if it cannot be moved, it is not necessarily not a constituent.

Another major test for constituency is Substitution. We should check to see whether *to leave London* in (52) can be replaced by a proform.

Exercise

Can you think of a way to replace the string *to leave London* with a proform?

The following sentence shows that *to leave London* can be replaced by the pronoun *it*:

(69) Jim wanted *it*.

The fact that *to leave London* can be replaced by *it* entails that this string is a constituent.

Taking stock at this point, we have found that there is so far only semantic evidence, and one piece of syntactic evidence (namely Substitution) in favour of the analysis in (52) in which *to leave London* is a constituent.

We turn now to the tests introduced in Chapter 12.

Exercise

Construct one or more sentences in which *to leave London* is coordinated with *to travel to Sicily*.

Here are some possible results:

Coordination

(70)   Jim wanted [to leave London] and [to travel to Sicily].
(71)   [To leave London] and [to travel to Sicily] is Jim's dream.

Next we try to apply the Cleft and Pseudocleft tests.

Exercise

Try to construct Cleft and Pseudocleft sentences in which *to leave London* is in the focus position. Turn back to Chapter 12 if you've forgotten what Cleft and Pseudocleft sentences look like.

Here are some (im)possibilities:

Cleft and Pseudocleft

(72)   *It was [to leave London] that Jim wanted.
(73)   What Jim wanted was [to leave London].

Pseudocleft (73) again establishes the constituent status of *to leave London*, but you will have found that this string cannot be positioned in the focus position of a Cleft sentence, cf. (72). However, we already mentioned in Section 10.2.1 and 12.2 that there are general restrictions on which elements can appear in the focus position of Cleft sentences, and strings containing verbs generally cannot be focused on, so (72) should not be taken as evidence against the constituenthood of *to leave London*.

There are two remaining tests, the Somewhere Else Test and the Constituent Response Test.

Here are some possibilities:

The Somewhere Else Test

(74) [To leave London] was Jim's goal.
(75) It was Jim's goal [to leave London].

Here's an example:

The Constituent Response Test

(76) A: What did Jim want?
      B: To leave London.

All these tests, with the exception of the Cleft construction, show that *to leave London* functions as a constituent. We have already seen that the Meaning Test also suggests that the bracketed string in (52) is a unit. (Notice that the Insertion Test does not apply, because it refers to S-constituent boundaries.)

Concluding this discussion, we have seen that most of the constituency tests show that *to leave London* in (52) functions as a unit. The only exceptions are Movement and the Cleft construction. On balance the accumulated evidence suggests that the analysis in (52) is correct, and maybe the reason why *to leave London* cannot be moved is due to some as yet unclear factor which will have to be investigated in future research.

15.3.2 Pattern 2: V + NP + to-*infinitive constructions involving* allow

You will remember that in Chapter 13 we discussed V + NP + *to*-infinitive constructions involving the verbs *believe*, *persuade* and *want*, used in the first three example sentences of pattern 2 above. The main issue with regard to these constructions was the functional status of the postverbal NP: is it a Direct Object argument, or the Subject argument of a subordinate clause? In order to find an answer to this question we looked at ways in which argumenthood can be established. We concluded that although sentences involving these verbs superficially all conform to the pattern V + NP + *to*-infinitive, their analysis turns out to be different. Thus the VPs of sentences involving *believe* or *want* should be bracketed as in (77):

(77)   [$_{VP}$ V [NP + *to*-infinitive]]

The chief reason for this is the lack of a thematic relationship between the main verb and the NP that follows it. Rather, this NP is the Subject of a subordinate clause. The only difference between *believe* and *want* is that sentences with *believe* can be passivised, while sentences with *want* cannot (cf. *Jim was believed to be a loner by my sister* / * *Jim was wanted to stay by my friends*).

By contrast, the bracketing of the VPs of sentences with *persuade* was argued to be as in (78):

(78)   [$_{VP}$ V [NP] [*to*-infinitive]]

Here the NP *is* an argument of the verb that precedes it, if we persuade someone they are directly 'being acted upon'. If you don't remember the reasoning behind these analyses review Chapter 13.

Consider now the verb *allow*. As the following sentence shows, this verb too occurs in the V + NP + *to*-infinitive pattern:

(79)   The prime-minister [$_V$ allowed] [$_{NP}$ the finance-minister] [$_{to\text{-}inf.}$ to increase taxes].

Our discussion of the pattern in which *allow* occurs will follow the same procedure as the one we followed in the previous section. First we consider the semantics of this construction, then its constituency.

If we consider the meaning of (79), in an effort to find out which are the arguments of *allow*, we might be led to think that apart from a Subject argument (*the prime-minister*), this verb takes two further arguments, namely *the finance-minister* and *to increase taxes*. The rationale for this analysis would be that there seems to be a direct thematic relationship between *allow* and *the finance-minister*, because the latter is the person who is being given permission. This would make the NP *the finance-minister* an argument of *allow*. The *to*-infinitive would then be an additional argument. With regard to its argument-taking properties *allow* would thus appear to be like *persuade*. However, there is evidence which suggests that this is not correct. This evidence relates to sentences of the following type:

(80)   The prime-minister allowed it to become too hot in the room.
(81)   The prime-minister allowed there to be a tax-raising round.

These data undermine the view that NPs following *allow* are arguments of that verb: as we have seen several times now, dummy *it* and existential *there* cannot be analysed as Direct Objects when they occur in postverbal position, because they cannot enter into a thematic relationship with a verb. We can draw the same conclusion from the data below:

(82)   The prime-minister allowed the coast to be clear for his finance-minister to raise taxes.
(83)   The prime-minister deliberately allowed the fat to be in the fire for his finance-minister, by leaking the story to the press.

Here the Subject idiom chunks *the coast* and *the fat* occur after *allow*, again suggesting that the postverbal position is not a DO slot for this verb. (Review Section 13.1.2 if you've forgotten about dummy elements and idiom chunks.)

Exercise

Consider the two sentences in (84) and (85). With what kind of evidence do they provide us?

(84)   The prime-minister allowed the finance-minister to increase taxes. (= (79))
(85)   The prime-minister allowed taxes to be increased by the finance-minister.

This Passivisation evidence again suggests that there does not after all appear to be a thematic relationship between *allow* and the NP that follows it. The reason is that (84) and (85) mean the same, and this tells us that the NP following the matrix verb in these sentences is not one of its arguments. This view is supported by the fact that in (85) 'taxes' are not something one normally gives permission to. It seems, then, that the sentences in (80)–(85) show that *allow* is not like *persuade*, but like *believe*.

However, if we consider further data it turns out that we're still not home and dry. In the following set of sentences we have again passivised the postverbal string, deriving (87) from (86):

(86)   Tim allowed the police to interrogate his son.
(87)   Tim allowed his son to be interrogated by the police.

This time we cannot be quite so confident in saying that these sentences mean the same: in both cases the postverbal NP refers to an individual or individuals to whom permission can be granted or denied, and as such this NP can be regarded as an argument of *allow* in (86) and (87).

We have ended up in a situation in which there is conflicting evidence: on the one hand we have evidence for regarding NPs following *allow* as Subjects of subordinate clauses (cf. (80)–(85)) while on the other hand we have evidence for regarding these same NPs as arguments of this verb (cf. (86)/(87)). How do we resolve this matter? There are two possible courses of action. One is to say that there are two verbs *allow*, let's call them *allow¹* and *allow²*, which are homophonous (i.e. they sound the same), but differ in meaning. *Allow¹* could then be said to pattern with *persuade* and mean 'give permission (to someone to do something)', while *allow²* would pattern with *believe* and mean 'tolerate (a situation)'. The meaning difference between *allow¹* and *allow²*, if real, is slight. Bearing in mind Occam's razor (see Section 10.2.2), positing the existence of two verbs *allow* is unattractive.

The other possibility is to argue that the postverbal NP in *allow* + NP + *to*-infinitive constructions is in fact *never* an argument of this verb, but that we *construe* it as an argument because in certain cases (e.g. (79), (86) and (87)) it refers to an individual (or entity) to whom permission could in principle be given. Put differently, when we process sentences containing the string *allow* + NP + *to*-infinitive, we are inclined to take certain NPs to be arguments of *allow* only by virtue of the fact that they are juxtaposed to this verb. It is not unlikely that NPs in *allow* + NP + *to*-infinitive strings are initially processed by analogy with sentences like (88), where *allow* clearly takes two internal NP arguments, one an Indirect Object, the other a Direct Object:

(88)   They allowed her two books.

On further processing (79), however, it turns out that what is allowed is a situation, described by a proposition (e.g. a nonfinite *to*-infinitive clause). Thus, what is being allowed is 'that the finance-minister increases taxes', rather than permission being granted to an individual. Because it has more evidence to support it, we will assume that the second approach is correct, and that *allow* patterns with *believe*.

Semantic evidence pertaining to argumenthood has led us to the conclusion that either *allow* takes two NPs, as in (88), or an [NP + *to*-infinitive] Complement clause, so that (79) is analysed as in (89):

(89)   The prime-minister allowed [the finance-minister to increase taxes].

Let's now see if there is syntactic evidence for this analysis as well.

If we first look at Movement, then we soon realise that displacing the bracketed string in (89) is impossible. We cannot, for example, topicalise it, as (90) shows:

(90)   *[The finance-minister to increase taxes] the prime-minister allowed –

Other Movement tests like VP-Preposing and *Though*-Movement are useful only in establishing whether a particular string of words constitutes a VP or not, so they are of no use in a discussion about the bracketed string in (89).

The Substitution test looks more promising.

Notice that what the prime-minister allowed in (89) was a situation, and we can substitute the postverbal string by the pronoun *it*:

(91)   The prime-minister allowed *it*.

This shows that *the finance-minister to increase taxes* in (89) functions as a constituent.

What about the tests discussed in Chapter 12?

If we apply these tests to (79) we obtain the following results:

Coordination

(92)   The prime-minister allowed [the finance-minister to increase taxes] and [the transport-minister to increase rail fares].

Cleft and Pseudocleft

(93)   *It was [the finance-minister to increase taxes] that the prime-minister allowed.
(94)   *What the prime-minister allowed was [the finance-minister to increase taxes].

The Somewhere Else Test

(95)   It was impossible for [the finance-minister to increase taxes].

The Constituent Response Test

(96)   A   What did the prime-minister allow?
         B   *The finance-minister to increase taxes.

(Notice that the Insertion Test doesn't apply, because it refers to S-constituent boundaries, and in (79) we are dealing with VP-internal units.)

The syntactic constituency tests yield mixed results: some do, and some do not, identify the postverbal string in (89) as a constituent. What do we do in such a situation? For now, we will provisionally conclude that in (89) the semantic and syntactic evidence taken together fairly convincingly suggests that *the finance-minister to increase taxes* is a constituent. Clearly, however, the matter can only be satisfactorily resolved by doing more research so as to find further evidence that is relevant to the issue at hand. Not all linguists will agree with the provisional conclusion we have just drawn, and you should not be surprised to find different analyses in the literature. Let's turn now to a further case.

15.3.3   Pattern 3: V + NP + {NP/AP/PP}

Consider again the sentences below which involve what we called Small Clauses in Chapter 5:

(97)   I considered [Jim a dunce]. (= (57))
(98)   I considered [Jim foolish]. (= (58))
(99)   I want [the kids in the car]. (= (59))

We will again consider both semantic and syntactic evidence to show that the bracketed strings in each case are constituents. We will concentrate here on the V + NP + NP construction exemplified in (97). This section too will be interactive: you will be prompted at various points in the discussion to think of examples that could be used as evidence for or against a particular analysis.

Let's start with a consideration of the meaning of (97).

Exercise

What does (97) mean? Is it fair to say that in *I considered Jim a dunce* I was considering Jim?

Your answer to this question may well have been 'yes', but if you think about it a little more, you will realise that (97) does *not* mean that I considered *Jim*, but rather that I considered a proposition, namely the proposition that 'Jim is a dunce'. Indeed, we can paraphrase (97) as in (100) or (101):

(100)   I considered *Jim to be a dunce.*
(101)   I considered *that Jim is a dunce.*

These considerations suggest a bracketing like that in (97).

Consider now (102) and (103):

(102) I consider it a fine day.
(103) The prime-minister considered the coast clear for tax increases.

Exercise

If you bear in mind the discussion in Chapter 13, what do these sentences show?

In these cases we have dummy *it* and a Subject-related idiom chunk following the main verb. As we saw in Chapter 13, the possibility of this happening indicates that the postverbal NP is not one of the verb's arguments. Again, we are led to the bracketing in (97) where the postverbal NP is analysed as the Subject of a Complement clause, rather than as the Direct Object of the main verb.

In short, if we consider a sentence like *I considered Jim a dunce* from a semantic point of view, we are led to the bracketing in (97).

Let's now turn to our syntactic constituency tests, starting with Movement and Substitution, as discussed in Chapter 11. Recall the following general principles: if we can move a string of words, and/or substitute a string of words by a proform, then that string must be a constituent. The question we must ask, then, is whether we can move the string *Jim a dunce* in (97), or replace it with a proform.

Exercise

Can you think of a sentence where such a movement has taken place, or where *Jim a dunce* has been replaced by a proform?

Movement of *Jim a dunce* is impossible. This string cannot be topicalised (cf. **[Jim a dunce] I considered – .*), and VP-Preposing and *Though*-Movement only prove the constituent status of the VP that contains *Jim a dunce*. As for Substitution, although we cannot interpret *it* in *I considered it* to substitute for *Jim a dunce* in (97), we *can* say *I considered this proposition*, where we have substituted the NP *this proposition* for *Jim a dunce*.

Our next test is coordination.

Exercise

Can we coordinate a string like *Jim a dunce* in (97) with a similar string?

Such coordination seems quite straightforward and unproblematic:

(104)   I considered *Jim a dunce* and *Pete a genius.*

Now let's try the Cleft and Pseudocleft Tests.

Exercise

Can *Jim a dunce* be in the focus position of a Cleft or Pseudocleft Construction?

It seems not, as (105) and (106) indicate:

(105)   *It was *Jim a dunce* that I considered.
(106)   *What I considered was *Jim a dunce.*

Exercise

Next apply the Somewhere Else Test to see if *Jim a dunce* can occur elsewhere as a constituent. You'll have to think hard!

An [NP NP] string like *Jim a dunce* can occur on its own in an interchange like the following:

(107)   A: I consider Jim a dunce.
         B: *Jim a dunce?* You must be joking. He nearly won the Nobel Prize for physics!

With [NP AP] and [NP PP] strings we can also have something like this:

(108)   *My mind free of worries,* I went out and had a drink.
(109)   She was too upset to say anything, *her thoughts in utter turmoil.*

The italicised strings function like Adjuncts here.
    [NP NP] strings can also occur as the complement of the preposition *with*:

(110)   With *Jim a vegetarian* we'll have to find another restaurant.

The same is true for [NP AP] and [NP PP] strings:

(111)   With *Isaac so unhappy* we can't really go on holiday.
(112)   With *her husband in France* Sally had a great night out with her friends.

Finally, we turn to the Constituent Response Test. (We're ignoring the Insertion Test, which does not apply.)

Exercise

Can [NP NP] strings like *Jim a dunce* function as a response to a question?

It would seem that the answer to this question is a negative one.

The conclusion we can draw from our deliberations must again be a provisional one: while not all the tests point to the bracketing in (97), the semantic and syntactic evidence *taken together* does seem to do so. Further research is needed to explain why some of the tests fail.

15.4   Subordinating Conjunctions and Prepositions

Consider the following examples:

(113)   She will have read the document before.
(114)   She will have read the document before the holiday.
(115)   She will have read the document before the holiday began.

Exercise

To which word class would you assign the word *before* in each of these examples?

Your answer was probably that in (113) *before* is an adverb heading an Adverb Phrase. In (114) *before* looks like a preposition, because it is followed by a NP, while in (115) *before* introduces a subordinate clause functioning as an Adjunct and is therefore maybe best classed as a subordinator. However, is this right? After all, the word *before* has the same shape each time. Given that this is the case, shouldn't our initial hypothesis be that these words belong to the same category? But how can we possibly maintain that analysis, given that we have said that words are assigned to categories on the basis of their distribution, and the distribution of each instance of *before* is different in the examples above? However, maybe we only arrived at this conclusion because we are holding on to mistaken views regarding the distributional properties of some of the word classes. For example, we might ask whether prepositions should always be followed by an NP, as traditional grammar has it. We saw in Section 10.2.2.1 that prepositions can be argued to be transitive (+ NP) or intransitive (−NP). If we apply this to the examples above we can say that in (113) *before* is an intransitive preposition, heading a PP, while in (114) it is a transitive preposition:

(116)   She will have read the document [PP [P before]].

(117) She will have read the document [$_{PP}$ [$_P$ before [$_{NP}$ the holiday]]].

But then what about (115)? Surely here we must analyse *before* as a subordinating conjunction? Well, this is indeed an analysis we find in many grammar books, but it is perhaps better to say that in this sentence, too, *before* is a preposition if we simply allow prepositions to introduce clauses:

(118) She will have read the document [$_{PP}$ [$_P$ before [$_{Clause}$ the holiday began]]].

But if we assign *before* to the class of prepositions, what about words like *although*, *because*, *while*, *when*, etc., words which I called adjunctisers in Chapter 3, occurring in such sentences as (119)–(121)?

(119) I didn't talk to Sally, *although* she was at the party.
(120) We didn't go to the Vatican Museum, *because* it was too expensive.
(121) *While* he was asleep, an intruder stole his iPod.

It has been argued recently that all the adjunctisers should be analysed as prepositions. This is a welcome strategy. After all, it was awkward in Chapter 3 that we had to single out *that*, *if*, *whether* and *for* as being special members of the class of subordinators. Although we haven't achieved an economy by reassigning the adjunctisers to the class of prepositions, we *have* attained a more elegant description (see Section 10.3.1) of the data.

15.5 Concluding Remarks

What we have seen in this chapter is that sometimes arguments regarding competing analyses are not very clear-cut, and don't lead us unambiguously to one account of a particular phenomenon and away from another. We are often faced with a situation in which there are arguments for two or more analyses of the same phenomenon. One way to proceed in such a situation is to be 'democratic', and accept as correct the analysis that has the most arguments in support of it. This is a dubious strategy to employ, because it assumes that all arguments have equal weight. That arguments are not valued in the same way became clear when we looked at the constituency tests of Chapters 11 and 12. We saw there that the Somewhere Else Test and the Meaning Test are less reliable than the Movement and Substitution Tests. When we are faced with conflicting evidence and with evidence of unequal importance, we have to consider our data carefully, make choices, and present our case in the way that seems the most appropriate. No analysis is ever final, and more often than not others will disagree with our conclusions. The challenge is then on us to find further independent evidence to support our claims. It is this search for the 'best' analysis that makes syntax and argumentation so exciting.

What I hope to have achieved in this book is to teach you the basics of English syntax, and how to argue cogently and coherently in favour of (or against) an analysis of a particular syntactic phenomenon, and also, in trickier cases, how to engage in a process of balancing different types of evidence.

Key Concepts in this Chapter

negated modal verbs
noun phrase structure
verb complementation
subordinating conjunctions and prepositions

Exercises

1. Consider (i).

   (i) She may write to you, but you never know: she may not – .

   What has been deleted at the tail end of this sentence? How is (i) a problem for our claim that negated modals are positioned in 'I'? Is there a way around this problem?

2. Consider the verb *promise* in the sentence below.

   (i) I promised her to take a day off.

   Assign function labels to the various constituents in this sentence. What is the understood Subject expression of the string *to take a day off*? How does *promise* differ from *persuade* in this respect?

3. Quirk et al. (1985) classify *persuade* as a ditransitive verb (i.e. a verb with an Indirect Object and a Direct Object). What do you make of this?

*4. Apply the argumentation we used in Section 15.3 to justify the bracketings shown in sentences (60)–(62) (patterns 4–6).

Further Reading

On *allow* see Huddleston (1984: 219–20), Schmerling (1978: 307–8) and Palmer (1987, Section 9.2). On Small Clauses, see Radford (1988) and Aarts (1992). The topics in Section 15.2 on the structure of the Noun Phrase are discussed in Akmajian and Lehrer (1976), Huddleston (1984: 236–9), Selkirk (1977) and Aarts (1998).

The latter is an article which contains a comprehensive list of references on BNPs. The analysis of words like *before* as prepositions was proposed by the Danish grammarian Otto Jespersen. For criticism of this idea, see Croft (2007) and my response in Aarts (2007b). Huddleston and Pullum et al. (2002) have suggested that all subordinating conjunctions, with the exception of the complementisers, should be analysed as prepositions.

Glossary

Cross-references are shown in **bold**.

absolute form   The form of an **adjective** (or **adverb**) that is not **comparative** or **superlative**. For example, in the following sequence the first form is the absolute form: *great - greater - greatest.*

active   A term applied to a **sentence** or **clause** in which the **Subject** is generally presented as the **Agent** of the action described by the **Predicate,** and the **Direct Object** as the **Patient**. For example, *The captain scored a goal.* See also **passive**.

adjective   One of the principal **word classes**; a word which has a modifying function in front of a **noun** (**attributive position**, e.g. *the beautiful beach*), or following a **linking verb** (**predicative position**, e.g. *the beach is beautiful*).

Adjective Phrase (AP)   A **phrase** headed by an **adjective**.

adjoin/adjunction   A syntactic process whereby one category is linked to another. Category B is adjoined to category A:

1.   by making B a sister of A and
2.   by making A and B daughters of a copy of the original node A

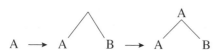

Adjunct   A **function** label which indicates the *where, why, when,* etc. in a **proposition** (e.g. *Last week, we finished all the work quickly.*). Adjuncts also act as modifiers inside phrases. For example, in the NP *the ugly duckling* the AP *ugly* functions as an **Adjunct**.

adjunctiser   A **subordinating conjunction** that introduces a **clause** functioning as **Adjunct**. See also **complementiser, conjunction**.

adverb   A **word class** which usually expresses manner, location, time, etc., for example, *quickly, secretly,* etc.

Adverb Phrase (AdvP)   A **phrase** headed by an **adverb**.

affix   An appendix added to the beginning or end of a word. For example, *-ness* is an affix, more specifically a suffix, which can be added to the adjective *happy*, deriving a noun, namely *happiness.* And *dis-* is an affix, more specifically a prefix, which can be added to the verb *like*, deriving another verb, namely *dislike.*

Agent   A **thematic role** which indicates the 'doer' or instigator of an action denoted by a **predicate** in a **proposition**.

agreement The phenomenon whereby a particular element harmonises with another with respect to a particular feature. For example, in the sentence *John likes warm weather* the third person singular form of the **verb** *like* (ending in *-s*) agrees with the third person singular **Subject** *John*.

argument A participant (role player) in a **proposition**.

argument structure A schematic representation which shows a **predicate** together with its **arguments**, and their categorial status. For example, the argument structure for the verb *devour* is as follows:

devour (verb)
[1 <NP>, 2 <NP>]

The underlined argument represents the **Subject** expression.

aspect A **semantic** notion which signifies the way in which a situation or event expressed by a **verb** in a particular sentence is viewed, for example as an ongoing process (**progressive aspect**), or as a process beginning in the past and extending up to, and including, the present (**perfective aspect**). In English aspect is syntactically expressed especially by **aspectual auxiliaries** (*be* and *have*).

aspectual auxiliary An **auxiliary verb** that expresses the **semantic** notion of **aspect**: in English the verbs *be* and *have* are aspectual auxiliaries.

attributive position The syntactic position in a **Noun Phrase** between the **Specifier** and **Head**. Elements occurring here have a modifying function. In the NP *the green bike* the **Adjective Phrase** *green* is in attributive position. See also **predicative position**.

auxiliary A verb which 'helps' the **main verb** in front of which it is placed from the point of view of **aspect, modality**, etc.

base form (of a verb) The form of a verb other than the third person singular.

Benefactive A **thematic role** which indicates the entity that benefits from the action or event denoted by the **predicate** in a **proposition**.

clause A sentence within a sentence. For example, *that he will be OK* is a **subordinate clause** functioning as a **Direct Object** within the sentence *I know that he will be OK*. See also **matrix clause**.

clause type A syntactic typology of **clauses** into four categories: **declarative, interrogative, imperative** and **exclamative**. See also the associated **pragmatic** notions **statement, question, directive, exclamative**.

cleft sentence A sentence which conforms to the pattern *it* + form of *be*+ Focus + *who/that*. For example, *It was in Brazil that I was so happy* is a cleft version of *I was so happy in Brazil*.

comparative form The form of **adjectives** (and some **adverbs**) that ends in *-er* (e.g. *quieter, faster*). Sometimes a periphrastic form is used, for example, *more competent* (rather than **competenter*).

Complement A functional label which denotes a constituent whose presence is required by a **verb, noun, adjective** or **preposition**.

complementiser   A word that introduces a **clause** that functions as a **Complement** to a verb. For example, *that* is a complementiser in the following sentence: *I believe that the sun will shine.* The string *that the sun will shine* functions as a Direct Object. There are four complementisers in English, which together form a subclass of the set of **subordinating conjunctions**: *that, if, whether* and *for*. See also **adjunctiser**.

conjoin   One element in a set of two or more items linked by a **coordinating conjunction**. For example, in the string *the sun and the moon* the NPs *the sun* and *the moon* are conjoins linked by the **coordinating conjunction** *and*.

conjunction   There are two types of conjunctions: **coordinating conjunctions** (principally *and, or* and *but*) and **subordinating conjunctions**. Of the latter there are two subtypes: **complementisers** (*that, if, whether, for*), which introduce **Complement** clauses, and **adjunctisers** (*although, because, in order that, since, when, while*, etc.), which introduce **Adjunct** clauses. Schematically, the word class of conjunctions can be represented as follows:

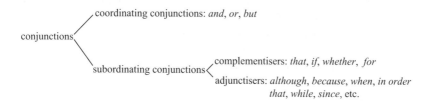

conjunctions

coordinating conjunctions: *and, or, but*

subordinating conjunctions

complementisers: *that, if, whether, for*

adjunctisers: *although, because, when, in order that, while, since*, etc.

constituent   A string of words which syntactically behaves as a unit.

constituency test   A test by means of which a string of words can be shown to behave as a unit. See, for example, **movement**.

Constituent Response Test   A **constituency test** which stipulates that only **constituents** can be used as responses to open interrogatives.

coordination   A syntactic configuration in which elements or strings of elements (**conjoins**) are juxtaposed by means of a **coordinating conjunction**. For example, *Bulgaria and Greece*.

coordinating conjunction   A linking word which connects units which are not subordinate to one another. In English the principal coordinating conjunctions are *and, or* and *but*.

copula   (Also known as linking verb.) Verbs like *seem, appear* and *be* which link a **Subject** to an expression which is predicated of it. For example, *He seems nice.*

cross-categorial generalisation   A generalisation that holds true for all syntactic categories. For example, **X-bar syntax** embodies the cross-categorial generalisation that all **phrases** are structured in an identical way.

declarative clause   A **clause type** with an unmarked word order, usually, though not exclusively, used to make a **statement**.

determinative   A class of words that occur before the **noun** functioning as **Specifiers** in **Noun Phrase** structure. For example, *the, this, that, those*, etc.

directive   A **pragmatic** label which denotes the main use of an **imperative clause**, i.e. getting someone to do something.

Direct Object (DO)   A **function** label which denotes an entity that undergoes whatever it is that the preceding **verb** expresses. For example, in the sentence *Greg hates estate agents* the **Noun Phrase** *estate agents* is the DO of the verb *hate*.

distribution   A term which refers to the arrangement of words, phrases, etc. in sentence structure. For example, in observing that in English sentences **Noun Phrases** typically occur in **Subject** position, **Direct Object** position, and as **Complements** of **prepositions**, we are talking about the distribution of NPs.

ditransitive verb   A **verb** that takes an **Indirect Object** and a **Direct Object**, as in the following sentence: *Simone sent me a letter*, where *me* is the IO, and *a letter* is the DO.

***do so*-substitution**   A syntactic process whereby a string of words is replaced by *do so*. For example, in *Maria bought a present for her daughter, and Sara did so too* the **proform** *do so* replaces the words *bought a present for her daughter.*

***do*-support**   This term refers to the insertion of the **dummy auxiliary** *do* to add emphasis, to form **interrogative sentences**, etc. in sentences which do not already contain an auxiliary. For example, if we want to change the following sentence into an interrogative form we need to add *do*: *Denise opened the file > Did Denise open the file?*

dominate   A node X dominates a node Y in a **tree diagram** if we can trace an upward path from Y to X along the branches of the tree. X immediately dominates Y if we go up only one step in the tree. In the following schematic tree X dominates all the **nodes** beneath it, but it only immediately dominates Y and Z.

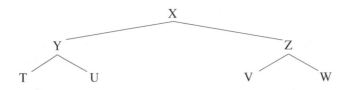

dummy auxiliary *do*   A meaningless auxiliary that is inserted by ***do*-support** to effect emphasis, to form interrogative structures, etc.

dyadic predicate See **two-place predicate**.

exclamation   A **pragmatic** notion which denotes the physical act of producing an utterance that expresses an emotion, for example surprise, anger, etc.

exclamative clause A **clause type** which is typically used to make an **exclamation**. For example, *What a great journey he made!*

existential *there* The ***there*** that we find in propositions that are concerned with the existence of people, things, etc. For example, *There is a cat in the garage.* See also **locative *there*, pleonastic elements**.

Experiencer A **thematic role** which indicates the entity that experiences the action or event denoted by a **predicate** in a **proposition**.

external argument The argument that functions as **Subject** in a **proposition**.

Extraposition The movement of a string of words to the left or to the right in a sentence. For example, in the sentence *It is wonderful to see you*, the **Subject** clause *to see you* has been moved to a sentence-final position, and **nonreferential** *it* has been put in its place.

finite A term applied to a **verb** to indicate that it carries **tense**. Also applied to a **clause** or **sentence** that contains a finite verb.

form This term refers to the syntactic categories we can assign an element or group of elements to. For example, *those cats* is a **Noun Phrase**, and within this Noun Phrase we distinguish a determinative, which **functions** as a **Specifier**, and a noun, which functions as **Head**. See also **function**.

function This term refers to such notions as **Subject, Direct Object, Adjunct**, etc. to which we can assign categories. See also **form**.

Goal A **thematic role** which indicates the location or entity in the direction of which something moves.

gradability This refers to the property of **adjectives** (and some **adverbs**) to express degrees of application of some notion. For example, the property of being *warm* can be graded, because we can have *warmer* and *warmest* (these are **comparative** and **superlative** forms, respectively) and also *very warm*, where the adjective is preceded by an intensifier.

grammaticalisation A process in grammar which takes place over time in which elements which formerly behaved like individual lexical items regroup and attain a particular grammatical function, for example **Specifier**.

Head A **functional** label which refers to the principal element in a phrase whose category determines the category of that phrase.

Heavy NP Shift (HNPS) Movement to the right of a **Noun Phrase** that is heavy by virtue of containing a postmodifying **Prepositional Phrase** or **clause**. For example, in the following sentence the NP *three bibles that were bound in leather* has been moved across the PP *to Rome* under HNPS: *I sent – to Rome [NP three bibles that were bound in leather]*.

idiom An idiom is an expression that is unique to a particular language. The meaning of an idiom cannot be derived from its constituent parts. For example, the phrase *paint the town red* means 'to have a good time while going out'. An idiom chunk is a portion of an idiom.

idiom chunk See **idiom**.

immediately dominate See **dominate**.

imperative clause   A **clause type** which usually lacks a **Subject** and is generally used to issue a directive. For example, *Go home*; *Leave your belongings in the cloakroom.*

Indirect Object (IO)   A **function** label which denotes an entity that expresses the **Benefactive** or **Goal** of whatever it is that the preceding **verb** expresses. For example, in the sentence *Greg sent the estate agent the document* the **Noun Phrase** *estate agent* is the IO of the verb *send*.

Inflection-node (I-node)   The **node** in a **phrase marker** that contains features carrying information about **agreement** and **tense**.

Inflection Phrase (IP)   A phrase headed by 'I'.

Insertion Test   A **constituency test** which stipulates that inserted parenthetical elements can only occur at S-constituent boundaries.

Instrument   A **thematic role** which denotes the medium by which the action or event denoted by the **predicate** in a **proposition** is carried out. For example, *The knife cut the bread* where the subject carries the role of Instrument.

interjection   A minor word class consisting of such words as *oh*, *ah*, *ouch*, *yuck*, etc.

internal argument   An argument that is positioned to the right of the verb in English, for example a **Direct Object** or an **Indirect Object.**

interrogative clause   A **clause type** characterised by **Subject–auxiliary inversion**, usually, though not exclusively, used to ask **questions**. For example, *Have you looked at this article?*

intonation contour   The melodic pitch pattern of an utterance.

intransitive

  preposition
    A preposition that takes no NP **Complement**, as in *He came in.*

  verb
    A verb that takes no **internal arguments**.

lexeme   The dictionary entry of a word. For example, the nouns *cat* and *cats* belong to the lexeme *cat*, and the verbs *sing* and *sings* belong to the lexeme *sing.*

Linguistically Significant Generalisation (LSG)   A generalisation that expresses a regular patterning observed in a particular language or across several languages.

linking verb   See **copula**.

Locative   A **thematic role** that specifies the place where the action or event denoted by the **predicate** in a **proposition** is situated.

locative *there*   The *there* that indicates a location. For example, *I live there.*

main verb   A verb that can stand on its own in a sentence without the need for an accompanying **auxiliary verb**.

matrix clause   The main clause, coextensive with the sentence as a whole, to which other clauses are subordinate. In *They felt that the result was deserved* the matrix clause is the whole sentence within which *that the result was deserved* is subordinate.

Meaning Test A **constituency test** which gives an indication as to how sentences can be carved up into units on the basis of meaning. For example, in the sentence *Jake wants Drew to stay* we can argue that *Drew to stay* is a constituent which functions as the **Direct Object** of *want*, and furthermore that *Drew* is not the DO, on the basis of the fact that Jake didn't want 'Drew', but what he wanted was for 'Drew to stay'.

modal auxiliary verb An **auxiliary verb** which expresses **modality**. For example, *can*, *could*, *may*, *might*, *must*, *will*, etc.

modality A **semantic** notion which is concerned with such notions as necessity, doubt, permission, intention, etc.

monadic predicate See **one-place predicate**.

morphology The study of the internal structure of words.

mother A **node** X is the mother of a node Y if X **immediately dominates** Y.

movement The displacement of linguistic material in a sentence to the left or to the right. Only **constituents** can be moved, so movement can be used as a **constituency test**. See also **NP-Movement**.

negated modal verb A **modal verb** with a negative element tagged onto it. For example, *can't*, *won't*, *mustn't*, etc.

NICE properties NICE is an acronym for the four properties that identify **auxiliary verbs**: negation, inversion, code and emphasis.

node A position in a **phrase marker** from which one or more branches emanate.

nonfinite A term applied to a **verb** to indicate that it does not carry **tense**. Also applied to a **clause** or **sentence** that contains a nonfinite verb.

nonreferential *it* The *it* that we find in expressions pertaining to the weather (e.g. *It is raining*) or in constructions which exhibit **extraposition** (e.g. *It is wonderful to see you.*). See also **referential *it***.

noun One of the major **word classes** which is usually said to denote a person, place or thing, but which is more adequately defined by reference to distributional criteria, for example, the fact that it can be preceded by a **determinative**, or that it can take certain types of **suffixes**, such as the plural ending *-s*, etc.

Noun Phrase (NP) A phrase headed by a **noun**.

NP-Movement The displacement of NPs in **raising** and **passive** constructions.

Occam's razor The principle that entities should not be multiplied beyond necessity. For example, we should not set up more **word classes** than we need.

one-place predicate A predicate that takes only one **argument**, namely an **external argument**. For example, *sleep* in the sentence *I was sleeping*. Also known as a monadic predicate.

***one*-substitution** A substitution process whereby an N-bar constituent is replaced by the **proform** *one*.

participle See **past participle, present participle**.

particle This **word class** label is given in some frameworks to the preposition-like elements in **phrasal verbs**, for example, *up* in *look up*. In this book we have argued that we can dispense with this word class.

passive   A term applied to a sentence or clause in which the **Subject** is presented as the **Patient** of the action described by the **predicate**, and the **Agent** is positioned in an optional **Prepositional Phrase** introduced by *by*, as in *This book was written by a politician*. See also **active**.

past participle   A main verb ending in *-ed*, other than the past **tense** form. For example, *I was fired*.

past tense   See **tense**.

Patient   A **thematic role** which is carried by the 'undergoer' of the action or event denoted by the **Predicate** in a **proposition**.

perfective aspect   A **semantic** notion which signifies that the action or situation expressed by the **verb** in a particular sentence is viewed as a process beginning in the past and extending up to, and including, the present. In English perfective aspect is syntactically expressed by the **aspectual auxiliary** *have* together with a main **verb** ending in *-ed* (the **past participle**), as in *I have lived in London since 1987*. See also **aspect, progressive aspect**.

Person   A three-level grammatical system, applied to pronouns and **referring expressions**, both in the singular and plural:

	singular	plural
1st person	I	we
2nd person	you	you
3rd person	he/she/it	they

Singular or plural referring expressions are also taken to be third person.

phrasal verb   A complex transitive or intransitive verb that consists of two parts: a verb and a **particle**, for example, *look up* (transitive; e.g. *He looked up the word/He looked the word up*), *give up* (intransitive; e.g. *She gave up.*). In this book we have argued that we can do away with phrasal verbs.

phrase   A string of words that behaves as a **constituent** and has a **Head** as its principal element. We distinguish **Noun Phrases, Verb Phrases, Adjective Phrases, Prepositional Phrases** and **Adverb Phrases**.

phrase marker   A graphic representation of the structure of a (subpart of a) sentence, alternatively known as a tree or tree diagram.

pleonastic elements   Words that have no **semantic** content and often act as **Subject** slot fillers. In English **nonreferential** *it* and **existential** *there* are pleonastic elements.

pragmatics   The study of language use, especially the effects of context on interpretation.

precede   A relationship between two **nodes** in a **phrase marker**: a node X precedes a node Y if X occurs to the left of Y.

Predicate   A syntactic label which denotes a **function**. The Predicate of a sentence is syntactically defined as comprising all the linguistic material to the right of the **Subject**. In this sense of the term, Predicate is on a par with such notions as **Subject, Predicator, Direct Object, Adjunct**, etc. See also the entry below.

predicate   A **semantic** label which denotes an element that requires the specification of the participants (**arguments**) in the proposition expressed. For example, in the sentence *We like parties* the predicate is the verb *like* which requires a **Subject** argument and a **Direct Object** argument. See also the entry above.

predicative position   The syntactic position that immediately follows a **linking verb**. For example, in the sentence *He is in love* the **Prepositional Phrase** *in love* is in predicative position. See also **attributive position**.

Predicator   A functional label applied to the **verb** in a sentence.

prefix   See **affix**.

preposition   One of the major **word classes**; a word which usually expresses a spatial relationship of some sort, either literally or metaphorically. For example, *by, in, at, through, with*, etc. They can be transitive or intransitive.

Prepositional Phrase (PP)   A phrase headed by a **preposition**.

prepositional verb   A **verb** that takes a **Prepositional Phrase** as its **Complement**. For example, *rely on NP, look at NP*, etc.

present participle   A main **verb** ending in *-ing*. For example, *I was singing.*

present tense   See **tense**.

proform   A word that can substitute for another word or string of words. The pronouns are examples of proforms, as is *do so* in *do so* **substitution**.

progressive aspect   A **semantic** notion which signifies that the action or situation expressed by the **verb** in a particular sentence is viewed as an ongoing process. In English progressive aspect is syntactically expressed by the **aspectual auxiliary** *be* together with a main **verb** ending in *-ing* (the **present participle**), as in *He is jogging*. See also **aspect, perfective aspect**.

pronoun   A subclass of **noun** which can denote people (personal pronouns; e.g. *he, she, they, we*, etc.), possession (possessive pronouns; e.g. *mine, hers, his*, etc.), and a number of further concepts.

proposition   A **semantic** notion which denotes a situation or action expressed by means of a sentence. The label is also used to designate the **thematic role** assigned to propositions.

pseudocleft sentence   A sentence which conforms to the following pattern: Wh-item +…+ Form of *be* + Focus, as in *What Janice did was laugh out loud.*

question   A **pragmatic** label which denotes the main use of an **interrogative clause**. For example, *Will you dance with me?* is an interrogative structure which can be used as a question to elicit either a 'yes' or 'no' response. Other **clause types** can also be questions, for example, the **declarative clause** *You will dance with me?* This would normally be used to make a statement, but can be used as a question if it is pronounced with a rising **intonation**.

raising   A process which involves the displacement of a **Noun Phrase** from the **Subject** position of a **subordinate nonfinite clause** to the **matrix clause** Subject position. For example:

— seems [Marlova to be happy] > Marlova seems [— to be happy]

referential *it*   The **pronoun** *it* that has referential content. For example, *Where is my coat? It is over there.* See also **nonreferential *it*, pleonastic elements**.

referring expression   A linguistic expression which denotes a person or entity in the real world. For example, in a particular context of utterance the referring expression *Nick* denotes an individual with the name Nick.

relative clause   A **clause** beginning in *which*, *who* or *that* (and a few other elements) which supplies additional information about the element it accompanies, for example, *the book that I bought*. Relative clauses can be restrictive or nonrestrictive.

Right Node Raising   A displacement process exemplified by the following sentence:

Pete bought –, but Hans read –, today's newspaper.

Here, the **Noun Phrase** *today's newspaper*, which acts as the **Direct Object** of both *buy* and *read*, has been moved to the right (raised from a right **node** position).

selectional restrictions   A **semantic/pragmatic** term that refers to the restrictions that are placed on lexical items (and their associated phrases) occurring in particular **argument** positions. For example, the meaning of the **verb** *sleep* dictates that it cannot take an inanimate entity as its **Subject** expression (cf. **The CD slept*).

semantics   The study of meaning.

sentence   The largest unit in **syntax**. It is usually, though not entirely satisfactorily, defined as a string of words which expresses a **proposition**, and that begins in a capital letter and ends in a full stop.

sister   Two **nodes** X and Y are sisters if they share the same **mother** node in a **phrase marker**.

Small Clause (SC)   A string of words without a **verb** that embodies a **Subject-Predicate** relationship. For example, in *I consider [him a difficult person]* the bracketed sequence is a Small Clause.

Somewhere Else Test   A **constituency test** which stipulates that a string of words is plausibly a **constituent** in a particular context, if it can occur as a constituent in a context other than the one under investigation.

Source   A **thematic role** that denotes the location or entity from which something moves.

Specifier   A functional label applied to elements positioned immediately under XP in a **phrase marker** and as a **sister** to X' (where X stands for N, V, A or P).

statement   A **pragmatic** label which denotes the main use of a **declarative clause**. For example, *We danced all night* is a declarative clause which is used as a statement.

subcategorisation   The requirement of a **predicate** to take a category (or categories) of a particular type as its **Complement**. For example, the verb *devour* subcategorises a **Noun Phrase**, as we cannot leave out the NP in a sentence that contains this verb: **The kids devoured*. The syntactic 'needs' of predicates are specified in **subcategorisation frames**.

subcategorisation frame   A graphic way of representing the **subcategorisation** requirements of a particular **predicate**. For example, the subcategorisation frame for the verb *devour* is as follows:

> *devour* (verb)
> [− , NP]

The '−' indicates the position of the verb, followed by the category it requires.

Subject   Often defined as the entity that carries out the action expressed by the **verb** in a sentence, for example, *Carrie* in *Carrie baked a cake*. However, because not all Subjects denote **Agents** (cf. e.g. *Carrie felt ill*), they are better defined by making reference to their distribution. Thus, for example, **Subjects** are entities that invert with **auxiliary verbs** in **interrogative sentences** (e.g. *Will she phone me?*), and they are repeated in tag **questions** (e.g. *She will phone me, won't she?*), etc.

subordinate clause   A clause which is dependent on another clause. For example, in the sentence *I believe that we will have a hot summer* the clause *that we will have a hot summer* is dependent on the **matrix clause**: it is the **Direct Object** of the **verb** *believe*.

subordinating conjunction (or subordinator)   A word that links a **subordinate clause** with the clause it is dependent on. There are two subtypes: **complementisers** (*that, if, whether, for*), which introduce **Complement** clauses, and **adjunctisers** (*although, because, in order that, since, when, while*, etc.), which introduce **Adjunct** clauses. See also **conjunction**.

substitution   The replacement of a word or string of words by a **proform**.

suffix   See **affix**.

superlative form   The form of **adjectives** (and some **adverbs**) that ends in *-est* (e.g. *quietest, fastest*). Sometimes a periphrastic form is used, for example, *most competent* (rather than **competentest*).

syntactic features   The features [± N] and [± V] which are used to characterise the major **word classes** as follows: **noun** = [+ N, − V]; **verb** = [−N, + V]; **adjective** = [+ N, + V]; **preposition** = [− N, − V].

syntax   The study of sentence structure.

tense   The grammatical encoding of the **semantic** notion of time.

thematic role (θ-role)   The particular role that the **arguments** in a sentence play, for example, **Agent, Patient**, etc.

thematic structure   A graphic way of showing the **thematic roles** associated with a particular **predicate**. For example, the thematic structure for the **verb** *devour* is as follows:

> *devour* (verb)
> [1 <NP, Agent>, 2 <NP, Patient>]

This shows that *devour* requires two **Noun Phrase** arguments, one of which (the underlined **external argument**, i.e. the **Subject**) carries the role of **Agent**, while the other (the **internal argument**, i.e. the **Direct Object**) carries the role of **Patient**.

Theme   A **thematic role** which is carried by an entity that is moved by the action or event denoted by the **predicate** in a **proposition**.

***Though*-movement**   A syntactic process which can be used as a **constituency test**. It is exemplified by the following sentence pair:

He said that he would leave them alone. > *Leave them alone* though he said he would...

This shows that the string *leave them alone* is a constituent (a VP).

three-place predicate   A **predicate** that takes three **arguments**. For example, *send* in *We sent her a birthday card*. Also known as a triadic predicate.

Topicalisation   The displacement of a phrase to a clause-initial position for emphasis or prominence. For example, *Films, I enjoy –*.

transitive

    preposition

        A preposition that takes an NP or clause as its **Complement**, as in *since the war (began)*.

    verb

    A verb that takes a **Direct Object** as its **internal argument**.

tree (diagram)   See **phrase marker**.

triadic predicate   See **three-place predicate**.

two-place predicate (or dyadic predicate)   A **predicate** that takes two arguments, namely an **external argument** and an **internal argument**. For example, in *She wrote a letter* the verb *write* is a two-place predicate; *she* is the external argument, and *a letter* is the internal argument.

utterance   A **pragmatic** term that refers to a sentence (phrase or word) used in a particular context.

V-bar deletion   The deletion of a V-bar **constituent**, as in the following example: *Henry will travel to South America, but Anna won't –*, where the V-bar *travel to South America* has been deleted.

verb movement   The displacement of a **verb** from inside the **Verb Phrase** to the **Inflection-node**.

verb   One of the major **word classes**. Verbs usually denote an activity of some sort (*shout, work, travel*, etc.), but can also denote states (*be, sit, exist*, etc.)

Verb Phrase (VP)   A phrase headed by a **verb**.

verb complementation   This term refers to the kinds of **Complements** that a **verb** can take. See also **subcategorisation**.

verb-preposition construction   A construction that involves a **verb** and a closely related **preposition**. For example, *look up, see through, throw out*. See also **phrasal verb, prepositional verb**.

VP-Preposing   The movement of a **Verb Phrase** to a sentence-initial or clause-initial position. For example:

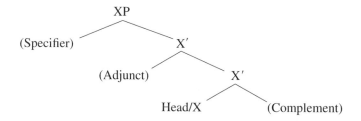

He said that he would go to Rio, and go to Rio he did — .

Here the VP *go to Rio* has been fronted under VP-Preposing.

wh-movement   The displacement of a phrase that contains an element that begins with the letters 'Wh'. For example, in *Which film did you see?* the Wh-phrase *which film* has been moved from a position immediately following the **verb** to the beginning of the sentence.

word   The smallest unit in **syntax**.

word class   A group of words the members of which can be shown to behave syntactically in the same way. For example, **nouns** occur as the **Heads** of **Noun Phrases**, they can be preceded by **determinatives**, etc.

X-bar syntax   A theory of syntax that treats all **phrases** as being structured in the same way, as follows:

```
                    XP
            _____/_____
(Specifier)                   X'
                        _____/_____
                (Adjunct)              X'
                                  _____/\_____
                            Head/X            (Complement)
```

X stands for N, V, A or P. Notice that optional **Adjuncts** are **sisters** of X' (here adjoined to the left, but they can also be adjoined to the right), while **Complements**, if present, are sisters of the **Head** X.

Yes–No interrogative   A syntactic term which refers to an **interrogative clause** that elicits either a 'Yes' or 'No' response. For example, *Are you cold?*

Yes–No question A **pragmatic** term that refers to an **utterance** that can be *interpreted* as eliciting a 'Yes' or 'No' response. As a rule, such an utterance would syntactically be a **Yes–No interrogative**, but it need not be, as in the following example: *She never went to San Francisco?* Syntactically this is a **declarative clause**, but pragmatically it has the force of a yes–no question.

Reference Works: Dictionaries, Encyclopedias, Grammars and Other Publications on the English Language

All linguists make use of a great number of technical terms, many of which you have become familiar with in this book. Unfortunately, they do not always use the terminology in the same way. Thus, very often a particular term is used in different senses by different linguists, and, to make things worse, different terms are often used to mean the same thing. There are now a number of dictionaries and encyclopedias to help you clear up such terminological confusions. Below I have listed some reference works which you may find useful. I have also listed a number of English grammars and other books on the English language which you might find helpful when studying syntax. Be aware of the fact that their approach might differ quite considerably from the one adopted here.

Dictionaries

The Oxford English Dictionary

> The largest and most comprehensive dictionary of the English Language in 20 volumes; also contains guidance on linguistic terminology. Your university or public library may subscribe to the online version. Check www.oed.com.

Chalker, S. and E. Weiner (1994) *The Oxford Dictionary of English Grammar* (Oxford: Oxford University Press).

> This book deals primarily with terminology from traditional/descriptive grammar. Phonetics is also covered. Available on *Oxford Reference*, which your university or public library may subscribe to. Check www.oxfordreference.com.

Crystal, D. (2002) *A Dictionary of Linguistics and Phonetics* (Oxford: Blackwell, 5th edn).

> This dictionary is the most comprehensive of the books listed in this section. It contains terminology from all fields of linguistics, ranging from syntax, morphology, semantics, pragmatics, phonetics and phonology to discourse studies

and functional linguistics. It contains both traditional and theoretical terminology. An absolute must.

Crystal, D. (2006) *Words, Words, Words* (Oxford: Oxford University Press).

Not a dictionary, but an informative and entertaining book on words.

Hurford, J. (1994) *Grammar: A Student's Guide* (Cambridge: Cambridge University Press).

Covers elementary grammatical terminology, and contains exercises. Useful in the early stages of your study of grammar, but somewhat basic after you've become more of an expert.

Leech, Geoffrey (2006) *A Glossary of English Grammar* (Edinburgh: Edinburgh University Press).

An excellent compact glossary of all the important terms in English grammar.

Leech, G., Benita Cruickshank, and Roz Ivanic (2001) *An A-Z of English Grammar and Usage* (London: Longman, 2nd edn).

A very useful and clearly written dictionary of descriptive grammatical terminology. Contains explanatory tables, diagrams and many examples.

Matthews, P. H. (2007) *The Concise Oxford Dictionary of Linguistics* (Oxford: Oxford University Press, 2nd edn).

A wide-ranging dictionary of key terms in linguistics, schools of linguistics, language theory, language families, etc. Available on *Oxford Reference*, which your university or public library may subscribe to. Check www.oxfordreference.com.

Swan, Michael (2005) *Practical English Usage* (Oxford: Oxford University Press, 3rd edn).

A classic reference work dealing with a wide spectrum of topics to do with grammar and usage.

Trask, R. L. (1993) *A Dictionary of Grammatical Terms in Linguistics* (London and New York: Routledge).

This book deals only with grammar in the narrow sense, i.e. syntax and morphology. It is written in a very clear style.

Trask, R. L. (1999) *Language: The Basics* (London: Routledge, 2nd edn).

Trask, R. L. (2000) *The Penguin Dictionary of English Grammar* (London: Penguin).

Trask, R. L. (2007) *Language and Linguistics: The Key Concepts* (London: Routledge, 2nd edn, ed. Peter Stockwell).

Encyclopedias

Asher, R. E. (ed.) (1993) *The Encyclopedia of Language and Linguistics* (Oxford, Pergamon Press).

A 10-volume mammoth work of reference containing articles written by specialists on just about everything that pertains to language and linguistics.

Bright, W. (ed.) (1992) *International Encyclopedia of Linguistics* (Oxford: Oxford University Press).

A sizeable one-volume work with shortish entries written by specialists.

Brown, Keith (ed.) (2006) *The Encyclopedia of Language and Linguistics* (Oxford: Elsevier).

Second, completely overhauled edition of Asher (1993), now in 14 volumes.

Collinge, N. E. (ed.) (1989) *An Encyclopedia of Language* (London: Routledge).

A one-volume encyclopedia in which topics are dealt with in fairly lengthy articles written by specialists. Not really useful for quick reference.

Crystal, D. (1997) *The Cambridge Encyclopedia of Language* (Cambridge: Cambridge University Press, 2nd edn).

A magnificent and delightful reference work dealing with all aspects of language.

Crystal, D. (2003) *The Cambridge Encyclopedia of the English Language* (Cambridge: Cambridge University Press, 2nd edn).

Like its sister volume on general language studies, this is a wonderful, comprehensive and quite indispensable book for anyone interested in the English language.

McArthur, T. (1992) *The Oxford Companion to the English Language* (Oxford: Oxford University Press).

McArthur, T. (2005) *The Concise Oxford Companion to the English Language* (with Roshan McArthur, Oxford: Oxford University Press).

These last two items cover the entire field of English language studies, including usage, style, varieties, the language of literature, etc. The concise companion is available on *Oxford Reference*, which your university or public library may subscribe to. Check www.oxfordreference.com.

Grammars and Other Books on the English Language

Aarts, F. and J. Aarts (1982) *English Syntactic Structures: Functions and Categories in Sentence Analysis* (Oxford: Pergamon Press).

Aarts, B. and A. McMahon (2006) *The Handbook of English Linguistics* (Malden, MA: Blackwell Publishers).

Berk, Lynn (1999) *English Syntax* (New York and Oxford: Oxford University Press).

Biber, D., S. Johanssson, G. Leech, S. Conrad and E. Finegan (1999) *Longman Grammar of Spoken and Written English* (London: Longman).

Biber, D., S. Conrad and G. Leech (2002) *Longman Student Grammar of Spoken and Written English* (London: Longman).

Börjars, K. and K. Burridge (2000) *Introducing English Grammar* (London: Arnold).

Brinton, L. (2000) *The Structure of Modern English: A Linguistic Introduction* (Amsterdam: John Benjamins).

Burton-Roberts, N. (1997) *Analysing Sentences* (London: Longman, 2nd edn).

Carter, R. and M. McCarthy (2006) *The Cambridge Grammar of English* (Cambridge: Cambridge University Press).

Collins, P. and C. Hollo (1999) *English Grammar: An Introduction* (Basingstoke: Macmillan – now Palgrave Macmillan).

Crystal, D. (2006) *The Fight for English: How Language Pundits Ate Shot and Left* (Oxford: Oxford University Press).

Dixon, R. M. W. (2005) *A Semantic Approach to English Grammar* (Oxford: Oxford University Press, 2nd edn).

Graddol, D., J. Swann and D. Leith (1996) *English: History, Diversity and Change* (London: Routledge).

Gramley, S. and Pätzold, K.-M. (2004) *A Survey of Modern English* (London: Routledge, 2nd edn).

Greenbaum, S. (1996) *The Oxford English Grammar* (Oxford: Oxford University Press).

Greenbaum, S. (2000) (ed. E. Weiner) *The Oxford Reference Grammar* (Oxford: Oxford University Press).

Greenbaum, S. and G. Nelson (2002) *An Introduction to English Grammar* (London: Longman, 2nd edn).

Greenbaum, S. and R. Quirk (1990) *A Student's Grammar of the English Language* (London: Longman). (This is a condensed version of Quirk et al. 1985.)

Haegeman, L. and J. Guéron (1998) *English Grammar: A Generative Perspective* (Oxford: Blackwell).

Hudson, Richard (1998) *English Grammar* (London: Routledge).

Huddleston, R. (1984) *Introduction to the Grammar of English* (Cambridge: Cambridge University Press).

Huddleston, R. (1988) *English Grammar: An Outline* (Cambridge: Cambridge University Press). (This is a condensed version of Huddleston 1984.)

Huddleston, R. and Geoffrey K. Pullum et al. (2002) *The Cambridge Grammar of the English Language* (Cambridge: Cambridge University Press).

Huddleston, R. and Geoffrey K. Pullum (2005) *A Student's Introduction to English Grammar* (Cambridge: Cambridge University Press).

Kuiper, K and W. Scott Allan (1996) *An Introduction to English Language* (Basingstoke: Macmillan – now Palgrave Macmillan).

Leech, G. and J. Svartvik (2003) *A Communicative Grammar of English* (London: Longman, 3rd edn).

Morenberg, M. (2002) *Doing Grammar* (New York and Oxford: Oxford University Press, 3rd edn).

Nelson, G. (2001) *English: An Essential Grammar* (London: Routledge).

Quirk, R., S. Greenbaum, G. Leech and J. Svartvik (1985) *A Comprehensive Grammar of the English Language* (London: Longman).

Rodby, Judith and W. Ross Winterowd (2005) *The Uses of Grammar* (New York Oxford University Press).

Svartvik, J. and G. Leech (2006) *English: One Tongue, Many Voices* (Basingstoke: Palgrave Macmillan).

Verspoor, M. and K. Sauter (2000) *English Sentence Analysis: An Introductory Course* (Amsterdam: John Benjamins).

Wardhaugh, R. (1995) *Understanding English Grammar* (Oxford: Blackwell).

Wekker, H. and L. Haegeman (1985) *A Modern Course in English Syntax* (London: Routledge).

Wierzbicka, A. (2006) *English: Meaning and Culture* (Oxford: Oxford University Press).

All the dictionaries are available in paperback and quite affordable. Most of the encyclopedias and some of the grammars are published in hardback and range in price from £25 to a couple of thousand pounds, and you may therefore need to consult them in a library.

Grammar on the Internet

The Internet Grammar of English (IGE) is an online grammar of English based at University College London. This unique resource is intended for those who want to learn about English grammar (or improve their existing knowledge of it) through self-study. It is also of use for teachers and researchers. *The Internet Grammar of English* consists of two modules: the Grammar Module and the Exercise Module. The first of these features descriptions of the English language, based on real language data. The Exercise Module offers interactive exercises which are linked to sections in the Grammar Module. The descriptive outlook of *IGE* is similar to that of this book, but beware of differences. The web address for *IGE* is:

http://www.ucl.ac.uk/internet-grammar/

Bibliography

Aarts, B. (1989) 'Verb-Preposition Constructions and Small Clauses in English'. *Journal of Linguistics*, **25.2**, pp. 277–90.

Aarts, B. (1992) *Small Clauses in English: The Nonverbal Types* (Berlin and New York: Mouton de Gruyter). Topics in English Linguistics vol. 8.

Aarts, B. (1995) 'Secondary Predicates in English', in: B. Aarts and C. F. Meyer (eds) *The Verb in Contemporary English: Theory and Description* (Cambridge: Cambridge University Press), 75–101.

Aarts, B. (1998) 'Binominal Noun Phrases in English'. *Transactions of the Philological Society*, **96.1**, pp. 117–58.

Aarts, B. (2007a) *Syntactic Gradience: The Nature of Grammatical Indeterminacy* (Oxford: Oxford University Press).

Aarts, B. (2007b) 'In Defence of Distributional Analysis, *pace* Croft'. *Studies in Language*, **31.2**, pp. 431–43.

Aarts, B. and A. McMahon (2006) (eds) *The Handbook of English Linguistics* (Malden, MA: Blackwell Publishers).

Aarts, Bas, D. Denison, E. Keizer and G. Popova (2004) (eds) *Fuzzy Grammar: A Reader* (Oxford: Oxford University Press).

Aarts, F. and J. Aarts (1982) *English Syntactic Structures: Functions and Categories in Sentence Analysis* (Oxford: Pergamon Press).

Adams, V. (1973) *An Introduction to English Word-Formation* (London: Longman).

Adams, V. (2001) *Complex Words in English* (Harlow: Pearson Education/ Longman).

Adger, D. (2003) *Core Syntax* (Oxford: Oxford University Press).

Aitchison, J. (2002) *Words in the Mind* (Oxford: Blackwell Publishers, 3rd edn).

Akmajian, A. and A. Lehrer (1976) 'NP-like Quantifiers and the Problem of Determining the Head of an NP', *Linguistic Analysis*, **2.4**, pp. 395–413.

Allwood, J., L.-G. Andersson and O. Dahl (1977) *Logic in Linguistics* (Cambridge: Cambridge University Press).

Bauer, L. (2004) *Introducing Linguistic Morphology* (Edinburgh: Edinburgh University Press, 2nd edn).

Birner, B. J., and G. Ward (2006) 'Information Structure', in: B. Aarts and A. McMahon, (eds) *The Handbook of English Linguistics* (Malden, MA: Blackwell Publishers), pp. 291–317.

Bolinger, D. (1977) *Meaning and Form* (London: Longman).

Burton-Roberts, N. (1991) 'Prepositions, Adverbs, and Adverbials', in: I. Tieken Boon van Ostade and J. Frankis (eds) *Language: Usage and Description* (Amsterdam: Rodopi), pp. 159–72.

Burton-Roberts, N. (1997) *Analysing Sentences* (London: Longman, 2nd edn).

Burton-Roberts, N. (1999) 'Language, Linear Precedence and Parentheticals', in: P. Collins and D. Lee (eds) *The Clause in English: In Honour of Rodney Huddleston*. (Amsterdam: John Benjamins), pp. 33–52.

Chalmers, A. F. (1999) *What Is This Thing Called Science: An Assessment of the Nature and Status of Science and Its Methods* (Milton Keynes: Open University Press, 3rd edn).

Chomsky, N. (1955/1975) *The Logical Structure of Linguistic Theory* (New York: Plenum Press).

Chomsky, N. (1965) *Aspects of the Theory of Syntax* (Cambridge, MA: MIT Press).

Chomsky (1970) 'Remarks on Nominalisation', in: R. A. Jacobs and P. S. Rosenbaum (eds) *Readings in English Transformational Grammar* (Waltham, MA: Ginn), pp. 184–221.

Chomsky, N. (1981) *Lectures on Government and Binding* (Dordrecht: Foris). (Now published by Mouton de Gruyter.)

Chomsky, N. (1986) *Knowledge of Language: Its Nature, Origins and Use* (New York: Praeger).

Croft, W. (2007) Beyond Aristotle and gradience: A Reply to Aarts. *Studies in Language*, **31.2**, pp. 409–30.

Crystal, D. (1967) 'Word Classes in English', *Lingua*, **17**, pp. 24–56.

Curme, G. O. (1935) *A Grammar of the English Language*, vol. II: *Parts of Speech and Accidence* (Boston: Heath).

Emonds, J. (1976) *A Transformational Approach to English Syntax* (New York: Academic Press).

Fabb, N. (1990) 'The Difference between English Restrictive and Non-Restrictive Relative Clauses'. *Journal of Linguistics*, **26**, pp. 57–78.

Fillmore, C. J. (1968) 'The Case for Case', in: E. Bach and R. T. Harms (eds) *Universals in Linguistic Theory* (New York: Holt, Rinehart & Winston), pp. 1–88.

Frawley, W. (1992) *Linguistic Semantics* (Hillsdale, NJ: Lawrence Erlbaum Associates).

Givón, T. (1993) *English Grammar* (Amsterdam: John Benjamins, 2 vols).

Gruber, J. (1976) (1965 MIT dissertation) *Lexical Structures in Syntax and Semantics* (New York: North Holland).

Haegeman, L. (1994) *Introduction to Government and Binding Theory* (Oxford: Blackwell Publishers, 2nd edn).

Haegeman, L. (2006) *Thinking Syntactically: A Guide to Argumentation and Analysis* (Oxford: Blackwell Publishers).

Horrocks, G. (1987) *Generative Grammar* (London: Longman).

Huddleston, R. (1984) *An Introduction to the Grammar of English* (Cambridge: Cambridge University Press).

Huddleston, R. and G. K. Pullum et al. (2002) *The Cambridge Grammar of the English Language* (Cambridge: Cambridge University Press).

Hudson, R. (1995) 'Competence without Comp?', in: B. Aarts and C. F. Meyer (eds) *The Verb in Contemporary English: Theory and Description* (Cambridge: Cambridge University Press), pp. 40–53.

Hurford, J. R., B. Heasley and M. B. Smith (2007) *Semantics: A Coursebook* (Cambridge: Cambridge University Press, 2nd edn).

Jackendoff, R. (1977) *X-Bar Syntax: A Study of Phrase Structure* (Cambridge, MA: MIT Press).

Katamba, F. and J. Stonham (2006) *Morphology* (Basingstoke: Palgrave, Modern Linguistics Series, 2nd edn).

Katamba, F. (2005) *English Words* (London: Routledge, 2nd edn).

Kortmann, B. (2006) 'Syntactic Variation in English: A Global Perspective, in: B. Aarts and A. McMahon (eds) *The Handbook of English Linguistics* (Malden, MA: Blackwell Publishers), pp. 603–24.

Levinson, S. (1983) *Pragmatics* (Cambridge: Cambridge University Press).

Lightfoot, D. (1982) *The Language Lottery: Towards a Biology of Grammars* (Cambridge, MA: MIT Press).

Matthews, P. (1993) *Grammatical Theory in the United States from Bloomfield to Chomsky* (Cambridge: Cambridge University Press).

McCawley, J. (1998) *The Syntactic Phenomena of English* (Chicago: University of Chicago Press, 2nd edn).

Morenberg, M. (1991) *Doing Grammar* (New York and Oxford: Oxford University Press; 2nd edn 1997, 3rd edn 2002).

Newmeyer, F. (1983) *Grammatical Theory: Its Limits and Its Possibilities* (Chicago: University of Chicago Press).

Ouhalla, J. (1999) *Introducing Transformational Grammar: From Principles and Parameters to Minimalism.* (London: Arnold, 2nd edn).

Palmer, F. (1987) *The English Verb* (London: Longman, 2nd edn).

Plag, I. (2006) *Word Formation in English* (Cambridge: Cambridge University Press).

Postal, P. and G. K. Pullum (1988) 'Expletive Noun Phrases in Subcategorised Positions', *Linguistic Inquiry*, **19.4**, pp. 635–70.

Radford, A. (1988) *Transformational Grammar: A First Course* (Cambridge: Cambridge University Press).

Rochemont, M. and P. Culicover (1990) *English Focus Constructions and the Theory of Grammar* (Cambridge: Cambridge University Press).

Schlesinger, I. M. (1995) 'On the Semantics of the Direct Object', in: B. Aarts and C. F. Meyer (eds) *The Verb in Contemporary English: Theory and Description* (Cambridge: Cambridge University Press), pp. 54–74.

Schmerling, S. (1978) 'Synonymy judgments as syntactic evidence', in: P. Cole (ed.) *Syntax and Semantics*, vol. 9 (New York, San Francisco and London: Academic Press), pp. 299–313.

Selkirk, E. (1977) 'Some Remarks on Noun Phrase Structure', in: P. W. Culicover, T. Wasow and A. Akmajian (eds) *Formal Syntax* (Orlando: Academic Press), pp. 285–316.

Spencer, A. (1991) *Morphological Theory: An Introduction to Word Structure in Generative Grammar* (Oxford: Blackwell).

Tallerman, M. (2005) *Understanding Syntax* (London: Edward Arnold, 2nd edn).

Taylor, John R. (2003) *Linguistic Categorization* (Oxford: Oxford University Press, 3rd edn).

Warner, A. R. (1993) *English Auxiliaries: Structure and History* (Cambridge: Cambridge University Press).

Webelhuth, G. (1995) 'X-Bar Theory and Case Theory', in: G. Webelhuth (ed.) *Government and Binding Theory and the Minimalist Program* (Oxford: Blackwell Publishers), pp. 15–95.

Index